The Political Economy of Health and Welfare

Proceedings of the twenty-second annual symposium of the Eugenics Society, London, 1985

Edited by

Milo Keynes
Department of Anatomy
University of Cambridge

David A. Coleman
Department of Social and Administrative Studies
University of Oxford

Nicholas H. Dimsdale
The Queen's College, Oxford

MACMILLAN PRESS

in association with
Palgrave Macmillan

First published 1988

Published by
THE MACMILLAN PRESS LTD
Houndmills, Basingstoke, Hampshire RG21 2XS
and London
Companies and representatives
throughout the world

British Library Cataloguing in Publication Data
Eugenics Society. *Symposium (22nd:*
1985: London)
The political economy of health and
welfare: proceedings of the twenty-second
annual symposium of the Eugenics Society,
London, 1985. — (Studies in biology,
economy and society).
1. Social medicine   2. Medical economics
I. Title   II. Keynes, W. Milo   III. Coleman,
David A.   IV. Dimsdale, Nicholas H. I.   V. Series
362.1′042   RA418
ISBN 978-1-349-09646-6   ISBN 978-1-349-09644-2 (eBook)
DOI 10.1007/978-1-349-09644-2

STUDIES IN BIOLOGY, ECONOMY AND SOCIETY

General Editor: Robert Chester, Department of Social Policy and Professional Studies, University of Hull

The study of eugenics today has the aim of increasing understanding of our own species and of the rich complexity of the biosocial fabric, so that professional workers, decision-makers in the community and the public at large may be well informed in areas of concern to the whole society. The Eugenics Society promotes and supports interdisciplinary research into the biological, genetic, economic, social and cultural factors relating to human reproduction, development and health in the broadest sense. The Society has a wide range of interdisciplinary interests which include the description and measurement of human qualities, human heredity, the influence of environment and the causes of disease, genetic counselling, the family unit, marriage guidance, birth control, differential fertility, infecundity, artificial insemination, voluntary sterilisation, termination of pregnancy, population problems and migration. As a registered charity, the Society does not act as an advocate of particular political views, but it does seek to foster respect for human variety and to encourage circumstances in which the fullest achievement of individual human potential can be realised.

Amongst its activities the Eugenics Society supports original research by its Stopes Research Fund, co-sponsors the annual Darwin Lecture in Human Biology and the biennial Caradog Jones Lecture, and publishes the quarterly journal *Biology and Society*. In addition, the Society holds each year a two-day symposium in which a topic of current importance is explored from a number of different standpoints, and during which the Galton Lecture is delivered by a distinguished guest. The proceedings of each symposium from 1985 constitute the successive volumes of this series, Studies in Biology, Economy and Society. Although the balance between different disciplines varies with the nature of the topic, each volume contains authoritative contributions from diverse biological and social sciences together with an editorial introduction.

Information about the Society, its aims and activities and earlier symposium proceedings may be obtained from The General Secretary, The Eugenics Society, 69 Eccleston Square, London, SW1V 1PJ.

STUDIES IN BIOLOGY, ECONOMY AND SOCIETY

General Editor: Robert Chester, Department of Social Policy and
Professional Studies, University of Hull

Published

Milo Keynes, David A. Coleman and Nicholas H. Dimsdale
(*editors*)
THE POLITICAL ECONOMY OF HEALTH AND WELFARE

Peter Diggery, Malcolm Potts and Sue Teper (*editors*)
NATURAL HUMAN FERTILITY

Milo Keynes and F. Ainsworth Harrison (*editors*)
EVOLUTIONARY STUDIES: A Centenary Celebration of the Life of
Julian Huxley

Contents

List of Tables

List of Figures

List of the Contributors

Roy M. Acheson is Professor of Community Medicine, University of Cambridge.

Ellie Breeze is Research Assistant, Department of Community Medicine, St Thomas's Hospital, London.

David A. Coleman is University Lecturer in Demography, Oxford.

Partha S. Dasgupta is Professor of Economics, University of Cambridge.

Nicholas H. Dimsdale is Fellow and Tutor in Economics at The Queen's College, Oxford.

A. J. Fox is Professor of Social Statistics, City University, London.

Walter W. Holland is Professor of Clinical Epidemiology and Social Medicine, St Thomas's Hospital, London.

John A. Kay is Director of The Institute for Fiscal Studies, London.

D. A. Leon is Lecturer in Epidemiology, London School of Hygiene and Tropical Medicine.

Nicola Madge is Research Fellow, Department of Community Medicine, University College Hospital, London.

Anthony F. Shorrocks is Professor of Economics, University of Essex.

Richard M. Smith is University Lecturer in Historical Demography, Oxford.

A. P. Thirlwall is Professor of Applied Economics, University of Kent at Canterbury.

Richard G. Wilkinson is Research Fellow, Centre for Medical Research, University of Sussex.

J. M. Winter is Lecturer in History, University of Cambridge.

1 The Political Economy of Health and Welfare

David A. Coleman and
Nicholas H. Dimsdale

The political economy of health and welfare is at the centre of a number of separate but related controversies, ranging across the spectrum from academic analysis of the causes of historical mortality differences to political arguments on the funding and efficacy of the NHS. This book is an attempt to explore some of them and their connections. This introduction sets the scene, reviews the papers and discusses briefly some more salient of the topics. Inevitably, many important and relevant topics could not be covered at the conference where the papers were presented.

The first papers look at the broader problem of welfare, particularly the pressures on individual and family resources from demographic and life-cycle changes, the causes of inequality, and some of the social and institutional arrangements that have arisen to minimise these risks. Others consider the narrower but related problem of health and sickness and the relative importance of individual behaviour and institutional support, and the distribution of income.

THE POLITICAL ECONOMY OF WELFARE

Inequality of income and 'welfare' has grown as a problem the further societies have moved from small-scale subsistence. Risks to family or individual welfare from extraneous circumstances including illness must be coped with, and more predictably, the threat to welfare posed by the inevitable changes in capacity for self-support associated with successive stages of the life-cycle. Traditional family and social structure in pre-modern societies are regarded as a response to these challenges.

In richer societies with a more interventionist state system and a more explicit system of obligations these needs may be met instead by more formal charitable arrangements. In the West patchy pre-modern monastic welfare was replaced by a much more radical

1

organised system of redistribution which began in England with the Poor Law of 1601. This was developed continuously through the Poor Law legislation of the nineteenth century to the immensely elaborate structure of today's welfare state. The proportion of national income redistributed under the earlier Poor Law legislation was not small compared to that of the present day. It certainly caused continuous complaint throughout the nineteenth century. We are not dealing with entirely new problems, nor with new political controversies. Certainly no redistributive system, especially one disposing of such large absolute amounts of money and being responsible for such substantial confiscations of income, could ever be far from political controversy and interference. Social security in 1985 accounted for 30 per cent of government spending or about £42 billion, and the NHS another £14 billion.

Poverty is in a sense the spur to all concern about welfare. So it is appropriate that the first paper by Madge should begin by looking at the role of inheritance, chance and choice in its genesis. The motion of the 'cycle of poverty' was at first well received as a mechanism which seemed to explain how poverty could be concentrated in a sub-group of society. Eugenic and anthropological ideas encouraged the relative notion of a 'culture of poverty', together with a concept of multiple deprivation whereby various components of poverty overlapped in certain individuals and groups much more than expected by chance. There are hardly any good data on the genetical inheritance of characteristics affecting poverty except at the extremes, although there is some interesting material relating the IQ of siblings with their subsequent social mobility. The report commissioned by Sir Keith Joseph (1976) showed a very imperfect transmission; although it was clear for those at the high end of the income distribution. By contrast, Richard Easterlin's 1980 explanation for some of the social variation in income and opportunity, which emphasises the importance of the birth cohort size, is essentially a Malthusian, non-genetic theory. Chance gets its opportunity by filling in the gaps left by the relative failure of empiricism and analysis of risk factors to account adequately for the distribution of poverty. Although there are systematic social aspects of health, for example, bad luck comes into it too, both for individuals and for their parents. The accidents of unemployment and of regional distribution are important too.

In our society family size, marriage partner, divorce, savings and expenditure can all be regarded as choice to a greater or lesser degree. Upward social mobility reflects personal decisions, but most downward mobility must be in the teeth of personal choice. Madge regards choice as being only a marginal force. And choice, chance and inheritance together still do not tell the whole story. There are cycles of attitudes to the poor and in the sense of justice. The processes of society and politics form another side to the picture. Madge concludes that it doesn't help the poor to tell them that they are badly off because of their antecedents, their own choice or bad luck.

Economists have traditionally treated poverty as a consequence of inequality in the distribution of income. Dasgupta explores a causal link running in the opposite direction and argues that in developing countries inequality may result from poverty. His basic analogy is that of a lifeboat containing two survivors in which there is only enough food for one of them. The fair way to distribute the rations is to draw lots and to give all the food to the winner. Provided the lots are drawn fairly, there is *ex ante* equality, but inequality *ex post*, which results from the inadequacy of food supplies.

There are two more realistic economic examples which Dasgupta considers where inequality arises from poverty because of the relationship between food intake and productive capacity. In a developing country a large family owning only a small plot of land on which it depends for its subsistence will find it economically efficient to employ only a proportion of its members. They will be allocated a relatively high food input to ensure that their productive capacity is well maintained, while the remaining members of the family are unemployed and may suffer from malnutrition. Poverty due to a shortage of land, therefore, creates a situation in which inequality is aggravated.

A similar problem may arise in the labour market where firms offer money wages which correspond to the minimum efficiency wage. Lower money wages would reduce the production capacity of workers more than the wage bill and so increase labour costs. The problem is that at the minimum efficiency wage, the supply of labour exceeds the number of jobs which firms can offer. There will be no incentive for firms to reduce money wages despite excess supply of labour, and there will be persistent unemployment with those in employment having higher incomes than the unemployed. Those who are unemployed may tend to become less productive as a result of malnutrition, so that patterns of inequality and poverty will become persistent.

These examples illustrate the complexity of the relationship between poverty and inequality in developing economies. Important consequences follow from allowing productive capacity to be a function of food allocation, so enabling the effects of malnutrition on the labour supply to be analyzed systematically.

Theoretical criteria for assessing whether there is equality of opportunity are developed in Shorrocks' Galton Lecture, and then used to examine the results of empirical studies of factors affecting the inequality of earnings and evidence for inequality of opportunity.

Starting from the viewpoint of the economist, Shorrocks considers the circumstances under which opportunities can be said to be equal. He distinguishes at the outset between initial opportunities and actual outcomes, which result from the operation of both choice and chance. Equality of opportunity implies that individuals are equal *ex ante* in that they face the same set of options. Inequality of observed outcomes may merely reflect differences in preferences and not necessarily imply unequal *ex ante* opportunities. The issue is more complex if chance is present, since individuals will tend to envy those who are blessed with more fortunate outcomes. The principle of horizontal equity requires that differences in incomes due to chance rather than choice should not be ignored. This implies that *ex ante* equality of opportunity is fair only if risks are undertaken voluntarily, since differences in outcome due to rational choice are fair, but those due to pure chance are not.

Shorrocks combines this 'economic choice–theoretic approach to equality of opportunity' with a more traditional approach which emphasizes the conditions which may prevent equality of opportunity being realized. The first and weakest condition is the absence of discrimination on sex or race. Meritocracy requires that family influences and inherited wealth should not affect an individual's earnings prospects. This ensures that lifetime opportunities depend only on ability. By the more stringent criteria of *ex ante* equality of opportunity each individual faces the same lifetime opportunities. Anything which prevents this, such as discrimination, differences in natural talent, and family effects, is undesirable. Finally, the no-envy concept of inequality permits only differences in outcome due to choice and excludes differences due to pure chance.

Different concepts of inequality of opportunity have been used by empirical research workers and this goes some way towards explaining their differing conclusions on the degree to which opportunities are unequal. Shorrocks points out the serious difficulties which arise from attempts to reconstruct the set of opportunities facing individuals from observed outcomes. Equal opportunities do not imply equal outcomes, while equal outcomes do not imply equal opportunities. There are problems of allowing for non-pecuniary factors, which enter into opportunities, and of determining the rate at which they are exchanged for money income. Only in a few cases, as in the study of the choice between work and leisure, does such an economic approach seem workable. It is more common to adopt a less ambitious approach of relating estimates of income to the personal and family background of individuals. Each individual is regarded as possessing a collection of characteristics which are valued in the labour market and these attributes determine his or her expected earnings. Empirical work of this type is intended primarily to explain the determinants of earnings, but it also throws some light on the question of differences in opportunities.

Shorrocks cites one study to show that omitted variables which are correlated with observed characteristics may seriously bias the empirical estimates of the contribution of the included variables. Work on the existence of sexual discrimination in the labour market may also be affected by problems with omitted variables, but introducing marital status may provide a way of allowing for the reduced work motivation of married women. He accepts that the Sexual Discrimination Act of 1975 may have reduced the degree of discrimination in a comparison of the hourly earnings of married women and single men.

His final example, on the persistence of patterns in intergenerational relative earnings, is closely related to the question of equality of opportunity. Positive correlation between relative earnings of parents and children is evidence of unequal *ex ante* opportunities and Shorrocks suggests that intergenerational mobility may be taken as an index of equality of opportunity. Some of the results which have been reported suggest that the relationship between relative earnings of sons and fathers may be similar to that found by Galton between the heights of successive generations of the same family; a fitting conclusion to a Galton Lecture.

POPULATION AND WELFARE

Population change affects both the demand and the supply side of welfare. There is no room here to consider this great debate exhaustively. But the fertility and mortality regime under which societies operate helps determine the balance of consumers and producers of welfare and the pressure their population puts on their own resources. The Malthusian position claims that economic activity measured by real wages and fertility measured by birth rates mediated by marriage, are intimately related, especially in Western societies of stable technology. Rapid population growth in these circumstances impedes economic growth at the national and at the family level (see Coleman and Schofield 1986).

Thirlwall's paper on economic consequences of population change takes a sceptical view, pointing out that cross-section analysis revealed little correlation between rates of population growth and levels of increase of income. Indeed population growth, as Marxists insist, increases one of the major factors of production. None the less it can be responded that there are no rich countries which still have high rates of population growth. The response of better-off populations, and better-off sections of populations, has been to reduce their family size, often below the level that national governments feel is adequate for economic ends. Viewed longitudinally, not cross-sectionally, rapid growth can present poor countries with severe problems of capital formation and job creation, directly through growth in numbers and indirectly through a much more youthful age structure; as the classical analyses of Coale and Hoover (1958) and Kuznets (1973) demonstrate.

Much depends on the scale of population growth; 1 per cent is quite compatible with rapid economic growth; 3 per cent in a poor country is a different matter; 3 per cent in richer countries never happens. It is revealing that a high proportion of countries with growing economies have come to their own conclusions on this by introducing official policies to limit population growth; even Marxist regimes in China and Vietnam, otherwise ideologically strongly opposed to Malthusian analysis, and erstwhile pronatalist authoritarian regimes in Brazil and Mexico.

Consideration of the components of the demographic system brings us closer to specific policy questions relating to welfare. In his paper Richard Smith emphasises the importance of the dramatic demographic and economic changes which occur in the lifetime of individuals and families, which put them alternatively on the demand and the supply side of health and welfare, and the surprising antiquity of the policy response to the problems thus generated by demographic uncertainty. In the absence of state welfare the extended family is often portrayed as a social arrangement for spreading risk across lifetimes and individuals; a 'welfare republic' incapable of replication by the nuclear family. Exogenous demographic change affecting survival or growth rates disrupts this dynamic equilibrium.

The long history of the Western family challenges this model of intergenerational contract, and the notion of an evolutionary change from the extended to the nuclear family. Left to itself the nuclear family is certainly exposed to demographic problems, notably the 40 per cent of men who in high-mortality (eighteenth-century) low-fertility regimes leave no sons, and the loss of children at marriage often to remote locations for service in other households.

Smith suggests that modern patterns of family life may be leading to a divergence of satisfactions between different components of the nuclear family life cycle: for example the old (see Kay's paper) and the young. Twentieth-century political developments, including the consequences of the growth of the elderly population may make welfare advantages proportional to cohort size (*contra* Easterlin) outside the labour force, especially when public spending is high.

Smith concludes by reminding us that in the past European wealth flow has depended upon economically active families with few dependents giving through the welfare system to those with costly dependents or who were economically inactive, irrespective of kin resources either way. Such a system is highly susceptible to changes in age structure and to changes in real income. The bigger the role of transfers relative to earnings, the bigger the role of the collectivity (the parish or the country) relative to the nuclear family, and the more advantageous at least in the past in belonging to a larger cohorts.

The demographic process is not a constant one. Demographic regimes can last for centuries, but from time to time they change radically. The most radical of such changes is now in its final stages – the so-called demographic transition from moderately high birth and death rates and moderate growth, to low rates and negligible or even negative growth. The advent of birth control in marriage from the late nineteenth century has made possible an historically unprecedented reduction in fertility and brought with it a new opportunity for volatility in the tempo as well as in the quantum of childbearing. The most striking features of the erratic path of twentieth-century fertility – common to most western societies – has been the periods of sub-replacement fertility in the 1930s and at the present day, and the extraordinary bulge of fertility from the 1950s to the 1960s which followed the transient peak of fertility after World War Two. The latter is generally supposed to be an unrepeatable one-off event, a result of the historically unique combination of low levels of married women in the work force, a general reduction in average age at marriage following universal family planning, coupled to the traditional Malthusian effect of a strong period of unprecedented economic growth, *via* men's wages, upon family building (see Ermisch, 1983). The combination of these two periods of few births and the intervening period of many births will dominate the demography of welfare in the West well into the next century (Craig 1983; Daykin 1986).

From the viewpoint of pensions, now is the good time. The post-war bulge, although it has made unemployment worse, has created a large workforce to pay pensions to the modest numbers now entering pensionable ages (from the small 1920s and 1930s birth cohorts). But it promises an old age crisis throughout the West in about thirty years' time when the baby boom are in their wheelchairs, pushed by the small workforce from the small birth cohorts of the 1970s and 1980s – which shows no sign of increasing in the 1990s.

Kay's paper shows how this relates to two major changes in the political economy of welfare. The first of those is the need to achieve better integration of tax and social security transfers; the other that under the present government, retirement benefits have lost their priority in the welfare budget, in part as a realisation – presaged in Smith's paper – that pensioners are doing a lot better than they used to. Thanks to the demographic transition, the share of pensions in national insurance benefits has increased (see DHSS, 1984). He also points out how growth in real benefits has followed from growth in pensioner numbers since the 1930s, and the higher propensity of older people to vote in elections. These broke the original pension schemes, especially the connection between contribution and receipts, and precipitated the series of solutions of which the State Earnings Related Pensions Scheme (SERPS) and its recent modification is only the latest. The advantages of belonging to a larger cohort (mentioned in Smith's paper) have been amply confirmed by the victory of the pensioners pressure groups over the originally more radical proposals to eliminate SERPS altogether.

The scheme creates the prospect of a massive burden of state pensions after the year 2000. The burden would be less oppressive if the scheme were founded on conventional actuarial principles. This is not so, since earnings related pensions are paid to the retired from the contributions of those currently employed on the tacit understanding that the pension rights of today's workers will be honoured by their successors.

Kay argues that this form of finance is inherently fraudulent, but that is perhaps going too far. What is wrong with the pay-as-you-go principle is that it is vulnerable to a slowing down of either the rate of population growth or the rate of growth of productivity. A diminution of economic growth for either reason can lead to the accumulation of pension obligations which exceed the ability of the working population to discharge, making some form of default inevitable.

Kay correctly emphasises that the controversy over SERPS raises fundamental issues over the role of the state in pensions policy. It is questionable whether the state should intervene in the allocation of an individual's income over time. If poverty in old age is regarded as a serious problem it could be dealt with more appropriately by providing a basic flat rate pension. While private decisions over pensions may be myopic, the record of governments suggests that they are prepared to burden future generations excessively in order to benefit the current electorate. Some combination of private and state funded pension schemes is needed and present arrangements are in need of urgent reconsideration.

HEALTH

The last few decades have seen a revolution in our understanding of the relation between medicine, spending and health. In the past it was generally and not unreasonably assumed that more doctors and more hospitals meant better health. The violent assault by McKeown and his colleagues (1955, 1976) on this simple view has damaged it beyond repair. Although the champions of the eighteenth-century hospitals (Sigsworth 1972; Cherry 1980a, 1980b) and others have successfully counter attacked McKeown's exaggerations, it is now generally accepted that medical knowledge and practice, as opposed to nursing, did little directly to relieve suffering or to reduce mortality until this century. Instead, improvements in nutrition and housing, personal hygiene, and attitudes to children, developing in a richer, more liberal and enlightened society, are preferred as explanations. State action has its place too, in its ability and willingness to impose quarantines in the seventeenth century and onwards (Slack 1981), to make and analyse effective registers of deaths and their causes in the early nineteenth century (Lewes 1983), to invest in public health works to segregate sewage from drinking water, to impose minimum housing standards in the mid and late nineteenth century and to make mass immunisation compulsory (as against smallpox in 1854) as effective techniques emerged. Szreter (1986) suggests that one of the most important influences of all were the preventive health measures carried out by urban local authorities.

It seems reasonable to assume that the position must have changed today. We know that 60 per cent of the mortality reduction since 1840 occurred this century, not last. Medical science can now prevent and cure many infectious and parasitic diseases, as well as perform prodigious work to save lives following otherwise terminal accidents and heart attacks. Mortality from many childhood cancers has been dramatically suppressed, and many lives saved by pacemakers and bypass surgery, and new developments in paediatrics and obstetrics. Indeed some of the strongest and best publicised medical questions have centred on the adequacy of expenditure and emphasis on childbirth and child care (e.g. Committee on Child Health Services 1976; House of Commons Social Services Committee 1980) as instanced by Britain's declining place in the international league table of infant mortality. But in fact the controversy has not gone away. Western mortality in the twentieth century is dominated, as it was in the nineteenth, by diseases that cannot be cured – only they are different diseases. The rise of lung cancer and of heart disease was not a failure of medicine; their later decline in the USA and less dramatically elsewhere has owed little to specific medical intervention. This is not to say that in future clinical developments, especially in monoclonal antibodies, may not shift this balance in favour of curative medicine and the identification of individuals at risk.

Instead the rise of living standards, far faster in the twentieth than in the nineteenth century, may still be a more important contributor to better health in the twentieth, just as it was in the nineteenth century. Gross deficiencies of nutrition, living space and warmth have now been for the most part put right by economic growth and income redistribution. Thanks in part to these, access to medical care is now general: the nineteenth century could not have afforded a NHS nor provided an effective one. One of the themes of this book is whether continued late twentieth-century declines in mortality are now more to do with the satisfied material needs, better education, knowledge, and the enlightened lifestyles which follow from it.

According to this view disease and cancer should not be regarded as diseases of civilisation, but of immature affluence. Their numerical significance in later life is uncovered by the fall of premature deaths from infectious disease. Their age-incidence was then made worse earlier this century by the early progress towards the solution of material problems. The new ability to over-eat and to smoke cigarettes are two examples. The latter is almost entirely a twentieth-century fad. It was made possible by early affluence. It is now being set aside at least in the West by still richer, and better educated, later generations. A more literate and educated society can better understand the importance of exercise, healthy eating and the avoidance of obesity, although in the UK today, a quarter of young men and women are overweight, particularly in the less literate and educated sections of society (OPCS 1984).

The rise of these diseases and the beginning of their decline are contained well within the space of one century. They follow a characteristic pattern to some extent following income and fashion: first prominent among men in the middle-class, then among middle-class women, working-class men and then working-class women. Recent downward trends in all social classes in smoking habits in the UK and other Western countries (OPCS 1984) are highly encouraging. Now, while smoking is in decline in all these groups except the last, the habit is spreading in the richer population of the Third World.

This competition for the credit for health between political economy and medical science is paralleled by a rivalry between epidemiology and clinical medicine. Much of the preventive medicine of the nineteenth century depended on the official collection of statistics and their manipulation by demographic and epidemiological techniques, notably by Farr, Snow and others (OPCS, 1985a) and by the practical application of empirical findings, innocent of bacteriological knowledge, by Bazalgette and other engineers. Pre-statistical observation permitted the imposition of quarantines by states from the seventeenth century onwards and the development of inoculation and vaccination against smallpox by medical men in the eighteenth century. Physiological sciences were essential for the later development of immunisation, and after the 1930s, the cure of bacterial disease. But even now, quarantine is our first line of defence against rabies and other diseases. Epidemiological techniques remain at the front of activity in the modern control of infectious disease, including AIDS, and hopes for the elimination of such diseases as measles (Anderson and May 1985; May and Anderson 1987).

This is also true of the demographically more important diseases such as cancer and circulatory disease. Although rates of relief and cure of such diseases have improved, thanks to improvements in surgery, chemotherapy and radiation therapy, many classes of common cancer still have very poor survival rates (OPCS 1985).

Even though the carcinogens leading to many cancers cannot yet be precisely pinpointed, and we cannot specifically establish exactly how important habits of diet and exercise are in relation to circulatory disease (DHSS 1985), epidemiological science, diffusing into popular knowledge, has undoubtedly led to improvements in sickness and mortality rates. This is less true in the tropical parts of the world. There, it was medical intervention imposed by an effective administration in the form of mass vaccination against smallpox, the saline treatment of cholera and so on that brought down death rates, rather than the rise of living standards – which in any case improved but slowly until recently. But these earlier easy victories over tropical illness cannot be sustained today. Favourable trends in Third World mortality may now depend rather more on the pace of material progress (Gwatkin 1980). This, although fast in some developing countries, is slow or negative in others, notably in tropical Africa. The rapid increase of smoking in the Third World will be an additional burden.

In contrast to all this, much discussion of the political economy and the politics of national health and welfare in the UK still seems rooted in the medical assumptions of the nineteenth century. It pays little attention to the academic debate of the last three decades, so that health is assumed to equate with medicine and the activities of the health service. Indeed the alleviation of disease is by no means always at the centre of discussion about the NHS. Instead the terms of political debate have more often centred on the concerns of pressure groups and their vested interests, many of them internal to the health service. As the NHS is the biggest employer in Europe, perhaps this is inevitable. And its own internal health has created a considerable literature. Bosanquet explored aspects of the politics of the NHS in a paper given at the symposium which, unfortunately, he was unable to present for this volume. Inputs to the health service have been more salient than outputs, cure more than prevention. But it is fair to say that since the late 1970s this has changed somewhat, witnessed by a series of DHSS papers on the importance of disease avoiding behaviour in smoking, drinking and eating (DHSS 1981a, 1981b, 1985) following the pressures generated by the House of

Commons Expenditure Committee's 1977 report. Prevention is now prominent in the DHSS annual report (1985). But still the terms of the present debate tend to be of money spent, numbers of doctors and nurses employed, and of hospitals built. There has been less consideration, at least until recently, of how these inputs actually relate to levels and trends of sickness and mortality and other 'hard' performance indicators (Goldacre and Griffin 1983).

Official figures show that public spending on the National Health Service, for example, has increased by 21 per cent in real terms since 1979, including 43 major new hospital schemes, 47 000 more nurses (in terms of full time equivalents) and 4000 more doctors and dentists (DHSS 1985). Eighty per cent of the public claim to be satisfied with their treatment under the NHS, yet 81 per cent tell opinion pollsters that they disapprove of the way the NHS is being handled (Gallup Poll 1986). And although in volume terms the NHS has never treated more patients (823 000 in 1984), critics claim that this has only been made possible through such steps as shortening stay in hospital.

As Klein (1983) has pointed out, the demand for medical care is almost endless; contrary to the expectations of the early architects of the NHS, better provision has not absorbed a finite burden of sickness; instead it has changed the threshhold of expectations of health and its care. Despite all that, criticism speaks of cuts, not growth. The increases in staff, for example, are to some extent vitiated by the shorter hours and more favourable terms of leave granted to nurses and doctors. Their salary increases, and the wages of non-medical staff, have consistently exceeded the rate of inflation. The unions' success in doing this is undoubtedly helped by public approval of general settlements for medical staff, even though this then reduces the proportion of resources available to expand facilities.

The picture is more varied at the regional level because of the controversial reshuffle of resources by the Resource Allocations Working Party (RAWP 1976). The effect of their formula for resource allocation has been to move resources from the better off areas of London and the South East, with their concentration of teaching hospitals, to the North and Midlands, especially the great industrial conurbations. These tend to be areas of higher rates of death and sickness; particular concentrations are to be found in such towns as Oldham and Salford (OPCS 1979). In this respect the RAWP formula follows the orthodox assumptions about the primary role of hospitals and clinical medicine on the population's health. It is difficult to see what else they could do.

There are North/South gradients in almost all causes of death, almost all of them unfavourable to the North. Epidemiological evidence show that these survive correction for socio-economic class (Shaper *et al.* 1980; OPCS 1978, 1984). They may owe much to regional differences in smoking, drinking and eating habits (notably fruit and fibre), (Cummins *et al.* 1981; OPCS 1983, 1984, 1985; National Food Survey Committee 1985). It is open to question therefore whether the RAWP formula, which focuses so sharply on the primacy of curative medicine in levels of disease, does not itself help to create unnecessary hardship and resentment in the areas from which resources have been taken.

For example, the low mortality in the South East of England is not necessarily just because of its greater wealth, or any excess of doctors or hospitals which it may have enjoyed in the past. (For example, in Italy the richer North has higher mortality then the poorer South, and Greece has one of the most favourable levels of mortality in all Europe.) Instead it may be in part a consequence of more healthy habits of life in the South of England. Its residents smoke less, drink less and eat more rationally than their compatriots elsewhere. Changes of hospital provision may not be the most appropriate response.

The social class gradient in sickness and mortality in the UK puts the spotlight on the following questions:

1. How much does health depend on health services and public expenditure upon them?
2. How far are social class mortality differences caused by differential access to health service provisions?
3. Are social class mortality differentials a direct measure of the distribution of poverty in society, affecting health in ways for which the NHS cannot compensate?
4. Are they a function of different attitudes and behaviour between social classes, not so directly influenced by income or health service provision?

These questions are also related to such controversies as the relative importance of occupational mentality, especially in respect of certain carcinogens such as asbestos, which are not considered in these papers (e.g. Peto 1980).

In response to such questions, Fox and Leon's paper takes the political economy down to the small scale and, linking the themes of Wilkinson's and Winter's papers, shows the importance of appropriate methodology and data. Despite criticism they insist that the Registrar-General's Social Class index remains a valuable criterion in assessing risks of premature mortality. The longitudinal life cycle analysis made possible by the Longitudinal Study makes it much easier to find the causes of these differences and analyse them according to several criteria simultaneously, as the same individuals move between classes, regions and employment states. The importance of tracking movements between classes has been apparent since the time of Farr, but until recently it simply couldn't be done. In taking this further they look particularly at cancer deaths. The Longitudinal Study links various forms of disadvantage to social class. On the whole social mobility itself within generations does not seem to be a major contribution to social class mortality differences, despite the powerful case made by Stern's selection theory. But these effects may operate more on an inter-generational rather than an intra-generational basis. The Longitudinal Study also offers the interesting possibility of the simultaneous analysis by tenure as well as by area and class. This suggests a complex and an incompletely explored relationship between health and housing tenure which unfortunately remains out of reach of the data in Fox and Leon's paper.

The Black Committee was set up under the Labour government in 1978 specifically to look at the persistence of social class differentials. It comprised two medical men and two sociologists, and their report (1980) is available on request from the DHSS and in an abridged version (Townsend and Davidson, 1982). The report reviewed competing explanations and data in the social class differentials in mortality, although its conclusions do not all seem to follow very directly from the evidence. It recommended higher public spending to compensate for the poverty and deprivation which it claimed was the primary cause of higher mortality among the lower social classes. Its economic prescriptions for ending the health disadvantage of poorer people are not accompanied by any econometric analysis to demonstrate the effect on mortality expected from any given increase in expenditure, or a specification of what poorer people would spend more money on in order to find better health in an environment of social medicine.

Richard Wilkinson's paper in this book addresses these problems specifically and makes a forceful case for the importance of differential access to the National Health Service and the direct effects of income differences and absolute deprivation. He argues that class differences in health are an inevitable expression of structural inequalities in society and show up the failure of the modern social structure and how it should be changed – an argument from health and mortality to political economy.

These differentials have shown no tendency to narrow as the most recent decennial supplement has shown, although the mortality of all classes continues to improve (OPCS 1986a, b). If we are interested in the effects of income, social class differences are not a good guide because of the heterogeneity of each class in respect of income. But direct income data linked to mortality data are difficult to find, although he believes they would expand the differences.

These social class differences apply across almost all major causes of death (although varying considerably in gradient). Wilkinson emphasises work which shows the gradient is as steep for non smoking related diseases as for those known to be affected by smoking. The large number of possible causes of mortality do not act evenly over the population; the most favourable effects concentrate in the upper classes of society to give a hierarchy of advantage. It follows that inequalities in health can most effectively be reduced not by reducing changes in behaviour in specific classes but by changing society so that choices do not depend on social position. Acknowledging that radical change in this direction is unlikely, attention should be focused on health as the best social indicator of welfare and the need to take it into account in all aspects of social structure and social life, including work, as an objective measure of its satisfaction, and the avoidance of stress (although the latter clearly needs definition – see Harrison 1980, 1982). And it might be difficult to place too much reliance on social or family structures for support which Anderson (1983) suggests are both recent and transient. Wilkinson puts the first charge on income, its effect being particularly strong at low income levels. Redistribution of incomes is advocated to resolve the problem, although the substantial economic consequences of such large scale income redistribution and consequent increases in public spending are not likely to be agreed.

Wider international comparisons may throw some light on these problems. Initial progress in reducing mortality in the Third World depended more on the provision of modern medicine than on the growth of wealth, but this relationship has changed fast. Twentieth-century mortality rates in Third World countries generally improved faster than in the West; they did not do so in the early twentieth and nineteenth century despite close contact with the West at that time. But total GNP and total expenditure on health isn't everything;

equality of access to health services clearly have an important effect. Third World societies which have socialised medicine tend to have lower overall mortality rates (e.g. Cuba, some southern Indian states, Ceylon) than other countries with equivalent levels of poverty. These early advances may be bought at a cost of an economic and health system which cannot develop further, and which may inhibit future economic growth and the mortality improvement which eventually comes with it. There are certainly major examples of such failure – after initial advances – in most of Eastern Europe and the USSR.

In Eastern Europe the increase in expectation of life, commonplace elsewhere in the developed world, has ceased or gone into reverse since the 1970s, notably among middle-aged males and especially in the Soviet Union (Compton 1985; Feshbach 1982). The causes of this extreme Soviet response are controversial. They may in part reflect the maturing into high mortality ages of war-damaged cohorts (Dinkel 1985). But the undoubted failure of infant mortality to improve cannot be held to that cause. Instead, the uniquely high proportion of married women in the workforce, inadequate maternity leave, problems of collective care of children, exacerbated by the decline of the *babushka*, the low status of the medical profession (with a high proportion of woman doctors) may be social factors relating to the problem. But it must be said other social trends point to other explanations: especially the high and rising consumption of tobacco and (until recently) alcohol. Detailed data do not exist to enable a decision to be made between these competing hypotheses: of the low proportion of GNP spent on medicine and other welfare problems, and unhealthy habits unrelated to deprivation as such. But cause of death data show rapidly increasing risks of death from heart disease, lung cancer and alcohol-related conditions including accidents. More detailed data point to a similar situation in Hungary and Czechoslovakia (Compton 1985; Jozan 1986). While the relation of income and its distribution works in an obviously powerful way when subsistence is a problem, it does seem less obvious in conditions of relative affluence.

Improvement of health and survival and changes in fertility have had a major impact on welfare systems which were designed to suit earlier demographic regimes. A rather different kind of question relates to how far these advances in health have themselves depended on the advance of medicine and the increase of health expenditure. Professor Holland shows how difficult it has been to answer this question, and how the NHS, in contrast to some other health systems, has seldom if ever been involved with questions of performance but has tended to judge its merit in terms of coverage, input and expenditure. Most of the NHS's history has been a desperate scramble to meet a growing and apparently limitless demand for services, modulated by conflict between vested interest groups within the health service itself, generated by a system without negative feedbacks to the consumer at all, and whose costs are not a concern to the professional (for example, see Klein 1983). Like pensions, this has generated an official response to control costs from on top. An attempt by the Central Policy Review Staff in 1982 to think about a system which made the costs more visible to the consumer, was effectively destroyed by a leak, and questions of cost have only forced the monitoring of performance from about 1984. And as Holland points out, these indicators are still concerned too much with what are essentially inputs and their delivery systems, not genuine outputs (for a review, see Goldacre and Griffin 1983). Hard outcome indicators are restricted to infant mortality. Introducing others is difficult. The distribution of avoidable mortality between regions of the Health Service is clearly helpful when dealing with 'curable diseases'. But the diseases causing the bulk of mortality are not curable, although some are preventable and thus this performance indicator can only measure curative services dealing with a minor part of the total burden of sickness and death rates.

But Acheson insists treatment must remain the main concern of the National Health Service. In his view, the scope for preventive measures is often less than is thought, and the choice between prevention and cure depends very much on the specific disease. For example, cholera contradicts the conventional wisdom. Environmental manipulation cannot be done in Bengal at all, and immunological prevention is ineffective. But despite the failure of prevention, a cheap and effective cure is available and is clearly the best option at present.

Despite much research and enthusiasm, intervention trials have not yet shown the unequivocal success of preventive measures against for example, coronary artery disease. Hypertension is its most important risk factor. High blood pressure can be lowered with drugs, which can help to lower the risk of ischaemic heart disease in that minority of potential victims with severe high blood pressure. But major intervention trials applied to the general population, like the Multiple Risk Factor Intervention Trial (MRFIT), fail to show unequivocal evidence of a reduction of cardiovascular disease. We cannot yet invest in prevention of heart disease. But the prevention of stroke is easier through the control of hypertension, and it is more beneficial to the NHS because stroke has later onset and causes chronic debilitation.

The uncertainty over the role of salt in high blood pressure is instructive in relation to these circulatory diseases and points to the importance of genetical variation in the population. And it is not yet possible to prescribe a good general diet, although a bad one can be described and avoided. Acheson therefore prescribes caution. Don't knock high technology cures. Simple primary prevention is only useful for diseases of simple aetiology (usually infections) which are rarely likely to involve the NHS. Secondary protection is most important and here the NHS can help at least in theory, although in practice it cannot yet make a major contribution.

Jay Winter turns the question of performance indicators around to ask the central question of why and in what ways expectation of life has increased in England and Wales from this century up to the 1960s.

Contrary to expectation the two decades which include the First and the Second World Wars showed the greatest increase in civilian life expectation this century. Infectious (diarrhoeal) disease was responsible for most of the earlier decline, while a decline in respiratory disease is more important in the later decades (27 per cent of the total decline in women, and the infectious disease decline was only a third as important as in 1911–21).

The quasi-experimental position which two world wars imposed on British society, with their consequent contrasts in housing provision, medical care and the equality of food availability, make it possible to test theories on the political economy of health and welfare. McKeown's 'nutritional determinism' and its challenge by Preston, who claims that it minimises medical contributions by artificially narrowing the concept of medicine, are both judged too extreme, but data on cause of death, nutritional inputs and the level of medical care on the whole support McKeown's view more than Preston's. But both are deficient in the political dimension.

In the First World War the poorest families enjoyed the biggest improvements in mortality. In both world wars direct medical cover was substantially reduced – 60 per cent of the nation's doctors were serving in the Royal Army Medical Corps during the First World War. But food rationing improved the nutrition of the majority. This in particular helped to reduce diseases of gastro-intestinal origin. Respiratory disease nonetheless went up in the First War; a consequence of the wartime neglect of the housing stock and the unusual crowding together in factories experienced by a higher proportion of the population. A similar story applies in the Second World War except that penicillin and sulpha drugs made an impact in the later 1940s. Respiratory disease in particular declined. The country was living off its capital, and there was a striking redistribution of income to the working class. The buying power of poorer people is a neglected factor in theories which tend to concentrate on the aggregate resources rather than the ability of various sections of the population to gain access to them.

None of these papers specifically addressed the question of the effects on health of secular changes in average income – a peacetime analogue of the more severe crisis described by Winter – or the concomitant effects of unemployment, both of them relevant today. Some analysts (e.g. Brenner 1979) have claimed that the recession in the 1920s and 1930s worsened infant mortality and damaged a generation. However plausible that may seem, the effects of unemployment on health are in fact extremely difficult to unravel unequivocally (Stern 1983) and Brenner's claims seem to be poorly substantiated (Winter 1986). Both then and now general mortality – and indeed real incomes of those in employment – continue to improve. But the Longitudinal Study should enable attention to be focused on those out of work in a way which should put the answer beyond argument and is indeed beginning to show that unemployment leads to adverse effects upon health (Moser *et al.* 1986). This book has, unfortunately, no paper devoted to that topic. Neither can its papers claim to resolve all the questions they do consider. But it does indicate the great effort now being devoted by researchers into some of the most practically important as well as intellectually stimulating problems presented by the combination of modern medicine, modern affluence, democratic politics and the unique demography of the twentieth century.

References

Anderson, M. (1983) 'What is new about the modern family: an historical perspective', in *The Family* OPCS Occasional Paper no. 31 (London: Office of Population Censuses and Surveys).

Anderson, R. M. and May, R. M. (1985) 'Vaccination and herd immunity to infectious diseases', *Nature*, 318 (28 November) 323–9.

Black, Sir D., Norris, J. N., Smith, C. and Townsend, P. (1980) *Report of the Working Group on Inequalities in Health* (London: DHSS).

Brenner, M. H. (1979) 'Mortality and the national economy: a review and the experiences of England and Wales 1936–1976', *The Lancet* (September) 568.

Cherry, S. (1980a,b) 'The hospitals and population growth: the voluntary general hospitals, mortality and local populations in the English provinces in the 18th and 19th centuries, *Population Studies*, 36, 1, 59–76, 2, 251–66.

Coale, A. J. and Hoover, E. M. (1958) *Population Growth and Economic Development in Low-Income Countries* (Princeton, N.J.: Princeton University Press).

Coleman, D. A. and Schofield, R. S. (eds) (1986) *The State of Population Theory: Forward from Malthus* (Oxford: Blackwell).

Committee on Child Health Services (1976) *Fit for the Future: The Report of the Committee on Child Health Services* ('Court Report') Cmnd 6684 (London: HMSO).

Compton, P. A. (1985) 'Rising mortality in Hungary', *Population Studies*, 39, 71–86.

Craig, J. (1983) 'The growth of the elderly population', *Population Trends*, 32, 28–33.

Cummins, R. O., Shaper, A. G., Walker, M. and Wale, C. J. (1981) 'Smoking and drinking by middle-aged British men: effects of social class and town of residence', *British Medical Journal 283*, 1497–502.

Daykin, C. (1986) 'Projecting the population of the United Kingdom', *Population Trends*, 44, 28–33.

DHSS (1981a) *Avoiding Heart Attacks* (London: HMSO).

DHSS (1981b) *Drinking Sensibly* (London: HMSO).

DHSS (1984) *Population, Pension Costs and Pensioners' Incomes*. (A background paper for the inquiry into provision for retirement) (London: HMSO).

DHSS (1985a) *Committee on the Medical Aspects of Food Policy* (Report) (London: HMSO).

DHSS (1985b) *The Health Service in England, Annual Report* (London: HMSO).

Dinkel, R. H. (1985) 'The seeming paradox of increasing mortality in a highly industrialised nation; the example of the Soviet Union', *Population Studies*, 39, 1, 87–98.

Easterlin, R. A. (1980) *Birth and Fortune* (London: Grant McIntyre).

Ermisch, J. (1983) *The Political Economy of Demographic Change* (London: Heinemann).

Feshbach, M. (1982) 'The Soviet Union: population trends and dilemmas', *Population Bulletin*, 37, 3.

Gallup Poll, May, July, 1986.

Gardner, M. J., Winter, P. D., Taylor, C. P. and Acheson, E. D. (1983) *Atlas of Cancer Mortality in England and Wales 1968–1978* (London: John Wiley).

Goldacre, M. and Griffin, K. (1983) *Performance Indicators. A Commentary on the Literature* (Oxford: Oxford Unit of Clinical Epidemiology).

Gwatkin, D. R. (1986) 'Indications of change in developing country mortality trends. The end of an era?', *Population and Development Review*, 6, 203–12.

Harrison, G.A. (1982) 'Life-styles, well-being and stress', *Human Biology* 54, 2, 193–202.

Harrison, G. A. and Gibson, J. (1980) 'Urbanisation and Stress', in *Disease and Urbanisation*, ed. E. J. Clegg and J. P. Garlick (London: Taylor & Francis) 55–72.

House of Commons Expenditure Committee (1977) *Report on Preventive Medicine* (London: HMSO).

House of Commons Social Services Committee (1980) *Second Report. Perinatal and neonatal mortality* (Short Report) (London: HMSO).

Joseph, Sir Keith (1976) Report of speech given 29 June 1972 to the Conference of Pre-school Playgroups Association, in *Cycles of Disadvantage*, M. Rutter and N. Madge (London: Heinemann Educational Books).

Jozan, P. (1986) *Recent Mortality Trends in Eastern Europe.* Paper presented at the British Society for Population Studies conference 'Health for all in the year 2000: the case of Europe' (London: City University, 23 June).

Klein, R. (1983) *The Politics of the National Health Service* (Harlow: Longman).

Kuznets, S. (1973) *Population, Capital and Growth. Selected Essays* (New York: Norton).

Lewes, F. (1983) 'William Farr and cholera', *Population Trends*, 31, 8–12.

McKeown, T. (1976) *The Modern Rise of Population* (London: Arnold).

McKeown, T. (1979) *The Role of Medicine: Dreams, Mirage or Nemesis?* (Oxford: Basil Blackwell).

McKeown, T. and Brown, R. G. (1955) 'Medical evidence relating to English population changes in the eighteenth century', *Population Studies* IX, 119–41.

May, R. M. and Anderson, R. M. (1987) 'Transmission dynamics of HIV infection', *Nature*, 326, (12 March) 137–142.

Moser, K. A., Goldblatt, P. O., Fox, A. J. and Jones, D. R. (1986) *Unemployment and Mortality 1981–1983: Follow-up of the 1981 Longitudinal Study Census Sample.* Working Paper 43, Social Statistics Research Unit. The City University.

National Food Survey Committee (1985) *Household Food Consumption and Expenditure: 1983* (London: HMSO).

OPCS (1978) *Occupational Mortality 1970–1972.* Series DS No. 1 (London: HMSO).

OPCS (1979) *Area Mortality Tables: The Registrar General's Decennial Supplement for England and Wales 1969–1973.* Series DS No. 3 (London: HMSO).

OPCS (1981) *Cancer Statistics: Incidence, Survival and Mortality in England and Wales.* Studies in Medical and Population Subjects (London: HMSO).

OPCS (1983) *Drinking Behaviour and Attitudes in Great Britain*, Monitor SS.83/1. (London: HMSO).

OPCS (1984) *Adult Height and Weight Survey* (London: HMSO).

OPCS (1985a) *William Farr 1807–1883: Commemorative Symposium*, Occasional Paper No. 33 (London: OPCS).

OPCS (1985b) *Cigarette Smoking, 1972 to 1984*, Monitor GHS 85/2. (London: OPCS).

OPCS (1986a) *Cancer Survival 1979–1981 Registrations*, OPCS Monitor MB1 86/2 (London: OPCS).

OPCS (1986b) *Occupational Mortality for Great Britain, 1979–80, 1982–83*: Registrar General's Decennial Supplement Series DS No. 6 (London: HMSO).

Peto, R. (1980) 'Distorting the epidemiology of cancer: the need for a more balanced overview', *Nature* 284, 297–300.

Preston, S. (1976) *Mortality Patterns in National Populations with Special Reference to Recorded Causes of Death* (London: Academic Press).

Resource Allocations Working Party (RAWP) (1976) *Report: Sharing Resources for Health in England* (London: HMSO).

Shaper, A., Pocock, S. J., Walker, M. (1981) 'British regional heart study: cardiovascular risk factors in middle aged men in 24 towns', *British Medical Journal*, 283, 179–86.

Sigsworth, E. M. (1972) 'Gateways to death? Medicine, hospitals and mortality 1700–1850', in *Science and Society 1600–1900*, ed. P. Mathias (Cambridge: Cambridge University Press).

Slack, P. (1981) 'The disappearance of plague: an alternative view', *Economic History Review*, 34, 469–76.

Stern, J. (1983) 'The relationship between unemployment, morbidity and mortality in Britain', *Population Studies*, 37, 1, 61–74.

Szreter, S. (1986) *The Importance of Social Interaction in Britain's Mortality Decline c. 1850–1916: A Reinterpretation*, Centre for Economic Policy Research Discusssion Paper No. 121. (London: CEPR).

Townsend P. and Davidson N. (eds) (1982) *Inequalities in Health – the Black Report* (Harmondsworth: Penguin).

Winter, J. M. (1984) 'Unemployment, Nutrition and Infant Mortality in Britain 1920–1950', in *The Working Class in Modern British History*, ed. J. M. Winter (Cambridge: Cambridge University Press).

Part I

Economics, Poverty and Equality

2 Inheritance, Chance and Choice in the Transmission of Poverty

Nicola Madge

There can be little doubt that relative poverty stands among the most pervasive and fundamental social problems in Britain today. It has led to the despair, discomfort and humiliation of numerous adults and children, and also, as many would argue, it has contributed to a continuing and out-dated war between social classes, an increase in crime and delinquency, unprecedented levels of alcoholism and drug-taking, hostility between racial groups – and even rioting such as has occurred very recently in some parts of the country.

Life without much money can, for these and other reasons, be very grim indeed. *Who*, however, are we talking about? *Who* are the poor? What is it that determines *which* people and families have so much less in their basket of goods, as Rowntree put it, than the rest of us? The title of this paper, proposed by the organizers of the symposium, suggests three possible explanations which may be important either on their own or in combination. Perhaps inheritance – and by inheritance I am referring to both genetic and social inheritance – is partly responsible and some people with certain family backgrounds are heavily disadvantaged from the start. Alternatively, or possibly also, chance may play a significant role so that whether a person is poor or not is to some extent the luck of the draw. Thirdly, maybe it is neither determinism nor fate that plays the biggest part. Instead, it might be argued, there is a sense in which people make some choice about their economic status.

Is there any evidence to support the role of these three factors in the transmission of poverty?

Certainly there is widespread support for the possibility that inheritance may be involved. The 'cycle of poverty' thesis, according to which the poor tend to reproduce themselves from generation to generation so that poverty becomes a family problem concentrated within a small sub-group of society, is among the theories of poverty which have greatly interested social scientists and politicians alike. This is no new idea and the notion stemmed quite strongly from the early Eugenics Movement in the late nineteenth and early twentieth centuries. Sir Francis Galton was at that time very concerned about the reproduction of the unfit, and established registers of both what he called 'noteworthy' families and families who, he thought, should not be allowed to reproduce (Galton 1880). In this intellectual climate, Henry Goddard published a book in 1912 entitled *The Kallikak Family* (Goddard 1912), which seemingly endorsed the view of Galton and others. In his book, Goddard tells the story of Martin Kallikak who produced two lines of descendants, one the result of dallying with a feeble-minded girl from a local tavern, and the other through his marriage to an upright Quaker girl from a 'thoroughly respectable' family. Needless to say, the tavern girl gave birth to a rascal son who in turn produced 'paupers, criminals, prostitutes, drunkards and all forms of social pest with which modern society is burdened'. Equally unsurprisingly, the Quaker wife was the mother of useful citizens, prominent in all walks of life.

It is interesting how widespread these ideas were, and how their influence spread through the attention paid to them by nineteenth century novelists. Emile Zola, for instance, devoted twenty novels to studying the effects of heredity and environment on the members of a family, in a series entitled *Les Rougon-Macquart. Histoire naturelle et sociale d'une famille sous le Second Empire.* (Zola 1869–93). In these, he stressed the role of physiological determinism and illustrated the contrasts between the legitimate and illegitimate branches of the family, the Rougons and the Macquarts respectively. Although all members of the family as a whole shared voracious appetites for life, the former were intelligent, energetic and generally successful in life whereas the latter, who resulted from two lines of unstable and neurotic ancestors, were violent, criminal, lunatic and generally undesirable characters.

Similar notions have continued to attract the popular imagination. They have recently been reinforced by, for example, the well-publicised and detailed anthropological studies of small numbers of families in Puerto Rica and Mexico and elsewhere carried out by Oscar Lewis (e.g. 1959, 1961, 1966). Lewis's observations led him to claim that poverty is self-perpetuating within families and sub-cultures because children from poor families are exposed to common experiences and so come to share the values and attitudes of their parents. Indeed, he argued, sub-cultural influences are so strong that children cease to be affected by changing circumstances and opportunities once they reach the age of only about six or seven years.

Science in a broader sense, too, has contributed to the debate by carrying out large-scale empirical enquiries to establish how far poverty and income level are transmitted across family generations. One approach has been the direct investigation of heritability and another has been to examine social mechanisms in the hope that implications for social policy might emerge. The United States Government, for example, paid considerable homage to the idea in their 1964 War on Poverty legislative programme (see Moynihan, 1969) when they noted that 'the vicious cycle, in which poverty breeds poverty, occurs through time, and transmits its effects from one generation to another'. And in Britain the 'cycle of deprivation' thesis has recently come under close scrutiny since Sir Keith Joseph, as Secretary of State for Social Services in June 1972, pointed to the fact that social problems had not disappeared despite marked improvements in prosperity and community services since the Second World War (Joseph 1972). He suggested that many such problems, among them poverty, might be passed on from generation to generation through the family, and he set up a massive research programme to investigate this possibility. The European Community, too, has placed a significant emphasis on the notion of poverty persisting within families in the major poverty programme it has undertaken (Commission of the European Communities 1981).

It is significant to note how, in most of these examples, poverty in terms of a low income and poverty in terms of a range of social deprivations have come to be linked. This is really not surprising as there is a strong tendency for disadvantage to be cumulative. Berthoud (1983) has illustrated this empirically by an analysis of 1975 General Household Survey data to determine the overlap between deprivation in education (head of family left school at minimum age *and* had no formal qualifications), family (lone parent *or* divorced/separated *or* four or more children), housing (more than one person per room *or* lacked sole use of kitchen, bath/shower or inside WC), income (below 140 per cent of Supplementary Benefit entitlement), health (head of family long-term ill *or* currently not working through sickness), and work (head of family a semi or unskilled worker *or* unemployed *or* earned less than £30 per week full-time). Overall, Berthoud found a marked tendency for problems to go together so that people were more likely to be not deprived in any of these areas or deprived in several than they were to be deprived in just one or two. Thus, compared with the situation if problems had been randomly distributed, somewhat more people than expected had no problems at all (23.6 per cent v. 14.9 per cent), slightly fewer than expected had one, two or three problems (67.6 per cent v. 81.5 per cent) and rather more than expected had four, five or six problems (8.8 per cent v. 3.6 per cent). Financial circumstances were, moreover, fundamental to multiple deprivation as the risks of further problems were greatest for families disadvantaged in income or work.

Even if poverty is linked to social deprivation more generally, can we not study its transmission in the narrower sense? In other words, what have we learned from research about the genetic and social inheritance of income level *per se*? The answer, unfortunately, is very little.

This is undoubtedly true of studies of direct genetic inheritance which – and discounting Cyril Burt's contribution – are few and far between. The largest and most widely-reported study of this kind examined income and occupation in over 2000 pairs of American adult male twins and calculated heritability values which, although smaller than those generally found for intelligence, suggested some influence of genetics on income and occupation (Taubman *et al.* 1978). Reanalysis of these data by Fulker (1978) led to the further conclusion that any genetic association was likely to be due to the inheritance of temperament and specific abilities rather than intelligence. All the same, effects were small, and the research methodology has been severely criticised (Goldberger 1979). The findings, therefore, can be considered as no more than suggestive.

Few definitive conclusions emerge, either, from studies which, instead of looking *within* a generation, have looked *across* family generations. The problems of collecting useful data of this kind are enormous – even gaining comparable information at a similar stage in the life-cycle of both parents and their children can be a formidable task – and probably account for the paucity of findings. Rutter and Madge noted in 1976 that there was at that time really only one study that directly compared the incomes of fathers and their sons. This had been carried out by Soltow (1965) and referred to a static population of 115 pairs of fathers and their sons in one city in Norway. Its findings clearly have very limited generality, but it is still noteworthy that only a weak association emerged between net income in successive generations and that this was statistically insignificant even when the analysis was restricted to a sub-sample in which the ages of men in the two generations were matched and where income levels were dichotomised simply into high and low. Most of the other evidence commonly mentioned in support of cycles of poverty stemmed from anecdote, studies of poor communities (such as those written about by Oscar Lewis), and comparisons of earnings in one generation and some proxy for income – usually occupational status – in another. It seemed from all this that not much could really be said at that time (which was only some ten years ago) about cycles of poverty, and certainly there was – apart from popular imagination – little to support widespread cultures of income poverty, especially in Britain.

Some repair to this poor state of empirical knowledge was, none-theless, made by the programme of research on Transmitted Deprivation instigated by Sir Keith Joseph (see Brown and Madge 1982). In particular, Atkinson, Maynard and Trinder (1983) carried out a detailed follow-up study of the children of men studied by Rowntree and Lavers (1951) in York approximately a generation earlier. As good information on income was available on both generations at similar points in the life-cycle, inter-generational similarities could be fairly directly investigated. A less than clear picture emerged, however, as cases of family similarities were matched by plentiful examples of family change. Although the children of parents with income levels below the National Assistance scale (the poverty line drawn by Rowntree and Lavers) were one and a half times more likely to have low incomes (i.e. below the Supplementary Benefit level) than if there had been perfect income mobility across the generations, and half as likely to be 'comfortably off' (i.e. with incomes at or above 240 per cent of the Supplementary Benefit level), it was still by no means true that income levels in one generation predicted those in the next. Further data from this study are presented by Professor Shorrocks see p. 66). Atkinson and colleagues pointed to the fact that their findings suggested neither complete earnings mobility nor immobility across generations. They were, nonetheless, impressed by the conti-nuities they found, especially when these were examined alongside comparable relationships between education and other factors in successive generations. Interestingly, these were stronger at the higher than at the lower end of the income distribution.

The lack of a consistent relationship between the income of fathers and their sons raises the question of what affects inheritance. There is no space here to examine this in detail, but it does seem that influences range from the individual to the societal. At one extreme, personal characteristics such as IQ – which is probably the result of both genetic and environmental factors – are likely to be significant. Mascie-Taylor and Gibson's (1978) study of 85 father-son pairs showed that social mobility (a proxy for income mobility) was least where fathers and sons had similar IQs but increased steadily as the ability gap widened. And at the other extreme society and its structure are implicated. Easterlin (1980) suggests that time of birth makes a difference. He points out how whether one is born poor or rich has always been important in determining life chances but how, in the post-World War II economy, this has to be measured against the size of a generation. He describes the lower earnings, more unemployment, poorer career advancement and greater pressures on family life encountered by people born during a baby boom relative to those born when the national birth rate is low. According to his theory, these patterns encourage inter-generational change as parents in a prosperous generation tend to have large numbers of children who face greater competition and experience more poverty than they themselves had and who, in turn, have fewer children who then find it easier to achieve success . . . and so on. These and other theories and empirical data all lead to the same conclusion, namely that inheritance is only part of the story when it comes to the transmission of poverty.

Chance factors in the transmission of poverty are even more difficult to examine and draw conclusions about than inheritance. Intuitively, however, they would seem to play some role. On the one hand, the failure of empiricism to predict an individual's economic status with any confidence – even though 'risk' factors such as educational achievement, family background, occupational history, age, and so on can be quite successfully documented – attest to this view. Chance factors, by their very nature, will not be the same for everybody and thus there are no laws what they might be. They are illustrated best by personal biographies or case studies and operate where, for instance, an accident at work, a family bereavement or a pools win makes a major difference to income. As there is no universal pattern an illustration from a fictionalized account of real events is as good as any other, and the television play *Cathy Come Home* describes well what can happen. In this example a father's illness set up a vicious cycle of disadvantage resulting in job loss, homelessness and, eventually, marital breakdown and the reception of children into care. In other words a chance happening set off a chain of events resulting in poverty and deprivation.

Health is probably one of the more important personal characteristics mediating a relationship between chance and poverty. Nevertheless other factors are important too. *When* and *where* a person lives, for example, are also elements of chance which help to determine the opportunities likely to be available. Compare, for instance, the life chances of somebody seeking to establish himself in an occupation in the South of the country during the prosperous 1950s when we 'never had it so good' with someone in the North in the 1980s where the chances of unemployment and low wage levels are particularly high.

Finally, choice. Do people make choices which affect their income, and do any such choices play a part in the transmission of poverty?

In answer to the first part of this question, there are probably very few people at any income level who *never* make a choice which has a direct or indirect impact on their relative poverty. Many choices are indeed hard to avoid. Patterns of saving and expenditure and lifestyle are, for instance, rarely fully determined. Nor, too, are choices regarding family size, the selection of a marriage partner (e.g. with better or worse income prospects), and decisions about marital separation and divorce. Most people, moreover, have some degree of control over where they live, and whether they pursue opportunities for education and training. Some, too, may have the option to work or not to work, or may be in a position where they can decide to accept a job with a wage or salary below the level they could command.

Beyond this there may be some people who, by choice, make substantial changes to their lifestyle. Only very few will rise from humble origins to become millionaires, but many more will swap these same humble origins for middle-class comfort and respectability. Such mobility almost always reflects some degree of personal decision, typically the combination of clear goals and the determination, opportunity, dedication and ability to meet them.

Do these aspects of personal choice, however, imply that choice significantly influences the transmission of poverty? The answer can be 'yes' in a meaningful sense only if similar levels of choice are available to everybody. In other words choice does not really exist unless the poor have as many opportunities for self-determination as the better-off. Choice, in turn, implies equality of opportunity which, according to Tawney (1964), applies ' . . . in so far as, and only in so far as, each member of a community, whatever his birth, or occupation, or social position, possesses in fact, and not merely in form, equal chances of using to the full his natural endowments of physique, of character, and of intelligence'.

On these strict criteria it is unlikely that choice is a strong force in the transmission of poverty even if it does have *marginal* effects on personal and family income level. Freedom and decision-making are much more possible with greater than fewer assets – such as a house that can be sold, personal transport that can be used to take advantage of opportunities of many kinds, sufficient solvency to allow time to find a 'suitable' and not just the first job available, or to allow a financial mistake to be made – and it is hard to see how the exercise of choice can do anything other than tamper with the distribution of income and poverty. Even if one can choose to be poor, can one choose not to be poor?

These notions of inheritance, chance and choice, then, have some validity, but none tells the whole story. People *are* affected by their genetic and social inheritance, but many are influenced more strongly by other characteristics and experiences they may have. Chance, too, is worth mentioning, not least because it gives the poor hope that they may strike good fortune and escape from their dreary lot, even though on its own it is unlikely to explain much. Choice appears to be even less important for the transmission of poverty within the population as a whole.

Why do these factors not explain more? Perhaps the answer lies in the fact that these three types of explanation have one important element in common. They all imply that there is not much that can be done about poverty *except*, perhaps, by the poor themselves. Inheritance lays the blame with the family, choice suggests that the poor are responsible for their own fate, and chance implies that life is a lottery. Should other possibilities, then, be taken seriously?

Whether or not they *should* be, they only *will* be if they fit in with current social perceptions. And there have always been cycles of attitudes to the poor. They have been regarded as undeserving and as deserving, and they have been used to fuel genetic and cultural arguments as well as to found the Welfare State (see Brown and Madge 1982). Moreover their role has been seen as important in society – to serve as scapegoats, to do the dirty work, and to provide an example of what can happen to those who do not toe the line – just as it has been deplored. Even in the current climate there are ambiguous and mixed reactions to the poor.

I would suggest that we will not get very far in achieving any meaningful and motivated initiative to reduce or eliminate poverty today unless we clarify and make explicit what we really think about poverty as a social problem. Even then we will not get very far unless we are prepared to admit that society plays its role in determining the opportunities, social conditions and economic circumstances to which different people are exposed. It is not good enough to say to the almost one in four families currently living in or on the margins of poverty that they lack money because of their genetic and/or social background, because that is what they have chosen, or because they are suffering from plain bad luck. Inheritance, chance and choice are only one side of the picture. Society and its policies and sense of justice are the other.

References

Atkinson, A. B., Maynard, A. K. and Trinder, C. G. (1983) *Parents and Children: Incomes in Two Generations* (London: Heinemann Educational).

Berthoud, R. (1983) 'Who suffers social disadvantage?' in *The Structure of Deprivation*, ed. M. Brown (London: Heinemann Educational).

Brown, M. and Madge, N. (1982) *Despite the Welfare State* (London: Heinemann Educational).

Commission of the European Communities (1981) *Final Report from the Commission to the Council on the First Programme of Pilot Schemes and Studies to Combat Poverty* (Brussels).

Easterlin, R. A. (1980) *Birth and Fortune* (London: Grant McIntyre).

Fulker, D. W. (1978) 'Multivariate extensions of a biometrical model of twin data', in *Twin Research: Psychology and Methodology*, ed. W. E. Nance (New York: Alan R. Liss).

Galton. F. (1880) *Pocket Register for Anthropological Purposes* (Swansea: British Association Report).

Goddard, H. H. (1925) *The Kallikak Family* (New York: Macmillan).

Goldberger, A. S. (1979) 'Heritability' *Economica*, 46, 327–47.

Joseph, Sir Keith (1972) '*The Cycle of Deprivation*', Speech at Conference of Pre-School Playgroups Association, 29 June.

Lewis, O. (1959) *Five Families* (New York: Basic Books).

Lewis, O. (1961) *The Children of Sanchez* (New York: Random House).

Lewis, O. (1966) *La Vida* (New York: Random House).

Mascie, C. G. N. and Gibson, J. B. (1978) 'Social mobility and IQ components', *Journal of Biosocial Science*, 10, 263–76.

Moynihan, D. P. (1969) *On Understanding Poverty* (New York: Basic Books).

Rowntree, B. S. and Lavers, G. R. (1951) *Poverty and the Welfare State* (London: Longman).

Rutter, M. and Madge, N. (1976) *Cycles of Disadvantage* (London: Heinemann Educational).

Soltow, L. (1965) *Towards Income Equality in Norway* (Madison, Wis.: University of Wisconsin Press).

Taubman, P., Behrman, J. and Wales, T. (1978) 'The roles of genetics and environment in the distribution of earnings', in *Income Distribution and Economic Inequality*, ed. Z. Griliches, W. Krelle, H.-J. Krupp and O. Kyn (New York: Halstead Press).

Tawney, R. H. (1964) *Equality* (London: Allen & Unwin, new edn.).

Zola, E. (1869–93) *Les Rougon-Macquart. Histoire Naturelle et Sociale d'une Famille sous le Second Empire.* First book (pre-1870) *La Fortune des Rougon*; last book (1893) *Les Docteur Pascal* (Paris: Charpentier).

3 Poverty as a Determinant of Inequality

Partha Dasgupta

1. UTILITY VERSUS WORK CAPACITY

Two aspects of man have successively dominated the thinking of social philosophers over the past two centuries, each true in itself but sadly incomplete without the other. One sees him as a biological entity, a machine, an engine, capable of effort and work for which he requires fuel in the form of food and nourishment. The other sees him as a seat of 'utility' or 'satisfaction', possessing desires and aspirations which need to be fulfilled. Classical Political Economy, developed in the early stages of the industrial revolution, emphasised the first. The idea of a 'minimum subsistence wage' occurs in David Ricardo's writings, just as it does in the writings of Robert Malthus. It is however the latter aspect which has dominated social thought over the past hundred years and more. This too is understandable. With rising wealth in the industrializing economies the basic necessities of life were being met for the majority of the population. What remained of concern were the "higher pleasures". (For a thorough account of this see A. K. Dasgupta 1985.)

In the sense that I have distinguished these two aspects of man, political economy this century has for the overwhelming part been thoroughly 'utilitarian' in character. Individuals are seen as having preferences – which, to be sure, are seen as being socially conditioned – they choose from what are available to them, and their choice affects their welfare, their sense of well-being. The point I am trying to make here is not so much that individual choice is necessarily dictated exclusively by preference, or that what is chosen from the available set of options necessarily maximises the individual's sense of well-being, for both would be false claims. Rather, I am making the point that individuals make their appearance in economic models as seats of 'utility'; their capacity to work and to produce labour power is raw data, unexplained by theory. Thus, in what I shall call the standard model, an individual is seen as choosing some combination of consumption goods and leisure in the face of market

36

prices of commodities and work. The study of 'inequality' as a result reduces to a study of the inequality of 'utility' across people or, to have an operational account, a study of the inequality in *income*. The theory says nothing about the basic necessities of life and what transpires if food intake falls short of required needs. In short, the link between food intake and work capacity is for the most part absent in economics.

To locate the link one is tempted to turn to Classical Political Economy. But the picture portrayed there is woefully inadequate. For example, in his famous chapter on wages David Ricardo begins by saying: 'the natural price of labour is that price which is necessary to enable the labourers, one with another, to *subsist* and to perpetuate their race, without either increase or diminution' (Ricardo 1911, p. 52; emphasis added). This suggests a demographic principle, namely that the rate of population growth is dependent on the wage rate and that there is a critical, or threshold, wage, say w_0, at which population growth is nil. Viewing the matter over the long haul, including future generations, w_0 is the subsistence wage. Any wage below this spells doom for the labour force. But over the short and medium run the theory says nothing. It does not postulate anything about a person's capabilities for *work*. It is mostly a theory concerning a person's propensity to *breed*.

2. UNDERNOURISHMENT AS A PHENOMENON

The science of nutrition has shown that the matter is a great deal more complex and that we can say much more. Survival, and not just short-run survival, does not on its own say all that is needed about a person's raw productive capacity. A person can stay alive and remain undernourished. Indeed, there are different kinds and different degrees of undernourishment. Food-adequacy-standards depend on the climate, are activity-specific and person-specific. They depend on a person's prior nutrition-status. Moreover, a person's metabolic efficiency in the *use* of energy adjusts, up to a point, to alterations in his energy intake. Put another way, there are multiple metabolic equilibria for a person; in particular, even hungry people operate sometimes with 'metabolic slack' (see in particular, Sukhatme 1978, 1982). All of this makes the problem immensely complex.

The general effects of malnutrition vary widely. In children they are especially severe. It can cause muscle wastage and growth retardation (thus future capability), increased illness and vulnerability to infection. There is evidence that it can affect brain growth and development. Chronic malnutrition in adults diminishes their muscular strength, disease protection and the capacity to work. Persons suffering thus are readily fatigued. There are also marked psychological changes, manifested by mental apathy, depression, introversion and lower intellectual capacity (see e.g. Read 1977). Life expectancy among the malnourished is low, but not nil. Such people do not face immediate death. Malnutrition is this side of starvation. For this reason the world can and does carry a stock of undernourished people, living and breeding in impaired circumstances. The science of nutrition is a difficult one. But none of the complexity should obscure the fact that the concept of food-adequacy-standard for a person is an operationally meaningful one and that a nutrition status falling short of it implies impairment in a person's capacity to work due to illness or plain weakness.

Thus, even by the most conservative of estimates well over four hundred million people in the world are thought to be seriously undernourished today, (see e.g. Sukhatme 1978 and Lipton 1983). These estimates are based on calorie deficiency in the diet and so are on the conservative side, for a food-adequacy-standard must meet other requirements as well, such as protein, vitamins, carbohydrates and minerals. The problem of malnutrition is acute and widespread in low-income countries.

3.   POVERTY AND INEQUALITY

In this essay I wish to address the issue of inequality in food and work allocations both within a household and across households in the context of a formal construct which builds on the fact that at low nutrition levels there is a positive association between food intake and the capacity to work. In the following section, where household allocations will be discussed, I shall argue that absolute poverty is doubly pernicious, in the sense that a poor family not only has to make do with little, it is also forced to share its poverty unequally among its members, even if it is egalitarian in outlook. Intra-family inequality in nutrition-status has been much documented in developing countries. The arguments in Section 4 below will provide a possible explanation for this. But the empirical literature has also noted that the brunt of the deprivation falls on female members (see e.g. Miller 1971). I do not know if there is an 'economic' reason for this gender-bias.

The discussion in Section 4 is restricted to a single decision unit: the family, or household. In Section 5 therefore I will look briefly at inter-family transactions via the familiar competitive market mechanism. It will be seen, in contrast to conventional economic theory, how under a wide range of circumstances inequality in opportunity and income is created among persons or families who, to begin with, possess equal potential. I should add that the mechanism which generates this inequality does *not* rely on exogenous chance factors. Inequality is created by the labour market which does not clear and thus resorts to rationing, that is, some are employed and are adequately nourished while others are kept out in the cold and are malnourished. (The wage does not fall to clear the market as in conventional economic models.) I will finally argue that this inequality has a tendency to reinforce itself: those who are initially at an advantage by having found employment gain cumulatively, possibly widening inequality in both income and nutrition status.

4. INEQUALITY IN POOR HOUSEHOLDS, OR, THE LIFEBOAT ETHIC

The point I want to develop is in its simplest form an implication of what social philosophers call 'lifeboat ethics'. Two people, stranded in a lifeboat, have enough food for precisely one. Equal sharing guarantees starvation for both. What should they do? The utilitarian answer, should the persons be similar, is to draw lots on who should throw himself overboard. Indeed, in recent months the need for unequal division of consumption because of minimum survival requirements has been demonstrated in a most terrifying manner by relief workers in famine-stricken Ethiopia.

If the decision on who should throw himself overboard in the lifeboat example is made on the toss of a fair coin there is equality, in the *ex-ante* sense: each person has equal chance of survival. But *ex-post*, that is, after the coin has shown its face, the treatment meted out is highly unequal.

Notice that this result depends critically on there not being enough for two: the lifeboat has only a small provision. If instead, there were sufficient food for both any egalitarian principle, such as utilitarian-ism, would recommend that the food be shared equally; that is, that there be *ex-post* equality.

This example brings out the essence of the general point I am trying to establish here; that absolute poverty is a cause of some of the inequality we observe. A poor family cannot even afford the luxury of equality. A rich family can. The example's limitation lies in that total available provision is given, it is not produced. Moreover, the options are survival and death, not alternative states of survival. Both these restrictions are removed in the model to which I now turn.

I begin by distinguishing labour *time* from labour *power* and observe that it is the latter which is an input in the production of goods and services. Suppose that in a given period the amount of labour power an individual can supply, or, to put it another way, the number of *tasks* of a certain basic unit the person can perform is functionally related to his food intake in the manner drawn in Figure 3.1 below, where c is his food intake and $k(c)$ is the maximum number of tasks he can perform. The key features of the functional relationship $k(c)$ are that it is positive but small and increases gently at low consumption levels, that it increases at a fairly accelerating rate at about the person's food adequacy standard and that it then

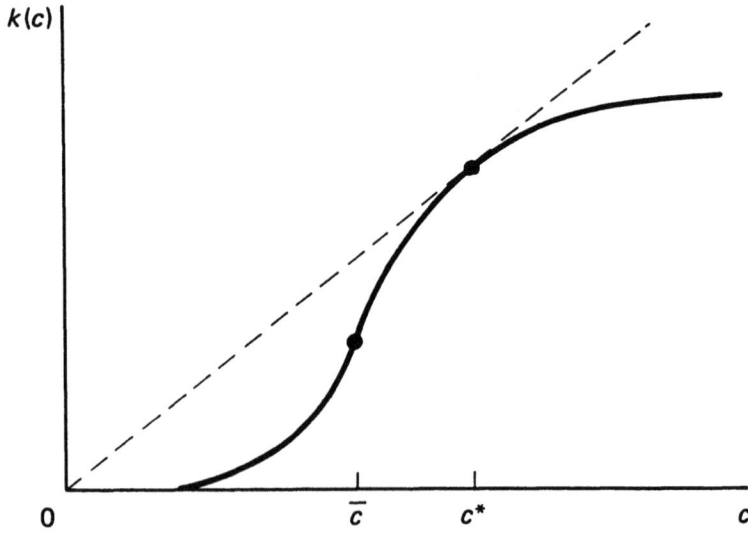

Figure 3.1   Food-productivity curve for an individual

flattens out, so that there are no biological advantages to further consumption. (I am ignoring obesity, since it is of no consequence to our analysis.)

Let c^* be the level of consumption at which average productivity per unit of consumption equals marginal productivity (as in Figure 3.1). Thus c^* is the solution of the equation $k(c)/c = dk(c)/dc$. For simplicity of exposition I want to assume that this curve is really steep just to the left of c^* (as shown) and that it is nearly flat almost immediately after, rather like a smooth approximation to a step-function. It would be as though c^* is a threshold level, and so is certainly the food-adequacy standard. Finally let $\bar{c}$ be the inflexion point of the curve, or the point at which $d^2k(c)/dc^2 = 0$.

Consider now a family of N members owning a small plot of cultivable land. If $c_i(i = 1, \ldots, N)$ is that i^{th} member's consumption level, $k(c_i)$ is the number of tasks he can perform. Assume that total output of food from the family plot is then given by the function $F(\Sigma k(c_i))$, where F is drawn in Figure 3.2 below. $F(\cdot)$ is an increasing function and it is assumed to increase at a decreasing rate since the family plot is fixed in size.

For simplicity of exposition I want to think of a timeless framework so that total family consumption is no greater than household

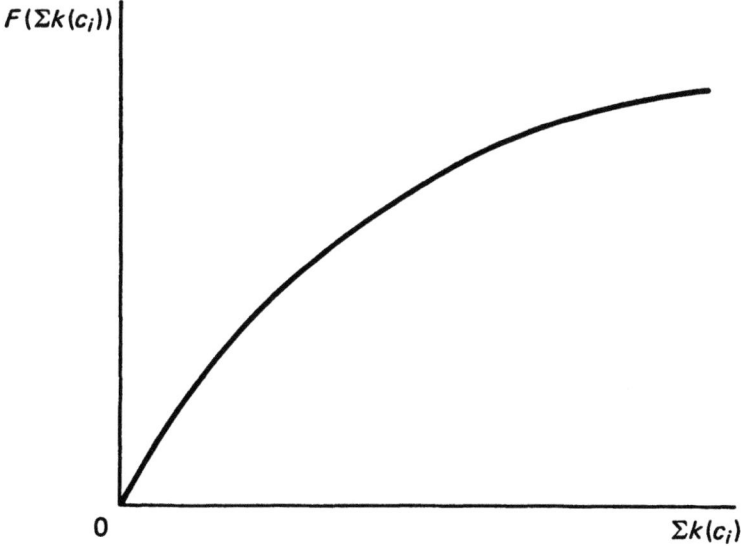

Figure 3.2   Household production function

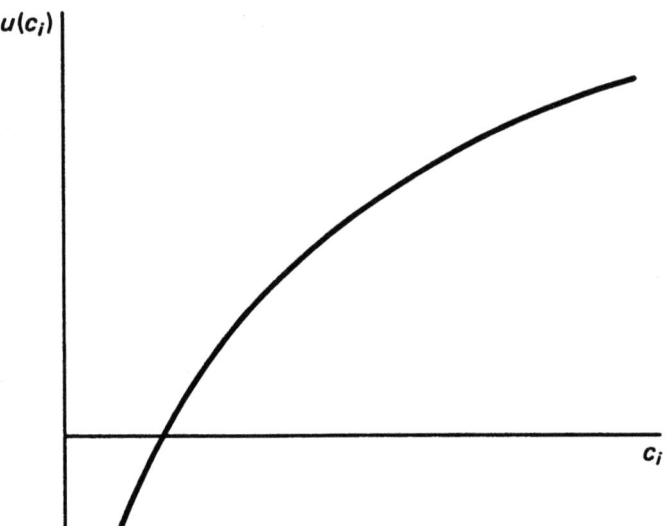

Figure 3.3   Individual utility function

production. (I am also assuming that there are no employment opportunities outside the family farm.) Family members are identical in their needs and tasks and I assume that the utility that member i derives from c_i is $u(c_i)$ where the utility function is drawn in Figure 3.3. Here, $u(c_i)$ is an increasing function of c_i and I take it, as did the classical utilitarians, that is increases at a diminishing rate.

The family is thoroughly utilitarian in its philosophy. It makes interpersonal comparisons blatantly. Thus it wants to solve the following food-allocation problem: it wants to choose $c_i(i=1,\ldots,N)$ so as to maximize $\sum_{i=1}^{N} u(c_i)$ subject to the leasibility constraint

$$\sum_{i=1}^{N} c_i \leqslant F\left[\sum_{i=1}^{N} k(c_i) \right]. \tag{1}$$

I want to consider the case of a poor family, that is, I want to assume that the family plot is small. By this I mean that food output F attains 'moderate' values only at relatively 'large' doses of labour power, or in other words, 'large' values of $\sum_{i=1}^{N} k(c_i)$. To be precise I want to suppose that the plot size is so small that it is not feasible to provide each member with a consumption level equal to or in excess of $\bar{c}$. This means that at least one member must consume less than $\bar{c}$. Given this it cannot be optimal to award all family members with the same nutrition-status. The reason is that with at least one member consuming less than $\bar{c}$, aggregate family *production* and thus total family welfare can be enhanced by differential treatment. In fact, a little reflection will show that the utilitarian-optimal allocation is to establish *two* nutrition norms in the family, say $\bar{c}$ and $\hat{c}$, award one group of family members with the nutrition status $\bar{c}$ each and the remaining group $\hat{c}$ each. Of course, by assumption, at least one group must be consuming below $\bar{c}$.

If on the other hand, the family plot is 'large', specifically, if it is feasible to award a nutrition status to each member at least as large as c^*, it will be a utilitarian-optimum to award all members the same consumption level. This follows from the assumption of diminishing marginal utility of consumption for each member *and* the assumption that all members *can* be fed at least to the extent of c^*, so that there are no *production* gains from differential treatment. I conclude that, as in the lifeboat example, a poor family is forced to mete out unequal nutrition treatment among its members.

5. UNEQUAL TREATMENT IN THE MARKET

Thus far an explanation of unequal treatment in poor families. But what happens in the market? In the standard economic model, like people are treated similarly by the market. People are considered identical if they have the same attitudes (i.e. same preferences) and own identical endowments of goods and services. In this case identical people face identical market opportunities. Given that preferences are the same, they choose identical baskets of goods and services.

The matter is a good deal more complex if we introduce the food-productivity curve of Figure 3.1 as an ingredient in our analysis of the market (for details of what follows, see Dasgupta and Ray 1986, 1987a). To see this, suppose there are a large number of landless (more generally, assetless) labourers. If such a person finds employment in the labour market his consumption is dependent wholly on his wages: he has by definition no non-wage income. Let us assume that if he does not find employment he survives by begging or by doing odd jobs and so forth, which keeps him malnourished; that is, his consumption is then less than c^*.

Consider now a profit maximising firm. It will wish to minimise its labour cost. What wage would it *ideally like* to offer a landless labourer? Not nil, because in this case the labourer will be useless in production (see Figure 3.1). If labour power is the input in production, the firm will ideally wish to pay the workers the wage at which the wage per unit of the worker's labour power is minimised, for at such a wage labour cost is minimised. If c is the wage then the firm would wish to minimise $c/k(c)$. But this is minimised at c^* (Figure 3.1). This is the worker's *efficiency wage* (see Mirrlees 1975, and Dasgupta and Ray 1986). If there are lots of firms, each will wish to offer landless workers the wage c^*. Given demand conditions for the firms' products presumably there is an aggregate market demand for landless labourers at c^*. Suppose this happens to be less than the total number of landless labourers. In the standard economic model there would be no wedge between demand and supply of labour since the wage would adjust. But in our economy this will not happen. No firm will lower the wage below c^*, since to do so would not be cost minimising.

But at c^* all landless labourers want to work – the alternatives of begging and so forth by hypothesis are less rewarding. So there is rationing in the labour market, for example by the use of a lottery, so that the number of workers employed precisely equals the number demanded in the market. The remaining workers are forced to beg. There is differential treatment of identical people. Inequality is created among them not *because* of chance factors – chance may be *used* to decide who gets a job, as in the case of a lottery – but because the market cannot 'afford' to employ all: total demand for landless workers is not large enough.

Notice that should a fair lottery be in use to determine who are employed, the market, like the fair coin in the lifeboat problem, metes out *ex-ante* equality. It is *ex-post* that the workers are divided into two groups: the employed and the unemployed. Now suppose the economy remains at a stationary state and suppose in every period a fair lottery is used. Then over the long haul each of these landless workers will be employed the same *number* of periods. (For example, if in each period 20 per cent of the landless workers are unemployed then in the long run each landless worker will be employed approximately 80 per cent of the time.) So then it would seem that once we introduce *time* into the analysis (approximate) equality of treatment reappears, even *ex-post*. Well, not really. If we introduce time, which we certainly should, we should introduce *history*. Suppose then, and the nutrition literature supports this, that a person's nutrition status in one period affects his productive potential the next period, even if ever so slightly. Thus a person with a better nutrition history has a higher value of k for every current level of consumption. Suppose the landless are all identical to begin with, just as we have been assuming so far. In the first period a fraction will be employed. Which particular people we cannot tell in advance because a fair lottery is in use. There is thus *ex-ante* equality. But in the next period the previously employed enjoy a slight advantage because of their better nutrition history. From then almost all of those who were previously employed will again find employment and all of those who languished in the first period, through bad luck, will continue to languish, no longer through bad luck but through the remorseless logic of cumulative causation. I conclude that once you introduce time a person's history can be pernicious. *Ex-post*, people who are identical in all relevant respects emerge with vastly differential opportunities and realisations, not through the usual chance factors, but by the weight of sheer economic logic in a poor environment.

6. CONCLUSIONS

In this essay I have argued that absolute poverty and inequality appear to be intrinsically linked in that poverty is itself a cause of some of the inequality that we observe in low income countries. In the case of a single decision unit, as in a household, unequal food and work allocation among members who are otherwise similar, can arise simply because of poverty. The economic logic is a generalisation of the lifeboat ethic (Section 4). In the market as well such unequal treatment arises when there is insufficient demand for labour. The real wage does not fall when nutrition intake affects a worker's productivity in the form of Figure 3.1. Here, too, insufficiency in demand can arise, not because the economy as a whole is desperately poor, but because there are too many landless persons; that is, too many people who are poor in assets (Section 5). The logic of the market-place is, to be sure, different from the logic operating within a household. But as regards the idea that absolute poverty is a cause of some of the inequality that we see in parts of the world, the two institutions would seem to be similar.

Notes

The literature using a food-productivity relation to obtain insights into labour and food allocation processes in poor economies is still lamentably small. Leibenstein (1957) was the first to use the idea in recent years to discuss poverty traps. The analysis of the household presented in Section 4 is based on the important work of Mirrlees (1975), that of the market Section 5 on Dasgupta and Ray (1986, 1987a) which presents a substantial number of additional results. The empirical literature on food-productivity relations is a lively one, since it is the basis upon which (absolute) poverty lines are drawn. It is therefore the basis upon which the incidence of malnutrition is assessed. Many of the articles addressing these empirical questions were published in *The Economic and Political Weekly* (Bombay). For a detailed discussion of the biological evidence, see Dasgupta and Ray (1987b).

References

Dasgupta, A. K. (1985) *Epochs of Economic Theory* (Oxford: Basil Blackwell).
Dasgupta, P. and Ray, D. (1986) 'Inequality as a Determinant of Malnutrition and Unemployment: Theory', *Economic Journal*, 96, 1011–34.
Dasgupta, P. and Ray, D. (1987a) 'Inequality as a Determinant of Malnutrition and Unemployment: Policy', *Economic Journal*, 97, 177–88.
Dasgupta, P. and Ray, D. (1987b) 'Adapting to Undernourishment: The Biological Evidence and its Implications', forthcoming, in J. Dreze and A. Sen (eds), *Poverty and Hunger: The Poorest Billion* (Oxford University Press).
Leibenstein, H. (1957) *Economic Backwardness and Economic Growth* (London and New York: John Wiley).
Lipton, M. (1983) *Poverty, Undernutrition and Hunger*, World Bank Staff Working Paper No. 597 (Washington, D.C.: World Bank).
Miller, B. (1971) *The Endangered Sex: Neglect of Female Children in Rural North India* (Ithaca, N.Y.: Cornell University Press).
Mirrlees, J. A. (1975) 'A pure theory of underdeveloped economies' in *Agriculture in Development Theory*, ed. L. Reynolds (New Haven, Conn.: Yale University Press).
Read, M. S. (1977) 'Malnutrition and human performance' in *Malnutrition, Behaviour and Social Organization* (New York and London: Academic Press).
Ricardo, D. (1911) *The Principles of Political Economy and Taxation* (London: Dent).
Sukhatme, P. (1978) 'Assessment of adequacy of diets at different economic levels, *Economic and Political Weekly*, special number, August.
Sukhatme, P. (1982) *New Concepts in Nutrition and Their Implications for Policy* (Pune: Maharashtra Association for the Cultivation of Science).

4 The Galton Lecture for 1985: Inequality of Economic Opportunity

Anthony F. Shorrocks

'Equality of opportunity' is one of the few objectives of social policy that can be said to find support across the whole spectrum of public and political opinion. Karl Marx, John Rawls and R. H. Tawney as well as Milton Friedman, Sir Keith Joseph and many others, all appear to rally around the same banner in a rare display of unity. Thus Rawls, for example, advocates a system in which 'offices and positions [are] open to all under conditions of fair equality of opportunity', while Friedman praises the fact that 'wherever anything approaching equality of opportunity has existed, the ordinary man has been able to attain levels of living never dreamed of before'.[1] Yet this apparent consensus in favour of an equal opportunity objective is largely a mirage. It is achieved only because the concept of equal opportunity is capable of supporting many different interpretations.

The aim here is to consider the extent to which opportunities can be said to be equal, drawing together material from a variety of sources and examining a number of different aspects. The focus of attention is on practical issues: the means by which evidence can be assembled, the conclusions that might be drawn, and the problems raised by each of the procedures. However, to make sense of the evidence that is often claimed to indicate opportunity differences, it is first necessary to discuss some of the alternative conceptions of equal opportunity, and to provide a framework in which they may be compared.

The perspective offered is one of an economist, which has two practical consequences. Firstly, the opportunities considered are those that relate to the economic sphere of life. More specifically, the focus of interest is the earning and income potential of individuals. Since the criteria for success and failure are closely allied to income, this preoccupation is not a severe limitation. But it clearly neglects other important aspects of human life, like legal and political rights, social status, and power, inasmuch as these are not reflected in income opportunities. The second component of the economic perspective is the framework of analysis and the methods of investigation: in effect, the mental apparatus brought to bear on the question in hand. It is in this respect that the economic perspective differs most from that of other disciplines, and, as a consequence, has most to offer.

In the economic view of the world, centre stage is occupied by the economic incentives confronting individuals and firms, and by the behavioural responses to the structure of rewards. The behaviour of economic agents is typically assumed to be governed by rational decision making: agents are faced with sets of options and select the ones best suited to their tastes. In the context of certainty – shopping in a supermarket, for example – the process of choice provides a direct link between the set of options, or opportunities, and the observed outcome. However when uncertainty is present, the act of choice ensures only an uncertain prospect, and chance plays a role in determining the final outcome. Thus in economics it is natural to distinguish opportunities from outcomes via the twin operations of choice and chance. It is also natural to interpret 'equality of opportunity' as meaning that individuals are equal *ex-ante*, in the sense of facing the same set of options, and to contrast this with equality of the *ex-post* outcomes.

By way of illustration, consider a situation in which individuals are confronted with a number of sure prospects, each of which involves a level of money income Y paired with some quantity of another characteristic X. The shaded area in Figure 4.1 represents the set of options. It may be helpful here to regard X as leisure (or non-working) time, in which case the options might correspond to a variety of employment prospects offering different combinations of work hours and earnings. But X might just as well stand for many other non-pecuniary factors, such as working conditions, job satisfaction, or the attractions of the geographical location. Two persons A and B with different tastes for, say, leisure versus income might well choose the different income–leisure combinations indicated by the points a and b. Since point a is associated with a higher money income than point b, inequality is observed in the *ex-post* incomes. However, in the circumstances described, when rational choice is the only source of differences, there is little cause for concern regarding the observed inequality. Equality of opportunity, rather than equality of outcome, seems the appropriate social goal.

The situation of equal opportunity and unequal outcome depicted

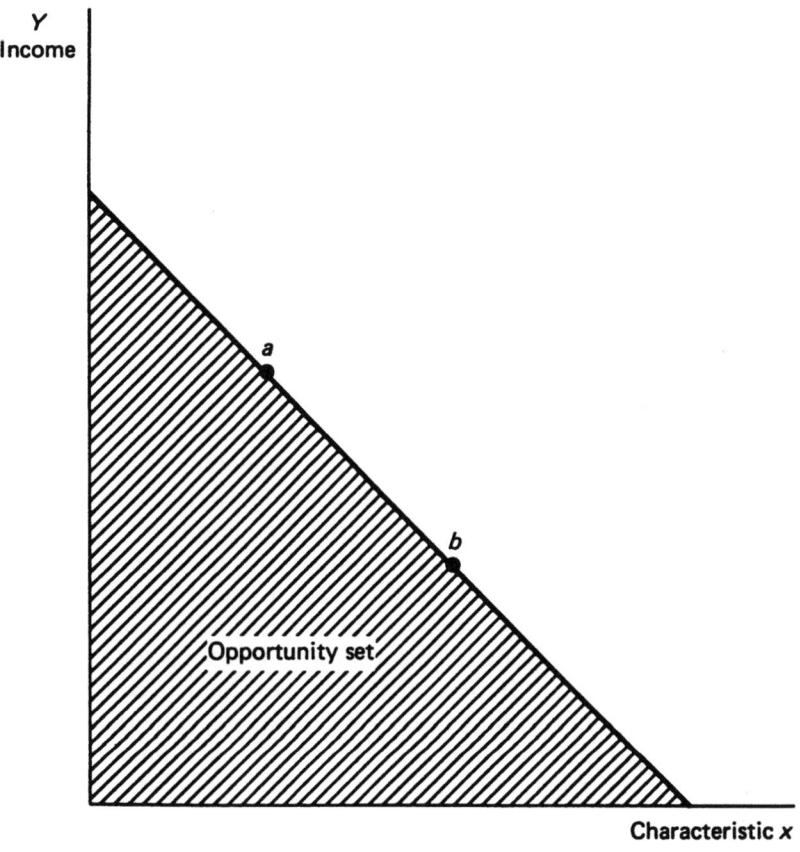

Figure 4.1   Choice between sure prospects

in Figure 4.1 can be characterised in several other useful ways. To begin with, we note that the observed income differences are exactly compensated by differences in the other characteristic *X* valued at the 'price' determined by the potential trade-off between *X* and *Y*. We may therefore describe the situation as one in which income differences are entirely due to 'compensating differentials'. Another characterisation sees the position as one in which there is 'no envy', in the sense that no individual wishes to exchange their *X–Y* combination for that of any other person.[2] This is true of the *a* and *b* outcomes portrayed in Figure 4.1, since the two individuals are already assumed to have considered and rejected the outcome chosen by the other. It will also be true, however many individuals select rationally from an identical set of certain prospects. Thus, equal opportunity and rational choice over sure prospects lead to an absence of envy. For this reason the 'no envy' notion of equal opportunity will be said to apply if, as portrayed in Figure 4.1, outcomes differ only by choice.

When chance comes into play, equality of opportunity no longer guarantees the absence of envy: the unlucky individuals will wish to trade their outcomes with those of the more fortunate. Thus the natural economic interpretation of equal opportunity as a situation in which individuals face the same mix of sure and risky prospects *ex-ante*, goes beyond the 'no envy' conception. This increase in generality is, however, accompanied by doubts as to whether equal opportunity is the appropriate social objective. The issues here are complex, and the discussion often confused. But a central point concerns whether the chance outcomes are avoidable or unavoidable.

In the case of the ever present and unavoidable risks encountered in the normal course of daily life, the limitations of the equal opportunity objective are exposed. Consider, for instance, the risk of serious physical handicap. It may be true that all have the same opportunity of being handicapped, and are, in this sense, equal *ex-ante*. But this is a poor justification for dismissing the claims of those who are disabled. In these circumstances, clearly, concern with the distribution of outcomes takes precedence over the distribution of opportunities. The explanation for this response ultimately rests, I believe, with the great moral force of the 'horizontal equity' principle, which requires that 'equals should be treated equally'. By their very nature, the effects of chance are horizontally inequitable, and cannot simply be ignored as the goal of equal opportunity suggests.

The effects of risks which are accepted voluntarily, or against which it is possible to insure, are viewed rather differently. Here, the principle of horizontal equity, which sees no merit in random influences, clashes with the principle of consumer sovereignty, which demands that the consequences of rational decisions be respected. As a result, our instinctive jealousy towards the good fortune of some, and our sympathy with the plight of others, is tempered by the knowledge that we were free to accept the same risks as the lucky ones, and that the unfortunate persons could have declined their invitation. This is the reason why a millionaire by virtue of a pools win is viewed in a different light to a millionaire by virtue of birthright; and why injuries sustained in a prize fight do not provoke the same response as similar injuries received in a mugging. Thus *ex-ante* equality may be regarded as the ultimate goal of social policy only insofar as the risks are undertaken voluntarily, or, in other words, only insofar as risky prospects and safe alternatives are present together in the set of options. Differences in outcomes due to rational choice are morally acceptable or fair; differences due to pure chance are not.

It may already be apparent that these two 'economic' definitions of equality of opportunity bear little resemblance to some of the other popular interpretations of the concept. These other interpretations are typically more restricted in outlook. Their advocates focus, not on the set of opportunities *per se*, but on the process by which opportunities are created, and the way in which opportunities may be exploited.[3] In essence, the demand is for freedom of choice and action, coupled with fair treatment, with the market place often being the arbiter of fairness.[4]

To capture some of the basic ideas it is necessary to examine the mechanism by which the opportunity set is created. Here, the opportunity set will be taken to mean the set of lifetime economic prospects, the potential that individuals have for acquiring and consuming resources over their lifetime. Figure 4.2 portrays a variety of influences on lifetime opportunities and lifetime outcomes. In the background are those factors which are common to all individuals: the state of technology, the institutional framework, and the laws and customs of society, particularly those governing property rights, economic relationships, and the pattern of taxes and subsidies. These, together with the general features of the economic system, determine the structure of markets and prices, and hence the incentives and rewards that influence the decisions of individuals and firms.

Within any given common environment, variations in personal circumstances can be traced to the four basic sources indicated in the corners of the figure. One of these sources covers factors that are not systematically related to the characteristics of individuals, and will be called 'random effects' or 'chance'.[5] The remaining three categories refer to different aspects of personal endowments: a 'genetic endowment' consisting of genetically determined individual traits; a 'family endowment' arising from the specific environment and advantages provided by the parent family; and an endowment of 'preferences' or 'tastes', which govern the selections made from sets of available alternatives. Note that individual preferences are themselves likely to be influenced by genetic characteristics and family background, as

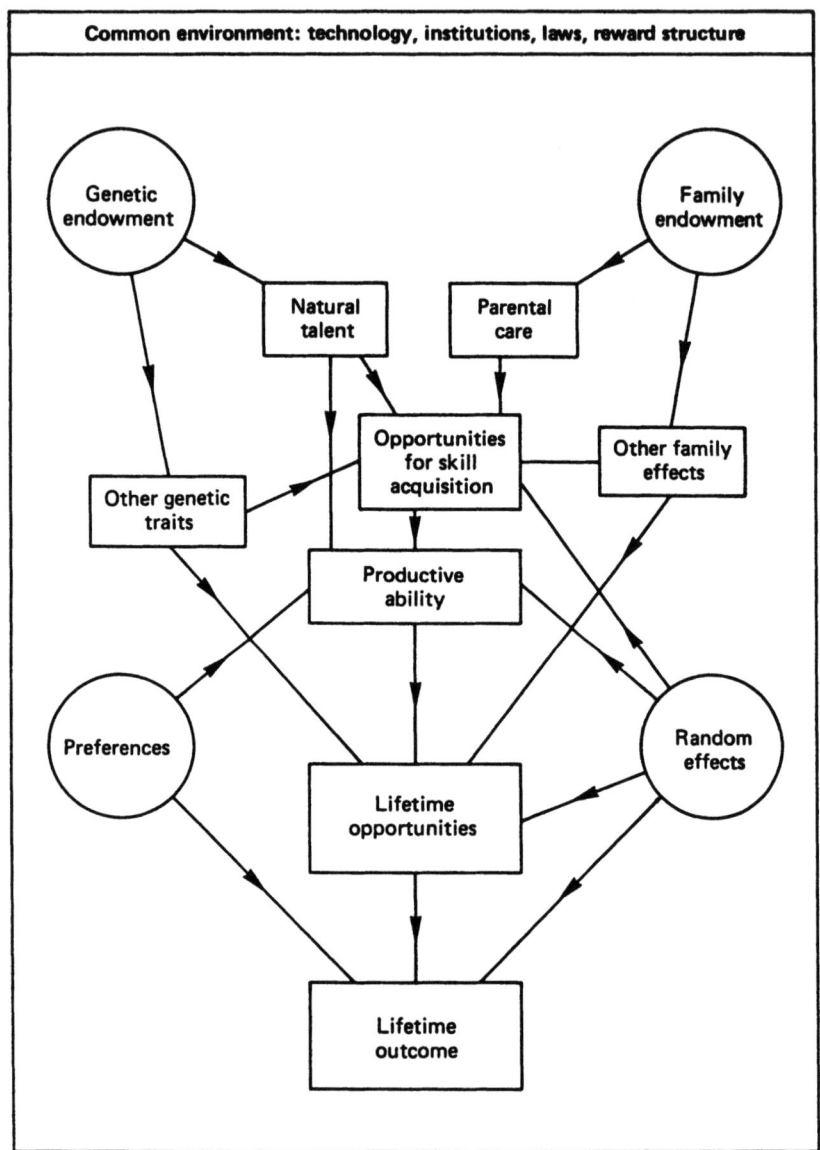

Figure 4.2   The determinants of lifetime opportunities and lifetime
          outcomes

well as by non-systematic or 'random' factors. They might therefore be subsumed under the other categories. However, given the importance attached to choice in economic analysis, and given the fact that personal preferences are generally regarded as sacrosanct, it seems appropriate to preserve the separate status indicated in the diagram. There is also likely to be a connection between the genetic and family endowments of individuals arising from the characteristics of the parent generation. This link has to be taken into account when explaining the correlated fortunes of successive generations, but for our purposes does not need to be explored.

The central part of Figure 4.2 illustrates the way that natural talent and skill acquisition together determine the productive capacities embodied in individuals. Here 'natural talent' refers to those productive abilities that are genetically inherited. Acquired skills arrive by a more complicated route. A principal feature is the opportunity for learning, determined by natural talent and family environment via such factors as parental care, financial support and residential location. Learning opportunities are also subject to a certain element of chance, and may be affected by 'other genetic traits' if sex or race discrimination influence access to, or. treatment during, training programmes. Individual choice regarding the extent and type of training, coupled with another liberal dose of random effects, then turn the opportunities for learning into the skills actually acquired. Further down the diagram we find that lifetime opportunities are affected by productivity, by 'other genetic traits' in the form of race and sex discrimination, and by 'other family effects' such as socioeconomic background and wealth inheritance. Finally these lifetime options are converted into the lifetime outcome through the process of choice and chance described earlier.

Although Figure 4.2 captures the influences on personal circumstances most frequently discussed, opinions differ widely on the importance attached to the particular links. Neoclassical economists, for instance, tend to emphasise the role of preferences and choice, while more radical commentators give prominence to the family endowment, and to the discrimination associated with genetic traits. There is no guarantee that the connections portrayed are quantitatively significant. Indeed, if current legislation against discrimination is completely effective, the contribution of 'other genetic traits' should not exist at all.[6]

Different conceptions of what is meant by equality and by equality of opportunity translate into arguments concerning the moral justification for the relationships portrayed in the diagram. A judicious simplification and rearrangement of the contributory influences will therefore allow us to identify and illustrate some of the more familiar positions. In Figure 4.3 the broken lines indicate that the factors shown above the line are undesirable sources of observed income differences. Moving in a downward direction means that additional factors are regarded as unacceptable, so the positions become progressively more egalitarian.

The top line represents the view that genetic characteristics other than natural ability should not influence either the opportunites for training, or the treatment of individuals capable of similar productive performance. This anti-discrimination position is perhaps the weakest version of the notion of equal opportunity, and its embodiment in legislation testifies to its widespread appeal. The next line broadly corresponds to the meritocratic argument that lifetime opportunities should be dictated only by ability. In addition to being against discrimination by gender or race, it would outlaw family effects which created conditions that are disadvantageous for the development or market worth of personal skills, and those rewards, such as inherited wealth, which are not merited by ability. The effects of chance on the acquisition and marketability of skills may also be ruled out on the grounds of horizontal equity, since they break the perfect correlation required between ability and reward.

Further down we come upon the concept of ex-ante equality already discussed. This seeks a situation in which all individuals face the same lifetime opportunity set, and hence regards as undesirable any factor that leads to a departure from this ideal, whether it be discrimination, natural talent, family effects or chance. Finally we arrive at the position previously described as the 'no-envy' concept of equality, which allows only those outcome differences due to rational choice. This is the position that most closely approximates the Rawlsian ideal.[7]

The different conceptions of equality of opportunity are reflected in empirical research, and help account for the bewildering variety of data that claim to provide information on the degree of unequal opportunity. It is therefore essential to recognise the different conceptions when it comes to assessing the empirical evidence. Figure 4.3 also helps us to understand the different methods that might be employed in obtaining relevant data on the set of lifetime opportunities. For we might attempt to reconstruct the opportunity set directly, working backwards from the set of outcomes and adjusting

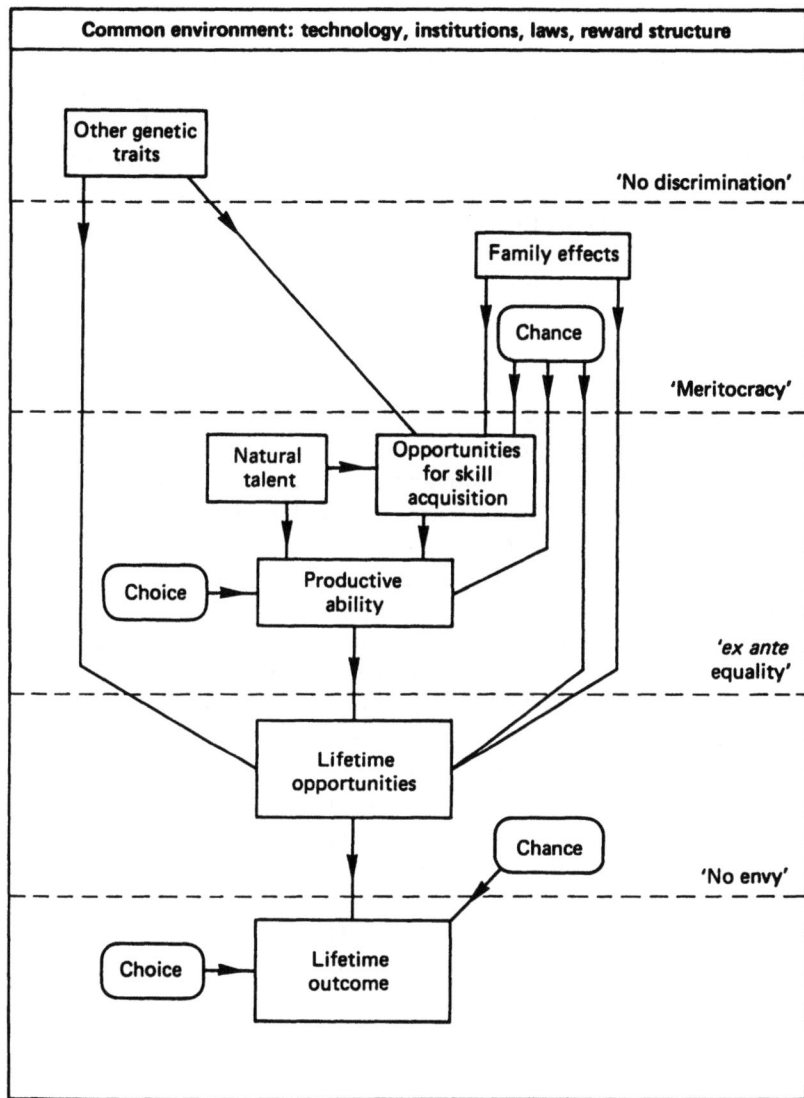

Figure 4.3   Alternative conceptions of equal opportunity

for the effects of choice and chance. Or else we might try to work from the basic sources, by identifying the separate links between the genetic and family endowments, and the set of opportunities. I intend to discuss a variety of methods that have been used to obtain evidence relevant to at least one of the conceptions of equal opportunity represented in the diagram. All of the methods have serious drawbacks, and one of the objectives is to outline the problems that arise in obtaining reliable information.

In principle, the simplest way of determining inequality of opportunity is to focus on the 'no-envy' conception and to work backwards from observed outcomes, by removing the element of choice. However, this is not easily accomplished. To examine the problems, consider Figure 4.4 which provides an expanded version of the earlier diagram representing the process of choice between income Y and some other characteristic X. Given the set of options bounded by the line O, individuals A and B are assumed to select the different combinations a and b. If the opportunity set expands, and the frontier become O', the same two persons are presumed to choose a' and b'. Thus the pair a and b, or the pair a' and b', represent equal opportunity, while the other combinations of observations do not. In particular, it should be noted, the pair a and b' correspond to the same observed income, but not the same set of opportunities. Equal outcomes do not imply equal opportunities any more than equal opportunities imply equal outcomes.

Now suppose we are faced with the income observations corresponding to a' and b. What can be deduced from this evidence? The diagram indicates that the higher income of person A does indeed reflect more opportunities, as well as a greater regard for money income *vis à vis* the non pecuniary characteristic. But to confirm this state of affairs it is necessary to reconstruct at least part of the opportunity frontiers O and O' passing through the points a' and b. This means, first of all, that we must be in a position to observe the other relevant factor X. Next, we have to be able to measure the quantity of this characteristic in some appropriate way. When this is done, the combinations a' and b can be plotted, as in the diagram. Finally we need to know the trade-off between Y and X: the income 'price' that must be paid to acquire further units of the other characteristic. This price determines the slope of the opportunity frontier, and hence allows the key parts of the opportunity sets to be established.

These informational requirements will occasionally be fulfilled.

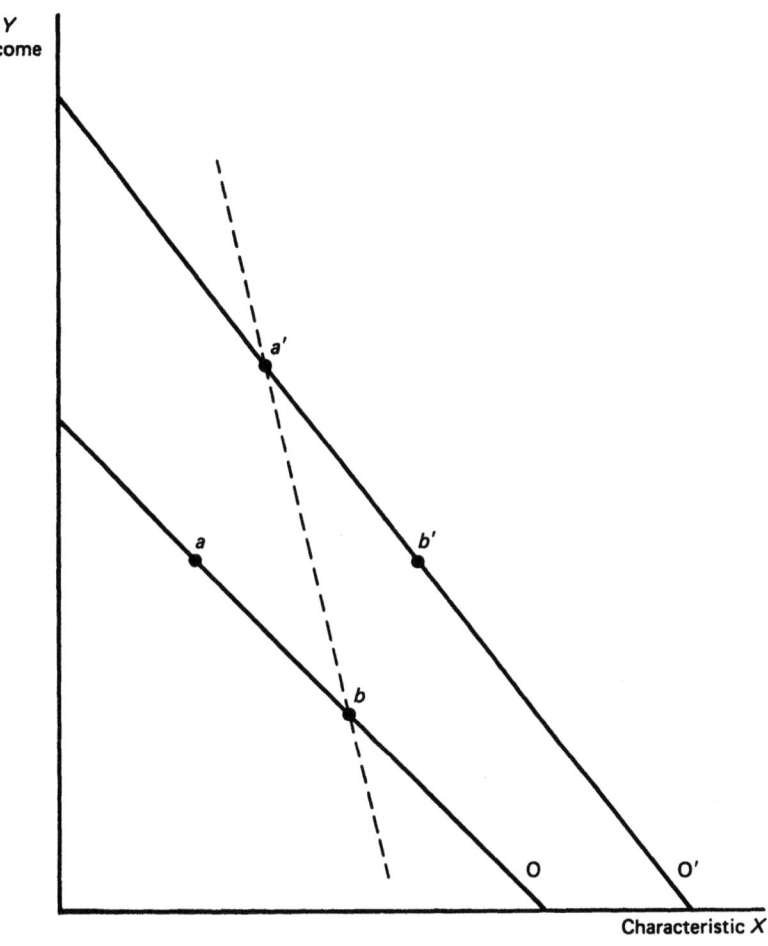

Figure 4.4   The reconstruction of opportunities from outcomes

For instance, in the choice between income and leisure, we can observe and measure non-working time reasonably easily. The price of leisure is more difficult to quantify, since marginal, rather than average, wage rates should be used, and since tax and social security contributions also need to be taken into account. Nevertheless, empirical research on the income-leisure decision is sufficiently well advanced to be able to provide a good guide to the impact of leisure choices on observed incomes.

In the case of other factors that might be traded off against money income, it may be virtually impossible to measure, or even observe, characteristics like job satisfaction. Even when an acceptable proxy is available, considerable doubt will surround the price that should be attached to the characteristic. This can have important consequences. For, as the diagram shows, the 'true' price of the characteristic leads to the true conclusion that person A choosing combination a' has more options than person B choosing combination b. However, if the estimated price corresponds to the broken line passing through the points a' and b, we would draw the incorrect conclusion that the two individuals experience equal opportunity.

Because of these very serious difficulties, few attempts are made to reconstruct the set of opportunities directly from the observed outcomes, except in respect of leisure differences and lifecycle variations associated with age. Instead, a more common practice is to base estimates of income, or earning, opportunities on the personal and family background traits of individuals. The general procedure regards an individual as a collection of characteristics related to factors such as intelligence, strength, motivation and education. To this collection of attributes the market is presumed to assign a value which reflects, amongst other things, supply and demand for each of the characteristics. It is this market value, plus or minus a chance effect, which determines an individual's income or earnings.

Although an enormous volume of empirical research falls within this general heading, very little is directed at the specific question of opportunity differences. More often the objective is to determine the extent to which variations in observed earnings can be accounted for by the personal characteristics under consideration, or to determine the reward associated with one particular factor, like education or union membership. Nevertheless, a detailed examination of the results enables some conclusions to be drawn regarding opportunity differences.

As an example, I draw upon a study of Taubman who examined the earnings experience of a group of male applicants to the US Air Force. The data set is particularly appropriate for our purposes, since the Air Force subjected the men to a wide range of aptitude tests. On various occasions they were also questioned about their family background, past history and current earnings. The contribution of each of the personal characteristics was estimated using standard econometric techniques. Table 4.1 covers some of the most significant influences and indicates the percentage income increment associated with each factor.[8]

Table 4.1   Percentage contributions to earnings

Education	BA/BSc	20
	MA/MSc	29
	PhD	43
	MD	82
Ability	Lowest 20%	−7
	Top 20%	7
Religion	Jewish	40
	Protestant	−9
Private School	Elementary	27
	Secondary	29
Self-Employed	Businessman	10
	Professional	31
Current Residence	Town	10
	Large City	27

Source: Taubman (1975), ch. 3.

Not surprisingly, educational credentials are seen to have a major impact on earnings. For instance a person with a bachelor's degree earned, on average, 20 per cent more than a similar person who did not go to college, while qualification as a medical doctor is estimated to increase earnings by 82 per cent. In contrast, the impact of the ability variable – a composite of the aptitude test scores – is relatively modest, raising the incomes of the most able 20 per cent of the sample by just 7 per cent, and lowering the incomes of the least able quintile by the same amount. This evidence appears to suggest that earnings depend much more on acquired skills than on natural talent. But it may be unwise to draw such a conclusion, given that the sample selection process restricted the ability range.

The next two characteristics relate to religious background and attendance at private school. The coefficient for the Jewish religion suggests a 40 per cent rise in earnings expectations associated with this factor, while a private school education at both elementary and secondary level is estimated to raise earnings by over 50 per cent. Both of these factors are best regarded as proxies for family effects, perhaps capturing the influence of wealth which is not observed directly.

The final pair of characteristics refer to self employment and residential location. Earnings are assumed to be 10 per cent higher for self-employed businessmen, and 31 per cent higher for self-employed professionals. Incomes are increased by a further 10 per cent for those living in towns, and by 27 per cent for those living in large cities. The effects here might be due to choice, with the self-employment differential compensating for the extra risk, and the residential premium compensating for the extra cost, or other disadvantages, of town and city dwelling. However, alternative interpretations are possible, and the results may again be picking up the effects of wealth.

Given the evidence presented in the Table 4.1, and the figures reported by Taubman for numerous other factors, we might begin the process of unravelling all the links between personal characteristics, choice, chance, opportunities and outcomes portrayed in the earlier diagrams. But there is one major drawback. The personal traits and family background variables typically explain no more than about one third of the total variation in earnings. This leaves a large residual to be allocated to chance, to the effects of choice not already captured in the observed variables, and to those personal characteristics which are not recorded. Unfortunately it is impossible to separate out the component contributions. As a consequence, any estimate of the quantitative significance of particular links, or any estimate of opportunity differences, will be subject to a wide margin of uncertainty.

The problems associated with the large residual component become less serious if the residual is, in effect, treated as pure chance, and if one is content with group, rather than individual experience. For, by the central limit theorem, aggregate chance effects will be negligible for a large collection of people. Therefore we need only analyse the impact of those systematic factors that have been identified. However, another serious difficulty raises its ugly head. It is possible, indeed likely, that observations on relevant personal characteristics are missing. If these omitted variables are correlated with the observed characteristics, the estimated contribution of the included variables can be biased, perhaps substantially. This is evident in the data reported in the table. The Jewish variable itself, for instance, cannot be the cause of the observed income differential: if I convert to the Jewish faith, I cannot expect an immediate 40 per cent jump in my earnings, as a naive interpretation of the results suggests. The contribution appears only because that variable is correlated with other, unobserved and influential, factors. Similarly, as already mentioned, the omission of observations on wealth may have affected a number of the estimated coefficients. Even the contributions of the education credentials may be grossly misleading. For the observed effect may be partly due to an inappropriate measurement of ability. Taubman himself, on another occasion, has concluded from data on identical twins that the observed rate of return to schooling may exaggerate the true rate of return by a factor of two or more.[9]

Problems concerned with omitted variables are also highly significant in the next topic on the agenda: sex discrimination. This topic has received a great deal of attention in Britain recently, prompted to some extent by the work of the Royal Commission on the Distribution of Income and Wealth, and given a subsequent impetus by the need to monitor the impact of laws against discrimination. There have been two major pieces of legislation: the Equal Pay Act of 1970, designed to achieve parity in the terms and conditions of employment of those in 'broadly similar' jobs; and the Sex Discrimination Act of 1975, which aims to ensure, amongst other things, that the hiring, promotion, training and dismissal practices of firms do not discriminate on the basis of either gender or marriage. 1975 was also the year in which the Equal Opportunities Commission began reviewing and enforcing the operation of the two acts.

A crude comparison of male and female earnings indicates that women, on average, earn little more than half that of men. But some of the difference reflects the shorter time at work. Since variation in work hours is generally regarded as a consequence of choice, discrimination is normally analysed in terms of differences in hourly wage rates, rather than earnings. Figures for the period from 1950 to 1970 show that female pay rarely exceeded 60 per cent of male wages. The relative position improved significantly in the years 1970–77, but has subsequently levelled off at around 67 per cent of male pay.[10] The *prima facie* evidence for sex discrimination is therefore strong, particularly for the period prior to 1970. However, just as differences in work hours contribute to differences in earnings, there may be other non-discriminatory factors that account for part, or all, of the observed differential in hourly wage rates. For example, women tend to have fewer educational qualifications and less work experience. Furthermore, they tend to congregate in particular kinds of industries and occupations. If – and it is perhaps a big if – these differences arise from free choice, rather than restricted opportunities, the associated pay differential is not discriminatory.

Empirical research on sex discrimination is usually viewed as an attempt to separate out those components of pay differences that can be attributed to choice and productivity related characteristics, leaving a residual that is interpreted as the effect of discrimination. Greenhalgh (1980) provides a good illustration of the arguments and techniques employed. This study is also interesting in that it refers to data for both 1971 and 1975, and hence spans the period when the Sex Discrimination Act took effect.

Greenhalgh uses more than 50 explanatory variables, of which a large number refer to occupation, industry, the level of education and the place of residence. The data are also reported separately for husbands, wives, single men and single women. Table 4.2 provides a small selection of the figures for husbands and wives.

The first two columns show the proportion of husbands and wives with the respective education levels, and the proportion found in the occupation and industry indicated. The last column gives the estimated percentage earnings contribution associated with each of these variables.[11] As expected, the sample reflects the tendency for men to acquire more educational qualifications. The percentage of men and women terminating their education with 'O' levels is roughly the same, at 12 per cent and 14 per cent respectively. But the husbands in this sample are three times more likely to stop with 'A' levels and six times more likely to gain a diploma. A similar proportion of husbands and wives happen to have degrees, but in this respect the data are not representative of the population at large. The figures in the last column show how the higher education level of men translates into higher earnings expectations, with the 13 per cent extra earnings corresponding to 'O' levels rising to a 60 per cent premium for a degree.

The evidence reported lower down in Table 4.2 is designed to illustrate the general tendency for women to be found in the lower paying occupations and industries. Husbands are five times more likely than their wives to have a professional occupation and three times less likely to have a junior non-manual job. Given the wide differences in the earnings contributions associated with occupations – an extra 55 per cent for professional jobs, for example, compared to the 7 per cent for the junior non-manual category – a significant proportion of the relative pay differential between men and women will be accounted for by differences in the distribution across occupations. The same applies to the distribution across industries. A higher proportion of husbands than wives are found in industries, like

Table 4.2 Male–female variations in personal characteristics and the associated contribution to wage rates

	Percentage of		Percentage contribution to wages
	Husbands	Wives	
Education			
O Level	12	14	13
A Level	6	2	22
Diploma	6	1	29
Degree	7	6	60
Occupation			
Professional	5	1	55
Junior Non-Manual	11	38	7
Industry			
Engineering	19	9	6
Distribution	8	17	–8
Services	11	41	–14

Source: Greenhalgh (1980), tables 2, A2, A4 and A5.

engineering, which the data associates with a positive premium. In contrast, the distribution and service sectors, in which the majority of women work, pay 8 per cent and 14 per cent less than average, respectively, according to these figures.

Once the influence of each variable on pay has been established, the observed average wage rate of the different groups can be adjusted to control for the mix of personal characteristics. Any residual difference has then to be explained in terms of some other factor, with sex discrimination being the obvious candidate in the male – female comparison.

One criticism which can be levelled against this general approach is that it identifies only part of the effects of discrimination. For instance, it takes into account the fact that women undertake less training, but does not investigate why this is so. If training opportunities are affected by discriminatory practices, it will clearly be inappropriate to regard skill qualifications as the consequences of choice. A similar argument applies, perhaps even more forcefully, to the selection of occupation and industry. For these reasons the conventional methods may understate the overall impact of discrimination.

Conversely, it can be argued that the unexplained residual exaggerates the true impact of discrimination, since other personal characteristics, excluded from the set of explanatory variables, may contribute to the observed pay disparity. For instance, psychological differences between men and women are often emphasised. These psychological differences – part innate, part conditioned by society and circumstances – may influence preferences, and hence account for systematic differences in choices; this is the rationale for regarding the selection of occupation and industry as non-discriminatory.

Psychological factors may also affect productivity. Of particular significance here is the impact of role specialisation within the family, which orients husbands towards the market place and wives towards the home. This may influence things like motivation, ambition and attachment to the labour market, which are subsequently rewarded or penalised in the market place. Thus productivity, as well as preferences, provides a route by which systematic psychological differences can affect earnings in a non-discriminatory manner.

Characteristics like motivation are, of course, notoriously difficult to measure. The empirical analysis of discrimination is therefore plagued with the same problem of omitted variables that arose earlier. However some concession to the problem can be made by considering the relative experience of groups distinguished by marital status as well as gender. The argument here is that marital status captures the motivational differences arising from the specialisation of family roles, while the pure discrimination effect is reflected in the comparison between single men and single women.

Table 4.3 summarises the results of Greenhalgh regarding the relative importance of the two contributory influences. All the figures refer to hourly wage rates, and are expressed as percentages of the pay of single men. The first column shows that in 1971 married men were paid, on average, 16 per cent more than single men, while single women were paid 14 per cent less, and married women 41 per cent less. By 1975, when the Sex Discrimination Act came into effect, pay differentials had narrowed, with the relative pay of married men moving downwards by 5 per cent, and the relative pay of single and married women moving upwards by 13 per cent and 10 per cent, respectively. The second and fourth columns report estimates of relative pay adjusted to compensate for the different mix of personal characteristics found in the four subgroups. This adjustment has no significant impact on the relative position of married and single men. But the observed characteristics of single women suggests that the

Table 4.3   The impact of gender and marital status on relative pay

	1971		1975	
	Relative pay	*Adjusted ratio*	*Relative pay*	*Adjusted ratio*
Married men	116	117	111	111
Single men	100	100	100	100
Single women	86	78	97	90
Married women	59	75	69	78

Source: Computed from Greenhalgh (1980), table 9.

labour market should treat them more favourably than single men. As a consequence, the adjusted figures show a larger differential than that evident in the raw data. In contrast, the educational qualifications, occupational distribution and industry of employment of married women are unfavourable, so the position relative to single men narrows when the compensatory adjustments are made.

The final adjusted figures in Table 4.3 give rise to the following possible interpretation. In 1971, pure discrimination, as represented by the comparison between single men and women, was about 22 per cent of single men's pay. Motivation, and other effects associated with marital status, leads husbands to earn a further 17 per cent more, and wives to earn a further 3 per cent less. Thus the 25 per cent differential between the pay of married women and single men breaks down into a 22 per cent differential due to discrimination and a 3 per cent differential due to marital status, all percentage figures again expressed relative to the pay of single men. By 1975 the impact of pure discrimination is estimated to have fallen considerably, from 22 per cent to 10 per cent. However this potential improvement in the relative pay position of wives is largely offset by an increase in the 'cost' attributed to marriage. As a consequence, the 22 per cent differential between married women and single men in 1975 splits roughly equally between pure discrimination and marital status effects.

Just how much confidence should be placed in these figures, and in the conclusions drawn for them, is a matter of personal judgement. There still remains a long way to go before the impact of discrimination can be said to have been identified and accurately measured. Nevertheless views regarding the impact of pure discrimination in Britain seem to be converging on a figure of about 10 per cent of earnings.[12]

The last topic to which we turn concerns intergenerational mobility. Evidence on mobility has long been regarded as relevant to the question of inequality of lifetime opportunities, and it is easy to see why. For if we discount any systematic influences on preferences, *ex-ante* equality of opportunity will ensure that lifetime outcomes are uncorrelated with any of the genetic or family background characteristics; it follows that there will be no relationship between the fortunes of successive generations. Thus any correlation observed in the lifetime experiences of parents and children provides strong evidence in favour of unequal opportunities, interpreted in the *ex-ante* sense. It is then a short step to the suggestion that intergenerational mobility be used as an index of the degree of unequal opportunity.

One of the problems with using evidence on mobility is that it provides little or no information on the precise causes of any observed intergenerational correlation. Its immediate relevance to policy issues is thus very limited.[13] A second problem is that appropriate data are not readily available. It is difficult enough to obtain observations on successive generations. But the problem is exacerbated when, as in the case of many economic variables, current observations are a poor guide to the long run or lifetime positions. It is for this reason that intergenerational mobility is most often examined in the context of occupational or social class data.[14]

Despite the general lack of data on earnings or income mobility across generations, some evidence has recently been provided by Atkinson, Maynard and Trinder (1983). The mobility matrix shown in Table 4.4 is drawn from their study and cross classifies the earnings of fathers and sons. The income classes are based on the quintile points of the UK earnings distribution corresponding to the year in which the earnings were observed. By definition, therefore, each income class is always occupied by exactly 20 per cent of the population. Each of the rows in Table 4.4 refers to the group of fathers falling within the income quintile indicated on the left hand side, and the figures in any given row represent the percentage of their sons occupying each of the income classes. Thus, for instance, if we take the group of middle quintile fathers, 35 per cent of their sons are indicated as also falling within the middle quintile, while 16 per cent are to be found in the top quintile and 12 per cent in the bottom category.

The use of income classes based on quintile points has great advantages in mobility analysis. One consequence is a 'bistochastic'

Table 4.4   Intergenerational earnings mobility

Income quintile of father	Income quintile of son				
	Top	*2*	*3*	*4*	*Bottom*
Top	48	40	6	0	6
2	14	14	21	36	14
3	16	16	35	22	12
4	13	13	23	27	23
Bottom	9	17	14	15	45

Source: Atkinson *et al.* (1983), table 6.7.

mobility matrix, with each row and column summing to 100 per cent.[15] This means that if there is equal opportunity, and hence zero intergenerational correlation, all of the entries in the table will be 20 per cent.[16] Conversely, a perfect (positive) correlation between the incomes of fathers and sons leads to a matrix in which all the off-diagonal elements are zero.

Neither of these benchmark cases is approximated by the figures in Table 4.4. Instead of identical entries, the numbers on and near the leading diagonal tend to be higher, and those in the opposite corners lower. In particular, the figures suggest that intergenerational links are strong at the very top and very bottom of the distribution, with almost half of the sons 'inheriting' their father's relative income position. At the same time, the evidence also points to substantial intergenerational movement across the class boundaries, and the situation in no way corresponds to that of perfect correlation.

For a variety of reasons, described in great detail in the Atkinson *et al.* study, it is unwise to place too much reliance on the figures reported in the table, or to regard them as necessarily representative of the UK population as a whole. The data will, however, allow me to refer, briefly and belatedly, to Galton's own work and to his continuing contribution.

In the classic study by Galton and Pearson, the (positive) correlation between the heights of fathers and sons was found to be about 50 per cent. This figure of 50 per cent also corresponds to the degree of 'regression towards the mean', defined as the coefficient in the simple linear regression of the son's height on that of his father, and implies that a son can expect to grow to a height midway between that of his father and that of the population at large. The Galtonian regression model, and the significance attached to the parameter representing the degree of regression towards the mean, remain central to many modern day studies of mobility, both between and within generations.[17] Atkinson *et al.* compute the regression parameter in the course of their work, and conclude that it is also about 50 per cent. Thus we have two very natural ways of interpreting the intergenerational correlation of earnings: a son can expect his earnings to be midway between that of his father and that corresponding to the average population figure; or, perhaps more revealingly, inheritance of earnings capacity seems to be on a par with the inheritance of height.

It is evident that the discussion of equal opportunity encompasses a wide variety of issues. I have tried to convey an impression of the diversity of the subject matter, and to highlight a number of the conceptual and empirical problems which need to be addressed. Now is the time to take stock and to draw some tentative conclusions.

The empirical evidence, derived from many different data sources using a variety of different procedures, points clearly to one conclusion: the situation in Britain and elsewhere falls some way short of any equal opportunity ideal. Incomes, after adjustment for age, work time and other compensatory characteristics, show a substantial degree of inequality. Furthermore, the observed correlation between the incomes of parents and children indicates that these income differences are due to more than just the influence of choice and chance. This evidence alone justifies the claim that lifetime prospects are far from similar: equal opportunity, interpreted in either the 'no envy' or '*ex ante* equality' sense, is not remotely achieved.

Narrower conceptions of the equal opportunity objective, such as the 'no discrimination' and 'meritocratic' positions, focus on the process by which opportunities are derived. Here relevant evidence may be obtained by detailed studies of the determinants of income, and these again suggest that equality of opportunity does not prevail. Research on male and female earnings shows that discrimination is still influential, while family background has an impact on both skill acquisition and incomes that is incompatible with a pure meritocracy.

These broad generalisations scarcely begin to do justice to the range of questions that ought to be answered. Yet they are, perhaps, as much as the current state of knowledge readily admits. Any attempt to proceed further brings us face to face with the numerous difficulties described earlier. We should like to know more about the extent to which lifetime opportunities differ, so that comparisons can be made across countries and over time. We also wish to know more about the policies that promote equality of opportunity, and the costs of implementing these proposals. But to answer these questions with any degree of confidence requires a better appreciation of the appropriate concept of equal opportunity and a better understanding of the process by which lifetime opportunities evolve. Whether this lack of knowledge will ever be satisfactorily rectified remains to be seen. Some progress can undoubtedly be made, and an eclectic approach, combining alternative viewpoints and exploiting information from different sources, offers the most promising means of advancement. However the lack of suitable data relating to the lifetime incomes, personal characteristics and family circumstances of individuals poses serious difficulties which will not be overcome by resourcefulness alone.

Notes

1. Rawls (1972) p. 83; Friedman and Friedman (1979), p. 146. For a variety of other statements see, for example, Tawney (1952), ch. 1; Williams (1962); Schaar (1967); Frankel (1971); and Letwin (1983).
2. See, in particular, Varian (1976).
3. Rae (1981) makes a similar distinction and refers to them as the 'prospect-regarding' and 'means-regarding' equalities of opportunity.
4. Thus, for example, Joseph and Sumption (1979) argue that: 'Equality of opportunity is a neutral concept. It does not set up any particular social arrangement as a desirable goal but merely requires the absence of artificial constraints on individual achievement' (p. 29); and later that 'Equality of opportunity is the corollary of the liberty of the individual' (p. 30).
5. The term 'chance' is a little misleading, since factors that appear to be random from the viewpoint of individuals may nevertheless be highly influenced by the common background conditions. Take, for example, so called 'positional goods' which are, by definition, limited in number. There may be a large element of randomness in the process by which, say, any particular individual comes to be appointed Prime Minister. Yet the fact that one, and only one, person holds this title at any given time is by no means a random event, but is instead dictated by the structure of the common environment.
6. This observation highlights the fact that legislation and policy proposals are often designed with the specific intention of weakening or eliminating some of the connections indicated in Figure 4.2.
7. Equal opportunity is not, of course, the only objective of social policy, so that policy recommendations will typically have to weigh the benefits of more equal opportunity against the costs of achieving the change. The popularity of anti-discrimination legislation in part reflects the fact that

the costs are likely to be small; indeed by removing artificial constraints on productive performance, the legislation appeals on the grounds of both equality and efficiency. Other equal opportunity objectives are likely to involve higher costs associated with the adverse incentive effects of the legislation, and these affect the degree to which equal opportunity is regarded as a desirable goal.

8. For details of the sample, the definition of the variables, and the statistical methods, see Taubman (1975). The data in Table 4.1 refer to earnings in 1969, when the men had an average age of 47.

9. See, for example, Taubman (1978), p. 386.

10. The relative pay of women during the period 1950 to 1981 is examined by Zabalza and Tzannatos (1985). For a wider perspective on both theoretical and empirical aspects of discrimination, see Sloane (1980; 1985).

11. The reported figures refer to contributions estimated from the sample of husbands, and differ from the estimates based on wives. The fact that the 'prices' attached to the characteristics appear to be different for men and women may be taken as further evidence of unequal treatment. On the other hand, they may also reflect econometric misspecification, perhaps due to omitted variables.

12. The position in North America appears similar: see the discussion in Sloane (1985), section 2.

13. However, a number of authors have attempted to describe and assess the intergenerational links: see, for example, Meade (1976), especially ch. IX; Conlisk (1977); Atkinson (1980).

14. For recent evidence on Britain, see Goldthorpe (1980).

15. This is true of Table 4.4, apart from rounding errors.

16. The benchmark in mobility tables based on social class or occupation is somewhat different, since the figures are affected by changes over time in the social class or occupational structure. This has led to a distinction between the 'structural' and 'exchange' aspects of mobility: see, for example, Goldthorpe (1980), pp. 73–4.

17. See, for example, Creedy (1985).

References

Atkinson, A. B. (1980) 'Income distribution and inequality of opportunity' *IHS Journal*, 4, 65–80.

Atkinson, A. B., Maynard A. K. and Trinder C. G. (1983) *Parents and Children: Incomes in Two Generations* (London: Heinemann).

Conlisk, J. (1977) 'An exploratory model of the size distribution of income', *Economic Inquiry*, 15, 345–66.

Creedy, J. (1985) *Dynamics of Income Distribution* (Oxford: Basil Blackwell).

Frankel, C. (1971) 'Equality of opportunity' *Ethics*, 81, 191–207.

Friedman, M. and Friedman R. (1979) *Free to Choose* (London: Secker & Warburg).

Goldthorpe, J. H. (1980) *Social Mobility and Class Structure in Modern Britain* (Oxford: Oxford University Press).

Greenhalgh, C. (1980) 'Male-female wage differentials in Great Britain: is marriage an equal opportunity?' *Economic Journal*, 90, 751–75.

Joseph, K. and Sumption J. (1979) *Equality* (London: John Murray).

Letwin, W. (1983) 'The case against equality', in *Against Equality*, ed. W. Letwin (London: Macmillan).

Meade, J. E. (1976) *The Just Economy* (London: Allen & Unwin).

Rae, D. (1981) *Equalities* (Cambridge, Mass.: Harvard University Press).

Rawls, J. (1972) *The Theory of Justice* (Oxford: Oxford University Press).

Schaar, J. H. (1967) 'Equality of opportunity, and beyond', in *Equality*, ed. J. R. Pennock and J. W. Chapman (New York: Atherton Press).

Sloane, P. J. (ed.) (1980) *Women and Low Pay* (London: Macmillan).

Sloane, P. J. (1985) 'Discrimination in the labour market', in *Labour Economics*, ed. D. Carline *et al.* (London: Macmillan).

Taubman, P. (1975) *Sources of Inequality in Earnings* (Amsterdam: North Holland).

Taubman, P. (1978) 'The relative influence of inheritable and environmental factors and the importance of intelligence in earnings functions', in *Personal Income Distribution*, ed. W. Krelle and A. F. Shorrocks (Amsterdam: North Holland).

Tawney, R. H. (1952) *Equalities* (London: Allen & Unwin, 4th edn).

Varian, H. (1976) 'Two problems in the theory of fairness'. *Journal of Public Economics*, 3/4, 249–60.

Williams, B. (1962) 'The idea of equality', in *Philosophy, Politics and Society* (Second Series), ed. P. Laslett and W. G. Runciman (Oxford: Basil Blackwell).

Zabalza, A. and Tzannatos Z. (1985) 'The effect of Britain's anti-discriminatory legislation on relative pay and employment', *Economic Journal*, 95, 679–99.

Part II

Population, Welfare and Economic Development

5 Population Growth and Economic Development

A. P. Thirlwall

INTRODUCTION

The relation between population growth and economic development is not an easy topic to write about. The connections are complex, and the historical quantitative evidence is ambiguous, particularly concerning what is cause and what is effect. Does economic development precede population growth, or is population growth a necessary condition for economic development to take place? The complexity of the subject is compounded by the fact that economic development is a multi-dimensional concept meaning different things to different people. For the purposes of this essay, I shall define economic development as a sustained increase in the level of per capita income, although bearing in mind Goulet's (1971) three core components of a wider meaning of development, namely life-sustenance, self-esteem and freedom.

The level of per capita income may be a reasonable proxy for life sustenance, but a poor indicator of the distribution of income and of educational and job opportunities which give people self respect, independence and freedom to choose. If the measure of development is to be translated into a measure of welfare, there are also complex philosophical questions involved relating to the meaning of welfare maximisation and the concept of an optimum population which have preoccupied welfare economists for centuries. If it could be shown, for example, that slower population growth leads to a higher rate of growth of per capita income, or less people means higher living standards, would this mean that if society adopted successful policies of population control it would be better off? The utilitarian approach to welfare would say not necessarily. The utilitarian adopts a total welfare criterion, as Sidgwick (1907) did in his *Methods of Ethics*:

> if the additional population enjoy on the whole positive happiness, we ought to weigh the amount of happiness gained by the extra number against the amount lost by the remainder. So that, strictly

conceived, the point up to which, on utilitarian principles, population ought to be encouraged to increase is not that at which *average*
[emphasis added] happiness is the greatest possible – as appears to
be often assumed by political economists of the school of Malthus –
but at which the product formed by multiplying the number of
persons living into the amount of average happiness reaches its
maximum.

On the other hand, instinctively and intuitively, most people are not
utilitarian.

In conditions of poverty, if increments to population reduce the
average standard of living still further, most people would no doubt
think it perverse to call this an improvement in welfare simply
because the number of people 'enjoying' such an impoverished state
had risen. As Cassen (1976) has put it: 'concern for the never born
(as opposed to those actually born, past and future) may be something of a luxury.' Rawls (1972) in *A Theory of Justice* invites us to
think of a rational observer having to choose membership in one or
other society from behind a veil of ignorance as to where in each
society he would find himself placed. With a moderate degree of self
interest, Rawls argues, he would likely choose the society which
rejects utilitarianism and adheres to the per capita criterion. And yet
a population policy based on maximising per capita income has
frightening implications (not entirely fanciful) for all sub-marginal
groups in society that may be deemed to be depressing the average
standard of life.

Where does all this leave the welfare basis for population control
programmes? A surer basis lies not in diminishing returns to population (indeed there may be increasing returns, in which case the
utilitarian debate becomes irrelevant), but in the divergencies between the private and social benefit from large numbers of children.
For example, each individual family may prefer to have fewer children if it knew all other families would have fewer children, but it is
not willing to limit the number of children in isolation. This is an
example of what is known in welfare economics as 'the isolation
paradox', and establishes a case for public intervention. It is the
children who suffer from more children because most of the costs
arise in the future. Present parents may enjoy their children, but their
children may wish their parents had had less, and, as I suggested
above, they probably would have had less if they could have been
sure that everybody else would have had less too.[1] A further reason

for public intervention in the field of population control may be market failure if it can be shown that families have more children than they actually want and that there is an unmet need for family planning services. It is interesting to note that surveys of desired family size in developing countries consistently put the figure at one or two lower than the actual family size. Apart from this, it could be argued that it is a basic human right to be able to choose freely and responsibly the number and spacing of children. This indeed was the resolution endorsed by Bucharest World Population Conference in 1974 which laid the foundation for the World Bank's increased support for population control programmes throughout the Third World.

In this essay my basic thesis will be that the deleterious effects of population growth on the growth of living standards are probably exaggerated; indeed, that population growth is almost certainly a positive growth inducing force (at least it has been historically). I shall spend most of the time arguing this case. This is not to deny, however, that curbing population growth may be desirable in many contexts to relieve overcrowding; to ease pressure on food supplies; to alleviate unemployment; to improve the distribution of income, and in general to raise the level of society's welfare. To be sceptical, therefore, about whether lower population growth rates would improve the average standard of life is not necessarily to pour cold water on population control programmes. On the contrary, I will conclude that given the uncertainty of the population growth – living standard relationship, it is preferable to run the risk of type II error (i.e. accept a false hypothesis), and proceed on the basis that limited population control will increase living standards, rather than do nothing.

Lest readers think at this point that I am beginning to suffer from economic schizophrenia, let me call to my aid John Maynard Keynes who addressed this Society in 1937 when he gave the Galton Lecture on 'Some economic consequences of a declining population' (Keynes 1937). He exhibited the same ambivalence to the effects of population growth on human welfare as I have indicated above. On the one hand, he recognized the Malthusian worry of excessive population growth on living standards. On the other hand, he was very doubtful, at least in the context of reasonably mature capitalist economies, whether a slow down of population growth, which was in prospect in the 1930s, would provide the stimulus to capital accumulation on which continued growth and full employment depend. Keynes concludes:

unquestionably a stationary population does facilitate a rising standard of life – but on one condition only – namely that the increase in resources or in consumption, as the case may be, which a stationariness of population makes possible, does actually take place. For we have now learned that we have another devil at our elbow at least as fierce as the Malthusian – namely the devil of unemployment escaping through the breakdown of effective demand. Perhaps we could call this devil too a Malthusian devil, since it was Malthus himself who first told us about him.[2] For just as the young Malthus was disturbed by the facts of population as he saw them round him and sought to rationalise that problem, so the older Malthus was no less disturbed by the facts of unemployment as he saw them round him and sought – far less successfully so far as his influence on the rest of the world was concerned – to rationalise that problem too. Now when the Malthusian devil P is chained up, Malthusian devil U is liable to break loose. When devil P of population is chained up, we are free of one menace; but we are more exposed to the other devil U of unemployed resources than we were before.[3]

So, you see, Keynes saw quite clearly the conflicting forces of population at work; that population can be both an impediment and a stimulus to economic development. Where does the balance lie? Before I proceed to my main argument, I shall outline by way of background some salient facts and figures concerning world population growth and trends.

WORLD POPULATION: FACTS AND TRENDS

The world's population is now approximately five billion. Every second, about five babies are born, and two people die, which means in the last minute alone, the world's population has increased by 180 persons. Over a year this adds up to an increase in population of over 90 millions; a yearly increase nearly double the population of Great Britain. The rate of growth of world population, of just under 2 per cent per annum, has no historical precedent. From the birth of Jesus to the advent of Britain's industrial revolution, world population grew on average at no more than 0.05 per cent per annum. During the next hundred years it grew at 0.5 per cent per annum, and even in the first half of the twentieth century it was growing at no more than 0.8 per cent per annum. The world's population explosion is a phenomenon of the last thirty years. Its root cause is no mystery. There has been a dramatic fall in the death rate in the developing countries of the Third World without a corresponding fall, at least until recently, in the birth rate. The present rate of increase will double world population every thirty-five years, and it can be fairly confidently predicted that unless there is a very rapid decline in the birth rate, or some catastrophe such as a nuclear holocaust, the world's population will be at least six billion by the year 2000. The explosive growth of world population is well illustrated graphically in Figure 5.1, which also shows the actual and projected crude birth and death rates for the developed and developing countries. The gap between the two rates gives the rate of population growth. For reference, the absolute level, and rate of growth, of population for all the countries in the world is shown in Table 5.1

In the developing countries the average rate of population growth is currently just over 2 per cent per annum, resulting from a birth rate of 32 per thousand and a death rate of 11 per thousand. This rate of increase is three times higher than in the developed countries. While the death rate in the developing countries has now fallen almost to the level in the developed countries, the birth rate is still considerably higher. The crude birth and death rates by country are shown in Table 5.2. There is a wide diversity of experience between countries, and also between sub-continents as shown in Figure 5.2. The death rate has fallen dramatically almost everywhere, but the birth rate continues to remain much higher in some countries and continents than others. In sub-Saharan Africa, for example, the birth rate has hardly changed at all, while in East Asia it has fallen by 25 per cent in the last twenty years. The conventional wisdom used to be that fertility decline would only come with rising levels of per capita income, urbanisation and industrialisation, but there is increasing evidence that it can occur with improvement in a wide range of socio-economic conditions: for instance, education and improved opportunities for women which delays marriage and makes women more receptive to contraceptive knowledge; the provision of health services and improved life expectancy; the level of literacy, and access to family planning services. In Figure 5.3, the negative association between the level of per capita income and fertility is clearly seen, but the downward drift in the curve over time can also be

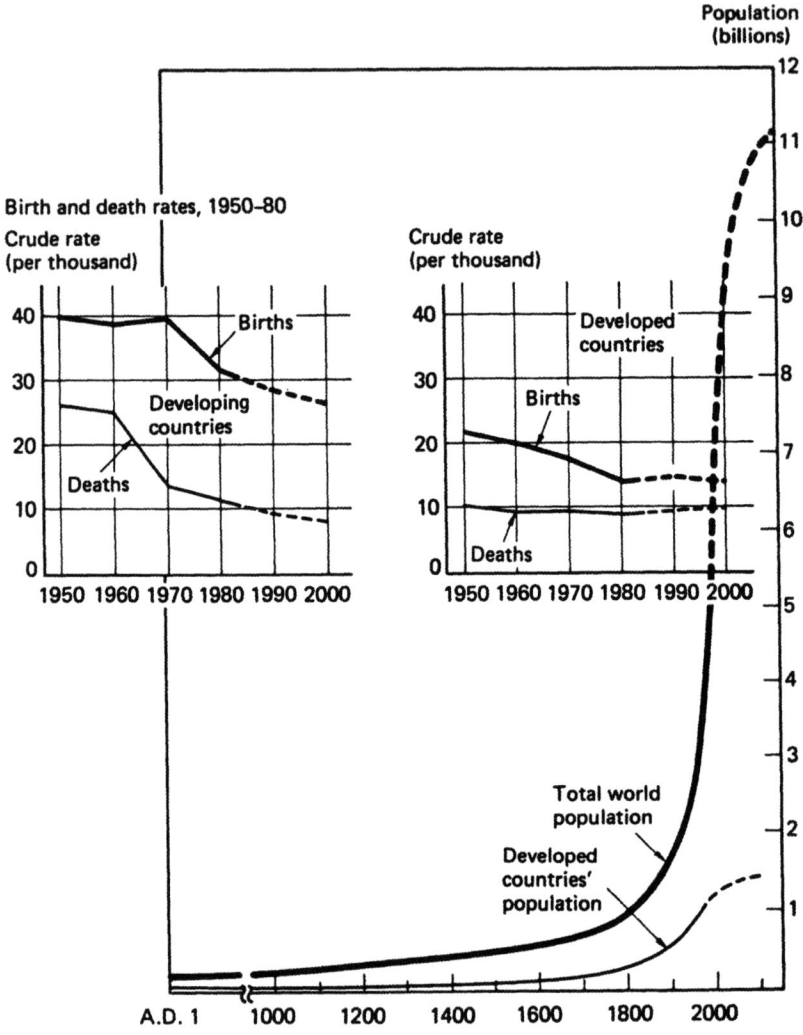

Figure 5.1   Past and projected world population, AD 1–2150

Source: *World Development Report 1984*

clearly discerned, as well as big differences in the fertility rate between countries at the same level of income, reflecting the influence of the factors mentioned above.

To summarise, we may say that the provision of public health

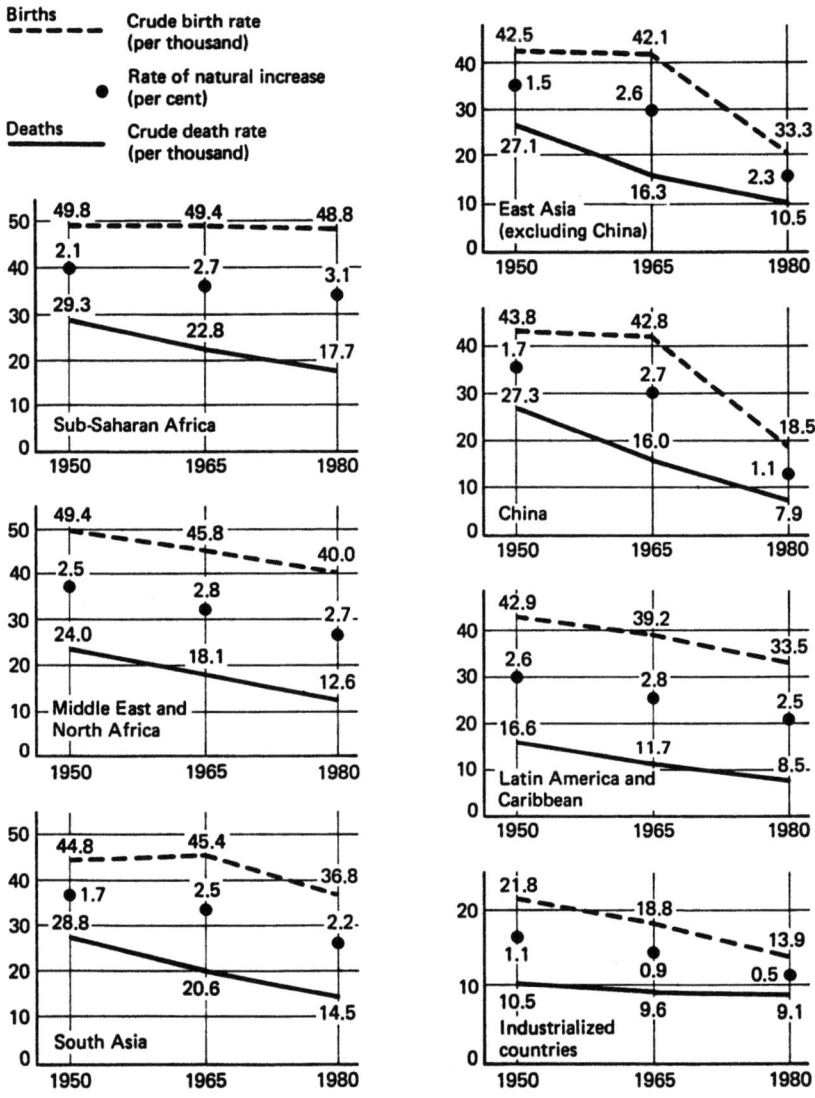

Figure 5.2 Birth and death rates and rates of natural increase by region, 1950, 1965, and 1980

Source: *World Development Report 1984*

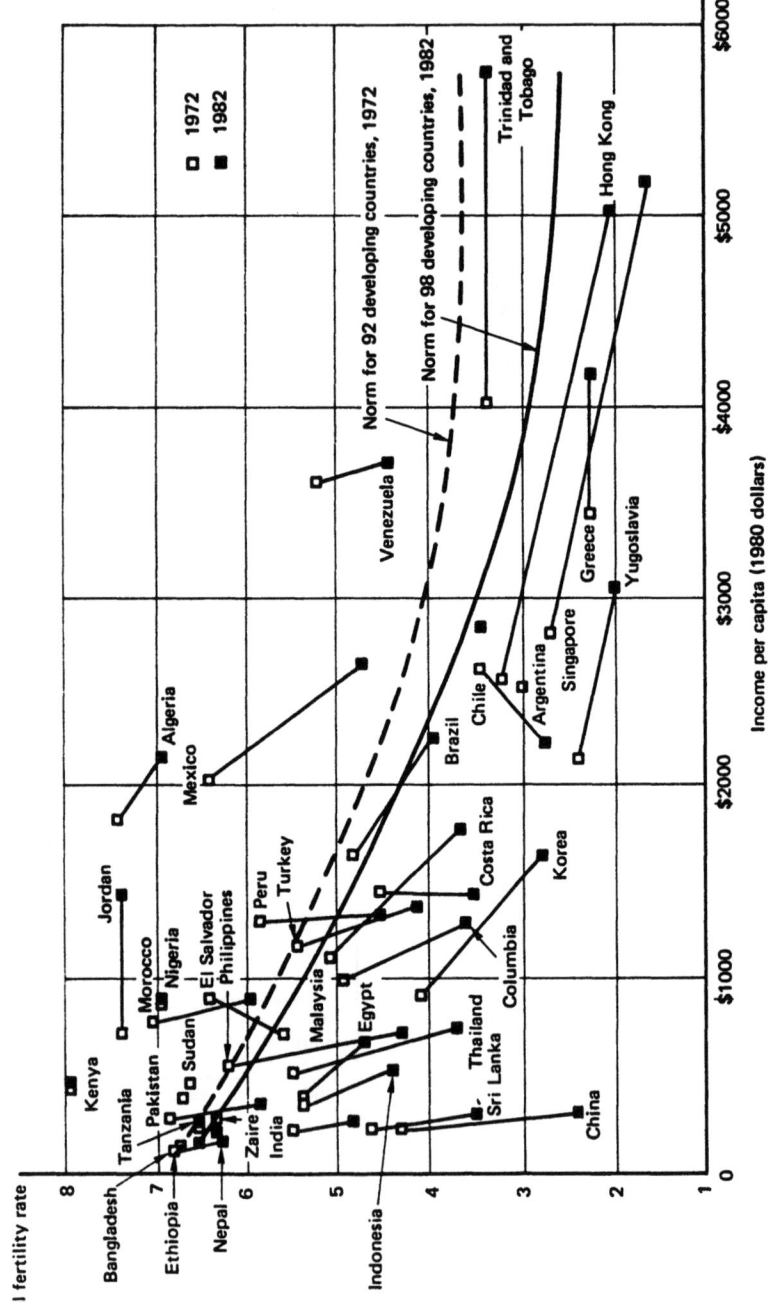

Figure 5.3   Fertility in relation to income in developing countries, 1972 and 1982
Source: World Development Report 1984

facilities and medical services in developing countries has reduced death rates suddenly and dramatically without time for the birth to adapt. This experience is also without historical parallel. In nineteenth-century Europe, birth and death rates tended to fall together. The death rate fell comparatively slowly and rising affluence was its own prophylactic. Population growth during the process of industrialisation in Europe was never more than 1 per cent over a sustained period.

THE PESSIMISTIC VIEW OF POPULATION

The conventional view is that high levels and rates of growth of population constitute a problem for the world as a whole and for the developing countries in particular. Population growth, it is argued, depresses human welfare because it reduces saving and dilutes the quantity of capital per man on which productivity growth and living standards depend. Population increase absorbs resources, spoils the environment, produces overcrowding and puts pressure on food supplies. The pessimistic view of population growth originated with Malthus, and in recent years has been revived by ecologists, environmentalists and various eco-doomsters of different persuasions. The pessimism of Malthus stemmed from the pervasive classical belief in the law of diminishing returns, and the underestimation of man's response to the challenge of diminishing productivity with the expansion of numbers through invention and innovation. According to Malthus there is a 'constant tendency in all animated life to increase beyond the nourishment prepared for it'. True, every mouth is accompanied by a pair of hands but every pair of hands produces less and less additional output. Technological progress (always grossly under-estimated by pessimists in general and by the classicists in particular) would not be rapid enough, it was thought, to offset the tendency. Parenthetically, it may be mentioned that Malthus became much less pessimistic between the first and fifth editions of his book and concedes at one point that if it were not for population increase 'no motive would be sufficiently strong to overcome the acknowledged indolence of man and make him proceed to the cultivation of the soil'.

The Malthusian position is a seductive one, especially in the face of immediate crises, such as the current famine in the Sahel, but taking the long span of history social scientists have always had difficulty in squaring the pessimism of classical theory with the observable facts. The world as a whole has grown progressively richer while population has expanded. Would the world be as rich today if population had been static? Would Great Britain have been the first country to industrialise if its population had been stagnant? Would the United States have become the wealthiest country in the world without the great influx of population from outside its shores to exploit its abundant natural resources? It is extremely difficult to answer these counter-factual questions without undertaking sophisticated simulation studies to estimate what might have been. The only counter-factual study I know is that of Kelley and Williamson (1974) for Meiji Japan which uses a simulation model to answer the question, what would have been the speed of economic growth had Japan sustained the high rate of population growth currently experienced in today's developing countries? Actual population growth in Meiji Japan was 0.9 per cent per annum. Assuming a rate three times faster over the period 1887–1915 makes very little difference to the growth of per capita income. Actual per capita income grew by 129 per cent, while the simulation estimate is 111 per cent. The small difference stems from the stimulus that population growth gives to capital formation. A more rapid population growth increases the share of profits in income and raises the aggregate savings ratio, and it slows the rise in the capital–output ratio; both effects contributing to a faster rate of capital accumulation.

Without simulation studies, we only have the actual facts to rely on which show that for individual countries over time, and comparing different countries at a point in time, there is no discernable negative relation between the rate of growth of population and the rate of growth of per capita income as a measure of living standards. For interest, I have plotted a scatter diagram in Figure 5.4 showing the relationship between the average rate of growth of per capita income and population growth in the developing countries over the years 1960–80 and there is clearly no relationship evident. Higher population growth by itself does not go hand in hand with a lower rate of growth of living standards. This does not prove that population growth does not impede progress; neither does it give ammunition to those who argue that it is beneficial. What the lack of correlation does indicate is that there is a complex interactive process and

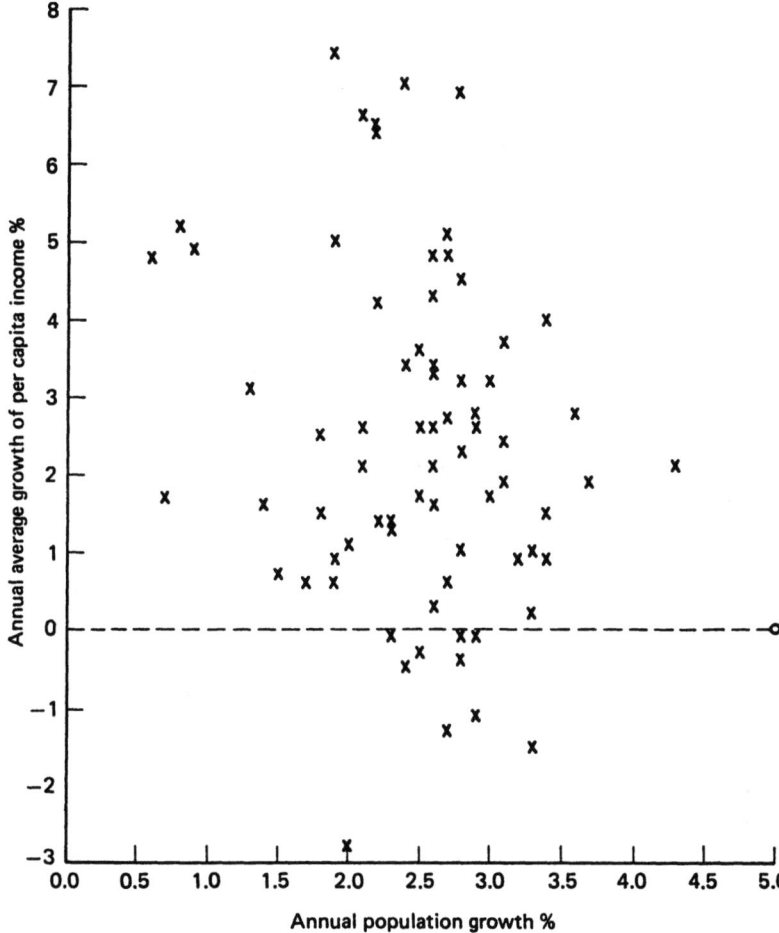

Figure 5.4   The relationship between the average rate of growth of per capita income and population growth in developing countries, 1960–1980

conflicting forces at work in which population is both an impediment and a stimulus to economic progress.

Notwithstanding the inconclusive statistical evidence, the popular, majority view, at least amongst the laity and policy makers, if not development economists, is still the old classical view that population growth is harmful to the long run development prospects of the developing countries. Three main reasons are advanced in support of this view. First, that rapid population growth, by raising the dependency ratio and reducing the level of per capita income, impairs the ability of countries to save and invest, on which growth depends. This is essentially an empirical question which can only be settled by an appeal to the facts. When I was interested in this topic myself in the 1970s (and when I was rather more 'scientific' than I am today), I conducted a cross section study of population growth and the growth of output and per capita income in a production function framework (Thirlwall 1972) in which I showed that it does seem to be true that the faster the growth of population, the lower the rate of capital accumulation. On the other hand, it also seems to be the case that the faster the growth of population, the faster the rate of growth of total factor productivity or technical progress. The fact that the one effect cancelled the other was the reason I adduced for the lack of any statistically significant association between population growth and the growth of living standards.

The second major reason why population growth is said to constitute a development problem relates to the question of employment. If population growth outstrips the capacity of the economy to absorb new labour in industry or in agriculture, urban unemployment or rural under-employment, or both, are exacerbated. Although there are more fundamental causes of growing urban unemployment in developing countries than the natural increase in population, such as the choice of techniques and the exodus from the land, the growth of unemployment must be taken very seriously. If the opportunity of employment and the reduction of unemployment are included in a definition of development, there may be grounds for regarding population growth as detrimental to welfare even though it may not retard the average rate of growth of per capita income.

The third major reason why population growth is regarded as a problem is the view, still held, that developing countries approximate to the type of world envisaged by Malthus; that the very rise in per capita income brought about, say, by technological progress, will itself induce a Pavlov-type response of further population growth such that any gains in living standards are eroded and per capita income will oscillate around a subsistence level, keeping countries in a so-called low-level equilibrium trap. The concept of Malthusianism and of a low level equilibrium trap have spawned many development theories and development strategies for countries to break out of this vicious circle of poverty, the most famous of which being those which argue for a critical minimum effort or big push to reach a level of per capita income such that the growth rate, via the ability to accumulate capital, exceeds for ever the rate of population growth. Not many economists these days believe in the necessity or the feasibility of a big push. If the Malthusian trap exists, it is possible to escape from it gradually. Those who still believe in the necessity of a big push, however, or who wish to speed up the time it takes to escape from the trap gradually, now focus their sights not on a massive capital investment programme, but on birth control.

The pessimistic view of population growth, leading to demands for a reorientation of development priorities towards a reduction in births, has been supported by the work of influential economists such as the late Professor Enke (1966; 1971) and Coale and Hoover (1958). Enke (1971) states:

> the economic danger of population growth lies in the consequent inability of a country both to increase its stock of capital and to improve its state of art rapidly enough for its per capita income not to be less than it otherwise would be. If the rate of technological innovation cannot be forced, and is not advanced by faster population growth, a rapid proportionate growth in population can cause an actual reduction in income per capita. Rapid population growth inhibits an increase in capital per worker, especially if associated with high crude birth rates that make for a young age distribution.

Coale and Hoover, in a study of population growth and development based on Indian experience, likewise remark:

> While greater numbers in the labour force add to the total product, faster growth of the labour force implies a lower output per worker than slower growth. The reason for this result is that with a faster growing labour force more capital must be directed to provide tools and equipment for the extra workers so that they will be as productive as the existing labour force, and thus less will be available, *ceteris paribus*, for increasing output per worker.

Enke's work and views led him to the conclusion that 'resources used to retard population growth can contribute perhaps one hundred times more to higher incomes per head than resources used to accelerate output growth' (Enke 1966).

The core of the argument is a simple numerical example comparing the impact on average income of equal expenditures either on conventional development projects intended to raise the national income, or on a birth reduction programme. For example, suppose $0.5 million is invested each year in conventional capital projects yielding a rate of return of 15 per cent per annum. This would give an annual output increase of $0.075 million. After ten years, $5 million will have been invested yielding an annual income flow of $0.75 million. If the initial level of income was, say, $500 million, the flow from the new investment represents a proportionate change of 0.0015. Now suppose $0.5 million is invested each year in a birth control programme fitting inter-uterine devices. If the cost per participant is $1, there would be 500,000 participants on average each year. Assuming that the live-birth fertility of a typical woman participant is 0.15 infants a year, the reduction in births over ten years is (500 000) (0.15) (10) = 750 000. If the initial population is, say, 5 million (which combined with the assumption of $500 million income gives a per capita income of $100), the proportionate change in population due to the annual investment in the birth control programme is 0.15. Thus if investment of $5 million in physical capital over ten years gives a growth rate of income of 0.0015, and $5 million invested over ten years in population control gives a proportionate reduction in population of 0.15, then investment to control births is 100 times more effective in raising the rate of growth of per capita income than investment in physical capital. Enke comments, 'it is staggering to encounter such ratios when comparing different economic policies.' General amazement could be reduced if it is noticed that this particular ratio is crucially dependent on the values taken for the initial levels of population and income. The lower the population and the higher the income (i. e. the higher the level of per capita income) the greater the relative return to birth control programmes – a conclusion opposite to the one Enke presumably wanted to reach. If the approach is sensible it also implies that the more investment in birth control programmes, the higher the ratio of effectiveness will become; a form of increasing returns to population control!

One weakness of the approach is that while Enke concedes that substantial bonuses may have to be paid to encourage the adoption of birth control practices, he does not recalculate the basic numerical example to take account of these additional expenditures. The excuse is that bonuses are simply transfer payments, but transfer payments have alternative investment uses. But the major, serious objection to the whole approach is that it treats changes in population and income as independent whereas they are interdependent. When population growth is reduced, output growth will also be reduced directly if the marginal product of labour is positive, and also indirectly if productivity growth in the economy falls as the population growth rate falls. A reduction in population growth may yield no long run increase in income per head. It is possible, of course, that an increase in income from investment in physical capital may induce population growth, nullifying also the gains from investment in physical capital in some crude Malthusian manner. But this is much less likely than the former possibility. If anything direct increases in income seem to have a depressing effect on the birth rate. Indeed many would argue that a precondition for any birth control scheme to be effective is that the level of income is first raised – a view summed up by the aphorism that affluence is the best contraceptive.

Enke also undertakes traditional cost-benefit analysis to estimate the rate of return to expenditure on birth control programmes. The benefit of a birth prevented is measured by the discounted value of the saved consumption (i.e. by increased saving). Up to the age of 15, when an addition to the population is not productive, Enke calculates a net gain in saving, discounting at 15 per cent, of $280 (at 1960s prices); and between the ages of 15 and 55, when the addition to population is productive, he calculates a net loss of saving $17, giving a total net benefit to society of a saved birth of $263. The cost of preventing a birth is estimated to be only $5, giving a very high net present value and a high social rate of return on capital invested. Within the framework of the model the most suspect feature of Enke's procedure is that the whole of a child's consumption up to the age of 15 is treated as a reduction in society's saving whereas, in fact, the child may work; the family to which it belongs may reduce their consumption on other things, or the family itself may work harder and produce more to support the child. When these considerations are taken into account, the net gain in saving or saved consumption from the prevention of a birth may be very much less. Also forgotten are the positive externalities that people may confer on one another, not to mention that great leaders, inventors and artists must come from the human stock. Who can say what the long run consequences of saving births will be with such intangible considerations involved? Moreover, to measure the benefits of a lower population simply in terms of additions to saving is extremely narrow in conception. Societies have never placed an infinite valuation on saving, not even Stalinist Russia. Taking the analysis to its logical conclusion, a social optimum would be achieved when consumption per head fell to zero, yielding maximum savings but at the cost of national suicide!

It would be misleading to give the impression, however, that all population economists are pessimistic about the influence of population growth on living standards and emphasise the overriding need for population control programmes. The pessimistic view has been challenged in a piecemeal fashion by a succession of economists over the years, although not with much impact. Professor Richard Easterlin (1967) has suggested that population pressure can affect favourably individual motivation and lead to changes in production techniques which overcome the consequences of large numbers. He also claims that a young age structure of a country makes it more amenable to change, more receptive to new ideas, more willing to shift resources from low productivity to high productivity sectors, and so on – all of which may raise income per head. Professor Hirschman (1958) points to the positive advantages of population increase: that it increases the supply of potential decision takers (which is the real scarcity in developing countries); expands markets, and leads to development via shortages. Professor Kuznets (1967) and Dr Colin Clark (1969) have pointed to the zero correlation between population growth and living standards, and Clark (a Catholic with a large family!) calls the population problem a development 'myth'.

A more recent challenge to the conventional wisdom has come in two stimulating and fascinating books by Professor Julian Simon (1977; 1981) whose major thesis is that 'the ultimate resource is people – skilled, spirited and hopeful people – who will exert their wills and imaginations for their own benefit, and so, inevitably, for the benefit of us all.' Simon brings together both the theoretical arguments and empirical evidence on both sides of the population debate and presents his own simulation results on the relation between population growth and living standards. He finds that the initial effects of population increase on per capita income are negative, but that in the longer term the positive feedback effects that result from the stimulus of population growth to technological progress and other factors which improve the rate of growth of productivity outweigh the negative effects. Simulations suggest that for countries already industrialised the initial negative effect of population is offset within fifty years. For less developed countries the conclusion is that moderate population growth is more favourable to the growth of living standards than either a stationary population or very fast population growth. An overall judgement on population growth, and whether it is beneficial or not, therefore depends very much on a weighing of the balance between the present and the future. In economics the present and the future are made comparable using the concept of a discount rate. Whether the positive long run benefits of population growth are considered to outweigh the short run negative effects depends very much on the discount rate and the time period taken. The less future benefits are discounted and the longer the time period taken, the more beneficial (less detrimental) population growth appears,and the shorter the time period considered and the more future benefits are discounted the less beneficial (more detrimental) population growth appears. There will be some time period and some discount rate at which additional population now is exactly on the borderline of having a negative or positive value.

What are the positive feedback effects that population increase exerts on economic progress which vitiates the classical prediction that population growth is uniformly depressing on living standards? In his simulation model of the relationship between population growth and per capita income in advanced countries, Simon attempts to capture the effect of additional children on such factors as the savings ratio; labour supplied by the parents; scale economies; and technical progress. In his simulation model for developing countries Simon considers the following important feedback mechanisms: the stimulus to new methods in agriculture; the supply response of families; the provision of social infrastructure (particularly transport); scale economies; and demand-induced investment. Let us briefly consider some of these factors.

A society under pressure from population growth may be expected to respond by finding new and more efficient ways of meeting given needs. In agriculture, the Malthusian view would be that improvements simply induce more population. Others would argue that even if population pressure does not induce the production of new techniques it certainly induces their *adoption*. There are many empirical examples of societies that have adopted new labour intensive agricultural techniques to replace land intensive methods as population pressure has exerted itself. Pierre Gourou (1965) cites various African cases where the change from shifting cultivation to settled agriculture can be clearly associated with density increases. And Ester Boserup (1965; 1981) has consistently argued that technological change needed to expand agricultural production often entails initially a greater labour input per worker and therefore will not be adopted voluntarily until necessity requires it. It is difficult to see where the stimulus to the green revolution would have come from without the pressure of numbers on food supply. Innovation, generally, may be linked to the number of people. Simon (1981) puts it thus: 'because improvements – their invention and their adoption – come from people, it seems reasonable to assume that the amount of improvement depends on the number of people available to use their minds. A larger population implies a larger amount of knowledge being created, all else being equal.'

Agricultural families may respond to the needs of additional children by changing methods, working harder and producing more. Studies suggest that the elasticity of output to increases in the number of children is about 0.5; that is, an increase in family size, say, from four to five (25 per cent) would result in a 12.5 per cent increase in output. Simon argues that population growth also has a large positive effect on agricultural saving, which tends to be overlooked because a large fraction is non-monetised.

Population pressure provides a stimulus to develop social infrastructure, transport and communication facilities, which have far-reaching external repercussions, extending beyond the additional numbers they were designed to serve. Population growth also makes these facilities more economical to provide because of the scale economies involved in their provision. Most studies find evidence of scale economies to population in the provision of transport, communications and other components of the economic infrastructure. A case study of roads by Glover and Simon (1975) shows a strong positive elasticity of roads per unit area with respect to population density (across countries and controlling for the level of per capita income). Simon (1977) sums up: 'if there is a single key element in economic development other than culture and institutions and psychological make-up, that single key element is transportation together with communications.' Adam Smith, an early contemporary of Malthus and much more optimistic about the development process, was impressed by the benefits of communications: 'good roads, canals and navigable rivers, by diminishing the expense of carriage, put the remote parts of the country more nearly upon a level with those in the neighbourhood of the town. They are upon that account the greatest of all improvements – they break down monopolies . . . they open new markets'. To the extent that population growth exerts pressure for these facilities to be provided, a significant output response is to be expected.

Increased population also has many other types of productivity effects which are subtle and indirect, yet nonetheless important. It is very difficult, for cxample, to improve health and sanitation in sparsely populated areas, but once sanitation and health improvement become feasible and economical with greater numbers, enormous benefits may result – more than in proportion to the increase in population. A growing population also facilitates change without disrupting the organisation and positions of those already established. Thus government and administration may be expected to improve and become more in keeping with the needs of development. Youth itself has positive advantages. Young people are more receptive to change and modernisation than older people. The younger a population the more education (or human capital) per head of the population. Young people tend to be more mobile which is an asset when structural change is required. With a growing population, investment is less risky. Many development economists believe that one of the major obstacles to development is not a shortage of saving but a lack of willingness to invest. An expanding market resulting from population growth provides an incentive to investment.

The great difference between the results of Simon and the results of Enke and Hoover and Coale cited earlier is that all the beneficial feedback effects of population on output mentioned above are omitted from the latter analyses. But any of the feedback factors referred to may partially or fully offset the capital-dilution effect of greater numbers in the short run which is the factor that the predictions of conventional models reflect. A complete analysis of the relation between population and living standards must have due regard to the longer term benefits that population expansion can confer on societies, as well as the short term costs.

So far, I have been deliberately iconoclastic to redress the bias in the popular literature in favour of the view that population growth is uniformly depressing on economic welfare and that a necessary, if not sufficient, condition for the eradication of Third World poverty is population control. I would concede, however, that rapid population growth can have adverse welfare consequences in inert societies that are unable, or find it difficult, to respond to the challenge. Particularly worrying is severe overcrowding in many of the major cities of developing countries; environmental pollution; the pressure of population on food supplies in particular parts of the world; and the lack of balance between the demand for labour and the increase in supplies. There is also convincing evidence of a positive association between population growth and the level of income inequality measured by the shares of income received by the poorest and richest households. None of these phenomena are the inevitable consequence of rapid population growth, but are seriously exacerbated in societies which lack the political will or resources to cope. It is for this reason that I began this essay by saying that it is probably preferable for societies to risk type II error even though I don't believe that a reduction in population growth in most developing countries would make any significant difference to the rate of growth of average living standards. Population plays a conflicting role in the growth process and there are many more fundamental determinants of the rate of economic progress than the population growth rate alone.

Notes

1. This leads Neher (1971) to his golden rule of reproduction that each generation should procreate for the future as it would have wished the past generation to procreate for itself!
2. It was Keynes who was to revive the concept of effective demand in his path-breaking book, *The General Theory of Employment, Interest and Money* (1936), in which he acknowledges a debt to Malthus.
3. Assuming a savings ratio of 8–15 per cent, and a capital-output ratio of 4, Keynes calculates the growth rate necessary for investment to fully absorb savings viz: 2–4 per cent. If technical progress is raising productivity at only 1 per cent, population (or labour force) growth must be between 1 and 3 per cent to ensure full employment. In this analysis of long run equilibrium, Keynes anticipates precisely Harrod's (1948) dynamic theory of the warranted and natural rate of growth and the conditions for a moving equilibrium through time. I develop this argument more fully in a paper 'Keynes, economic development and the developing countries' (1987).

References

Boserup, E. (1965) *The Conditions of Agricultural Growth* (London: Allen & Unwin).
Boserup, E. (1981) *Population and Technological Change: A Study of Long Term Trends* (Chicago: University of Chicago Press).
Cassen, R. (1976) 'Population and development: a survey', *World Development*, 4, 785–830.
Clark, C. (1964) 'The "population explosion" myth' *Bulletin of the Institute of Development Studies*, 1 (4), 19–20 (Brighton: University of Sussex).

Coale, A. J. and Hoover, E. M. (1958) *Population Growth and Economic Development in the Low-Income Countries* (Princeton, N. J.: Princeton University Press).

Easterlin, R. (1967) 'The effects of population growth on the economic development of developing countries', *Annals of the American Academy of Political and Social Science*, 371, 98–108.

Enke, S. (1966) 'The economic aspects of slowing population growth', *Economic Journal*, 76, 44–56.

Enke, S. (1971) 'Economic consequences of rapid population growth', *Economic Journal*, 81, 800–11.

Glover, D. R. and Simon, J. L. (1975) 'The effects of population density upon infra-structure: the case of road building', *Economic Development and Cultural Change*, 23, 453–68.

Goulet, D. (1971) *The Cruel Choice: A New Concept on the Theory of Development* (New York: Atheneum).

Gourou, P. (1965) *The Tropical World: Its Social and Economic Conditions and its Future Status* (London: Longman, 4th edn).

Harrod, R. (1948) *Towards a Dynamic Economics* (London: Macmillan).

Hirschman, A. (1958) *Strategy of Economic Development* (New Haven, Conn: Yale University Press).

Kelley, A. C. and Williamson, J. G. (1974) *Lessons from Japanese Development: An Analytical Economic History* (Chicago, Ill.: University of Chicago Press).

Keynes, J. M. (1936) *The General Theory of Employment, Interest and Money* (London: Macmillan).

Keynes, J. M. (1937) 'Some economic consequences of a declining population', *Eugenics Review*, 29, 13–17.

Kuznets, S. (1967) 'Population and economic growth', *Proceedings of the American Philosophical Society* III (Philadelphia: American Philosophical Society).

Neher, P. A. (1971) 'Peasants, procreation and pensions', *American Economic Review*, 61, 380–9.

Rawls, J. (1972) *A Theory of Justice* (Oxford: University Press).

Sidgwick, H. (1907) *Methods of Ethics* (London: Macmillan, 7th edn).

Simon, J. (1977) *The Economics of Population Growth* (Princeton, N. J.: Princeton University Press).

Simon, J. (1981) *The Ultimate Resource* (Princeton, N. J.: Princeton University Press).

Thirlwall, A. P. (1972) 'Population growth and the growth of output and living standards in a production function framework', *Manchester School of Economics and Social Studies*, 40, 339–53.

Thirlwall, A. P. (1987) 'Keynes, economic development and the developing countries', in *Keynes and Economic Development*, ed. A. P. Thirlwall, Proceedings of the Seventh Keynes Conference, University of Kent at Canterbury (London: Macmillan).

World Development Report 1984 (Oxford: Oxford University Press for the World Bank).

Table 5.1   Population growth and projections

	Average annual growth of population (%)			Population (millions)		
	1960–70	*1970–82*	*1980–2000*	*1982*	*1990*	*2000*
Low-income economies	**2.3** *w*	**1.9** *w*	**1.7** *w*	**2269**	**2621**	**3097**
China and India	**2.3** *w*	**1.7** *w*	**1.3** *w*	**1725**	**1938**	**2190**
Other low-income	**2.5** *w*	**2.6** *w*	**2.9** *w*	**544**	**683**	**907**
1 Chad	1.9	2.0	2.5	5	6	7
2 Bangladesh	2.5	2.6	2.9	93	119	157
3 Ethiopia	2.4	2.0	3.1	33	42	57
4 Nepal	1.9	2.6	2.6	15	19	24
5 Mali	2.5	2.7	2.8	7	9	12
6 Burma	2.2	2.2	2.4	35	43	53
7 Zaire	2.0	3.0	3.3	31	40	55
8 Malawi	2.8	3.0	3.4	7	8	12
9 Upper Volta	2.0	2.0	2.4	7	8	10
10 Uganda	3.0	2.7	3.4	14	17	25
11 India	2.3	2.3	1.9	717	844	994
12 Rwanda	2.6	3.4	3.6	6	7	11
13 Burundi	1.4	2.2	3.0	4	5	7
14 Tanzania	2.7	3.4	3.5	20	26	36
15 Somalia	2.8	2.8	2.4	5	5	7
16 Haiti	1.6	1.7	1.8	5	6	7
17 Benin	2.6	2.7	3.3	4	5	7
18 Central African Rep.	1.6	2.1	2.8	2	3	4
19 China	2.3	1.4	1.0	1008	1094	1196
20 Guinea	1.5	2.0	2.4	6	7	9
21 Niger	3.4	3.3	3.3	6	8	11
22 Madagascar	2.2	2.6	3.2	9	12	16
23 Sri Lanka	2.4	1.7	1.8	15	18	21
24 Togo	3.0	2.6	3.3	3	4	5
25 Ghana	2.3	3.0	3.9	12	17	24
26 Pakistan	2.8	3.0	2.7	87	107	140
27 Kenya	3.2	4.0	4.4	18	26	40
28 Sierra Leone	1.7	2.0	2.4	3	4	5
29 *Afghanistan*	2.2	2.5	2.3	17	20	25
30 *Bhutan*	1.3	2.0	2.2	1	1	2

31 *Kampuchea,*						
Dem.	2.5	–	–	–	–	–
32 *Lao PDR*	1.9	2.0	2.6	4	4	6
33 *Mozambique*	2.1	4.3	3.4	13	17	24
34 *Viet Nam*	3.1	2.8	2.5	57	70	88
Middle-income						
economies	**2.6** *w*	**2.4** *w*	**2.2** *w*	**1163**	**1404**	**1741**
Oil exporters	**2.6** *w*	**2.7** *w*	**2.5** *w*	**521**	**641**	**819**
Oil importers	**2.5** *w*	**2.3** *w*	**2.0** *w*	**642**	**763**	**922**
Lower						
middle-income	**2.5** *w*	**2.5** *w*	**2.4** *w*	**673**	**816**	**1023**
35 Sudan	2.2	3.2	2.9	20	25	34
36 Mauritania	2.3	2.3	2.6	2	2	3
37 Yemen, PDR	2.2	2.2	3.1	2	2	3
38 Liberia	3.2	3.5	3.5	2	3	4
39 Senegal	2.3	2.7	3.1	6	8	10
40 Yemen Arab						
Rep.	2.3	3.0	2.9	8	9	12
41 Lesotho	2.0	2.4	2.8	1	2	2
42 Bolivia	2.4	2.6	2.4	6	7	9
43 Indonesia	2.1	2.3	1.9	153	179	212
44 Zambia	2.6	3.1	3.6	6	8	11
45 Honduras	3.1	3.4	3.1	4	5	7
46 Egypt, Arab						
Rep.	2.5	2.5	2.0	44	52	63
47 El Salvador	3.4	3.0	2.6	5	6	8
48 Thailand	3.1	2.4	1.9	49	57	68
49 Papua New						
Guinea	2.2	2.1	2.2	3	4	5
50 Philippines	3.0	2.7	2.1	51	61	73
51 Zimbabwe	3.6	3.2	4.4	8	11	16
52 Nigeria	2.5	2.6	3.5	91	119	169
53 Morocco	2.6	2.6	2.5	20	25	31
54 Cameroon	2.0	3.0	3.5	9	12	17
55 Nicaragua	2.6	3.9	3.0	3	4	5
56 Ivory Coast	3.7	4.9	3.7	9	12	17
57 Guatemala	3.0	3.1	2.6	8	10	12
58 Congo,						
People's						
Rep.	2.4	3.0	3.8	2	2	3
59 Costa Rica	3.3	2.5	2.2	2	3	3

continued on page 98

Table *5.1   continued*

	Average annual growth of population (percent)			Population (millions)		
	1960–70	*1970–82*	*1980–2000*	*1982*	*1990*	*2000*
60 Peru	2.9	2.8	2.2	17	21	26
61 Dominican Rep.	2.9	3.0	2.2	6	7	8
62 Jamaica	1.4	1.5	1.4	2	3	3
63 Ecuador	2.9	2.6	2.6	8	10	13
64 Turkey	2.5	2.3	2.0	47	55	65
65 Tunisia	2.0	2.3	2.3	7	8	10
66 Colombia	3.0	1.9	1.9	27	32	38
67 Paraguay	2.6	2.6	2.3	3	4	5
68 *Angola*	2.1	2.5	2.8	8	10	13
69 *Cuba*	2.1	1.1	1.0	10	11	12
70 *Korea, Dem. Rep.*	2.8	2.5	2.1	19	22	27
71 *Lebanon*	2.9	0.5	1.3	3	3	3
72 *Mongolia*	3.0	2.9	2.4	2	2	3
Upper middle-income	**2.6** *w*	**2.3** *w*	**2.1** *w*	**490**	**588**	**718**
73 Syrian Arab Rep.	3.2	3.5	3.5	10	13	17
74 Jordan	3.1	2.5	3.9	3	4	6
75 Malaysia	2.8	2.5	2.0	15	17	21
76 Korea, Rep. of	2.6	1.7	1.4	39	45	51
77 Panama	2.9	2.3	1.9	2	2	3
78 Chile	2.1	1.7	1.4	12	13	15
79 Brazil	2.8	2.4	2.0	127	152	181
80 Mexico	3.3	3.0	2.3	73	89	109
81 Algeria	2.4	3.1	3.7	20	27	39
82 Portugal	0.3	0.8	0.6	10	10	11
83 Argentina	1.5	1.4	1.3	28	32	36
84 Uruguay	1.0	0.4	0.7	3	3	3
85 South Africa	2.4	2.8	3.1	30	39	52
86 Yugoslavia	1.0	0.9	0.6	23	24	25
87 Venezuela	3.8	3.6	2.6	17	21	26

88 Greece	0.6	1.0	0.4	10	10	11
89 Israel	3.5	2.5	1.6	4	5	5
90 Hong Kong	2.5	2.4	1.4	5	6	7
91 Singapore	2.3	1.5	1.0	3	3	3
92 Trinidad and Tobago	2.1	0.5	1.7	1	1	2
93 *Iran, Islamic Rep.*	3.4	3.1	3.1	41	53	70
94 *Iraq*	3.2	3.5	3.4	14	19	26
High-income oil exporters	**4.2** *w*	**5.0** *w*	**3.8** *w*	**17**	**24**	**33**
95 Oman	2.6	4.3	2.9	1	1	2
96 Libya	3.9	4.1	4.3	3	5	7
97 Saudi Arabia	3.5	4.8	3.7	10	14	19
98 Kuwait	9.9	6.3	3.5	2	2	3
99 United Arab Emirates	9.3	15.5	3.7	1	2	2
Industrial market economies	**1.1** *w*	**0.7** *w*	**0.4** *w*	**723**	**749**	**780**
100 Ireland	0.4	1.5	1.1	4	4	4
101 Spain	1.0	1.0	0.7	38	40	43
102 Italy	0.7	0.4	0.1	56	57	58
103 New Zealand	1.8	1.0	0.6	3	3	4
104 United Kingdom	0.6	0.1	0.1	56	56	57
105 Austria	0.5	0.1	0.1	8	8	8
106 Japan	1.0	1.1	0.4	118	123	128
107 Belgium	0.6	0.2	0.1	10	10	10
108 Finland	0.4	0.4	0.1	5	5	5
109 Netherlands	1.3	0.7	0.4	14	15	15
110 Australia	2.0	1.5	1.0	15	16	18
111 Canada	1.8	1.2	1.0	25	27	29
112 France	1.1	0.5	0.4	54	56	58
113 Germany, Fed. Rep.	0.9	0.1	−0.1	62	61	60
114 Denmark	0.8	0.3	0.1	5	5	5
115 United States	1.3	1.0	0.7	232	245	259
116 Sweden	0.7	0.3	0.1	8	8	9
117 Norway	0.8	0.5	0.2	4	4	4
118 Switzerland	1.5	0.1	0.1	6	6	6

continued on page 100

Table *5.1   continued*

East European nonmarket economies	1.1 *w*	0.8 *w*	0.6 *w*	384	407	431
119 Hungary	0.3	0.3	0.1	11	11	11
120 Romania	0.9	0.9	0.7	23	24	25
121 *Albania*	2.8	2.5	1.8	3	3	4
122 *Bulgaria*	0.8	0.4	0.3	9	9	10
123 *Czechoslovakia*	0.5	0.6	0.4	15	16	17
124 *German Dem. Rep.*	–0.1	–0.2	0.2	17	17	17
125 *Poland*	1.0	0.9	0.7	36	39	41
126 *USSR*	1.2	0.9	0.7	270	288	306
Total				4556	5205	6082

Figures in italics are for years other than those specified. *w* means weighted average.

Source: *World Development Report, 1984.*

Table 5.2 Demographic and fertility-related indicators

	Crude birth rate per thousand population		Crude death rate per thousand population		Percentage change in:		Total fertility rate	
					Crude birth rate	Crude death rate		
	1960	1982	1960	1982	1960–82	1960–82	1982	2000
Low-income economies	44 w	30 w	24 w	11 w	**-34.2** w	**-54.7** w	**4.1** w	**3.2** w
China and India	43 w	25 w	24 w	9 w	**-42.6** w	**-61.5** w	**3.4** w	**2.4** w
Other low-income	47 w	44 w	24 w	16 w	**-7.2** w	**-32.8** w	**6.1** w	**5.2** w
1 Chad	45	42	29	21	-6.6	-27.7	5.5	5.6
2 Bangladesh	47	47	22	17	0.2	-24.7	6.3	5.1
3 Ethiopia	51	47	28	18	-7.0	-35.9	6.5	6.1
4 Nepal	46	43	26	19	-6.5	-27.3	6.3	5.3
5 Mali	50	48	27	21	-3.2	-23.0	6.5	6.0
6 Burma	43	38	21	13	-11.3	-37.9	5.3	3.6
7 Zaire	48	46	24	16	-4.1	-34.2	6.3	5.8
8 Malawi	56	56	27	23	0.2	-15.7	7.8	7.1
9 Upper Volta	49	48	27	21	-1.5	-20.1	6.5	6.0
10 Uganda	49	50	21	19	1.4	-11.6	7.0	6.4
11 India	48	34	24	13	-28.3	-46.8	4.8	2.9
12 Rwanda	53	54	27	20	0.9	-27.4	8.3	7.6
13 Burundi	45	47	25	19	2.9	-23.7	6.5	6.0
14 Tanzania	47	47	22	15	0.8	-33.4	6.5	5.8
15 Somalia	48	48	29	25	0.2	-12.3	6.5	6.1

continued on page 102

Table 5.2 Demographic and fertility-related indicators

	Crude birth rate per thousand population		Crude death rate per thousand population		Percentage change in:		Total fertility rate	
					Crude birth rate	Crude death rate		
	1960	1982	1960	1982	1960–82	1960–82	1982	2000
16 Haiti	39	32	19	13	–17.4	–35.7	4.6	3.7
17 Benin	51	49	27	18	–2.5	–32.2	6.5	5.9
18 Central African Rep.	43	41	26	17	–3.9	–35.4	5.5	5.6
19 China	39	19	24	7	–52.8	–71.9	2.3	2.0
20 Guinea	48	49	35	27	1.8	–22.6	6.5	6.1
21 Niger	52	52	27	20	0.7	–24.5	7.0	6.4
22 Madagascar	47	47	27	18	–0.1	–33.0	6.5	5.9
23 Sri Lanka	36	27	9	6	–25.7	–34.8	3.4	2.3
24 Togo	51	49	23	19	–2.7	–17.6	6.5	5.9
25 Ghana	50	49	20	13	–1.8	–35.7	7.0	6.3
26 Pakistan	49	42	23	15	–13.6	–34.3	5.8	4.8
27 Kenya	55	55	24	12	0.2	–47.9	8.0	7.1
28 Sierra Leone	49	49	34	27	–0.2	–20.6	6.5	6.1
29 Afghanistan	50	54	31	29	7.4	–6.5	8.0	5.6
30 Bhutan	43	43	25	21	–0.2	–15.3	6.2	5.1
31 Kampuchea, Dem.	45	–	21	–	–	–	–	–
32 Lao PDR	44	42	23	20	–4.7	–12.0	6.4	5.9
33 Mozambique	–	49	–	16	–	–	6.5	5.9
34 Viet Nam	47	35	21	8	–24.9	–62.3	5.0	3.1

	43 w / 47 w / 40 w	35 w / 38 w / 31 w	17 w / 21 w / 15 w	10 w / 12 w / 9 w	−22.0 w / −19.1 w / −24.5 w	−39.6 w / −42.9 w / −37.0 w	4.7 w / 5.3 w / 4.2 w	3.6 w / 4.0 w / 3.3 w
Middle-income economies	**43** w	**35** w	**17** w	**10** w	**−22.0** w	**−39.6** w	**4.7** w	**3.6** w
Oil exporters	**47** w	**38** w	**21** w	**12** w	**−19.1** w	**−42.9** w	**5.3** w	**4.0** w
Oil importers	**40** w	**31** w	**15** w	**9** w	**−24.5** w	**−37.0** w	**4.2** w	**3.3** w
Lower middle-income	**46** w	**37** w	**20** w	**12** w	**−21.2** w	**−42.0** w	**5.0** w	**3.9** w
35 Sudan	47	45	25	18	−3.4	−29.9	6.6	6.0
36 Mauritania	51	43	27	19	−14.3	−28.3	6.0	5.9
37 Yemen, PDR	50	48	29	19	−5.6	−33.9	6.9	6.3
38 Liberia	50	50	21	14	−0.3	−30.6	6.9	6.2
39 Senegal	48	48	26	21	–	−22.5	6.5	6.0
40 Yemen Arab Rep.	50	48	29	22	−2.8	−25.1	6.8	6.2
41 Lesotho	42	42	23	15	–	−35.8	5.8	5.2
42 Bolivia	46	43	22	16	−7.2	−28.7	6.3	4.2
43 Indonesia	44	34	23	13	−23.9	−43.2	4.3	2.8
44 Zambia	51	50	24	16	−2.2	−36.5	6.8	6.1
45 Honduras	51	44	19	10	−14.2	−45.1	6.5	4.1
46 Egypt, Arab Rep.	44	35	20	11	−22.1	−44.6	4.6	3.0
47 El Salvador	48	40	17	8	−17.4	−52.1	5.6	3.3
48 Thailand	44	28	15	8	−36.2	−48.1	3.6	2.6
49 Papua New Guinea	44	34	23	13	−22.3	−43.1	5.0	3.6
50 Philippines	47	31	15	7	−34.0	−53.4	4.2	2.7
51 Zimbabwe	55	54	17	12	−1.8	−25.0	8.0	7.1
52 Nigeria	52	50	25	16	−4.7	−35.6	6.9	6.3
53 Morocco	50	40	21	15	−19.8	−30.7	5.8	3.8
54 Cameroon	38	46	21	15	21.2	−30.7	6.5	6.4

continued on page 104

Table 5.2 *continued*

	Crude birth rate per thousand population		Crude death rate per thousand population		Percentage change in:		Total fertility rate	
					Crude birth rate	Crude death rate		
	1960	1982	1960	1982	1960–82	1960–82	1982	2000
55 Nicaragua	51	45	18	11	-11.3	-39.8	6.3	4.0
56 Ivory Coast	49	48	24	17	-2.7	-28.2	7.0	6.4
57 Guatemala	48	38	18	9	-21.0	-49.1	5.2	3.4
58 Congo, People's Rep.	40	43	18	10	6.8	-46.0	6.0	5.7
59 Costa Rica	48	30	8	4	-36.8	-51.3	3.5	2.3
60 Peru	47	34	19	11	-27.4	-42.1	4.5	3.2
61 Dominican Rep.	49	34	17	8	-31.1	-54.0	4.2	2.7
62 Jamaica	42	27	9	6	-35.0	-36.4	3.4	2.3
63 Ecuador	47	37	17	8	-20.5	-49.3	5.4	3.5
64 Turkey	43	31	16	9	-28.0	-43.4	4.1	2.7
65 Tunisia	47	34	19	9	-27.0	-51.9	4.9	3.1
66 Colombia	47	29	17	7	-38.8	-57.5	3.6	2.6
67 Paraguay	43	31	13	7	-27.2	-44.6	4.2	2.7
68 Angola	50	49	31	22	-1.8	-28.6	6.5	6.0
69 Cuba	31	16	9	6	-46.7	-36.7	2.0	2.0
70 Korea, Dem. Rep.	41	30	13	7	-25.9	-42.0	4.0	2.6
71 Lebanon	43	29	14	9	-33.2	-40.2	3.8	2.4
72 Mongolia	41	34	15	7	-17.0	-52.7	4.8	3.1

Upper middle-income	40 w	31 w	13 w	8 w	−23.2 w	−36.4 w	4.2 w	3.1 w
73 Syrian Arab Rep.	47	46	18	7	−1.5	−62.1	7.2	4.0
74 Jordan	47	45	20	8	−5.5	−59.3	7.4	5.2
75 Malaysia	44	29	15	6	−34.1	−57.0	3.7	2.4
76 Korea, Rep. of	43	23	14	6	−46.7	−53.3	2.7	2.1
77 Panama	41	28	10	5	−31.9	−47.6	3.5	2.3
78 Chile	34	23	13	7	−32.8	−46.8	2.7	2.2
79 Brazil	43	31	13	8	−26.9	−37.4	3.9	2.6
80 Mexico	45	34	12	7	−25.3	−41.5	4.6	2.8
81 Algeria	51	47	20	13	−7.8	−36.7	7.0	6.1
82 Portugal	24	18	11	10	−26.4	−8.3	2.3	2.1
83 Argentina	23	25	9	9	6.5	3.4	3.4	2.5
84 Uruguay	22	18	10	9	−17.4	−5.2	2.6	2.2
85 South Africa	39	40	15	9	1.3	−43.2	5.1	4.4
86 Yugoslavia	24	15	10	9	−36.6	−10.1	2.0	2.1
87 Venezuela	46	35	11	6	−24.4	−50.9	4.3	2.7
88 Greece	19	14	7	9	−24.3	19.2	2.3	2.1
89 Israel	27	24	6	7	−12.3	19.3	3.1	2.3
90 Hong Kong	35	18	7	5	−47.2	−20.9	2.1	2.1
91 Singapore	39	17	6	5	−55.3	−16.1	1.7	2.1
92 Trinidad and Tobago	38	29	8	7	−22.1	−17.2	3.3	2.4
93 Iran, Islamic Rep.	53	41	19	10	−23.8	−48.7	5.6	4.2
94 Iraq	49	45	20	11	−9.2	−46.2	6.7	4.9

continued on page 106

Table 5.2 *continued*

	Crude birth rate per thousand population		Crude death rate per thousand population		Percentage change in:		Total fertility rate	
					Crude birth rate	Crude death rate		
	1960	1982	1960	1982	1960–82	1960–82	1982	2000
High-income oil exporters	**49** w	**42** w	**22** w	**11** w	**−12.9** w	**−49.8** w	**6.9** w	**5.8** w
95 Oman	51	47	28	15	−7.0	−47.1	7.1	4.0
96 Libya	49	45	19	11	−7.1	−42.9	7.2	6.3
97 Saudi Arabia	49	43	23	12	−11.2	−45.8	7.1	6.3
98 Kuwait	44	35	10	3	−21.4	−65.2	5.7	3.0
99 United Arab Emirates	46	28	19	3	−39.1	−82.1	6.0	4.8
Industrial market economies	**20** w	**14** w	**10** w	**9** w	**−31.4** w	**−5.4** w	**1.7** w	**2.0** w
100 Ireland	21	20	12	9	−5.1	−18.3	3.2	2.1
101 Spain	22	15	9	9	−29.5	1.1	2.2	2.1
102 Italy	18	11	10	11	−37.0	9.4	1.6	1.9
103 New Zealand	27	16	9	8	−40.4	−8.0	1.9	2.0
104 United Kingdom	18	13	12	12	−27.4	3.5	1.8	2.0
105 Austria	18	13	13	12	−30.2	−5.5	1.6	1.9
106 Japan	17	13	8	7	−25.4	−13.2	1.7	1.9
107 Belgium	17	12	12	12	−28.4	−4.8	1.6	1.9

108 Finland	19	14	9	9	−25.9	–	1.6	1.9
109 Netherlands	21	12	8	8	−42.3	6.5	1.4	1.8
110 Australia	22	16	9	8	−28.1	−9.3	2.0	2.0
111 Canada	27	15	8	7	−43.4	−11.5	1.8	2.0
112 France	18	14	11	11	−23.5	−3.5	1.8	2.0
113 Germany, Fed. Rep.	18	10	12	12	−42.3	–	1.4	1.8
114 Denmark	17	10	10	11	−38.0	13.7	1.5	1.9
115 United States	24	16	10	9	−32.5	−9.5	1.8	2.0
116 Sweden	14	11	10	11	−19.0	9.0	1.7	1.9
117 Norway	17	12	9	10	−28.3	9.9	1.7	1.9
118 Switzerland	18	11	10	9	−35.2	−3.1	1.9	2.0
East European nonmarket economies	23 w	18 w	8 w	10 w	−20.5 w	34.4 w	2.3 w	2.1 w
119 Hungary	15	13	10	14	−15.0	32.4	2.0	2.0
120 Romania	19	17	9	10	−9.4	11.5	2.4	2.1
121 *Albania*	43	28	10	6	−35.9	−47.1	3.6	2.2
122 *Bulgaria*	18	15	8	10	−18.0	28.4	2.1	2.1
123 *Czechoslovakia*	16	15	9	12	−4.4	27.2	2.2	2.1
124 *German Dem. Rep.*	17	15	14	13	−14.7	−6.6	1.9	2.0
125 *Poland*	23	19	8	9	−14.2	21.1	2.3	2.1
126 *USSR*	25	19	7	10	−23.7	42.3	2.4	2.1

w means weighted average. Figures in italics are for years other than those specified. See notes.

Source: World Development Report, 1984.

6 Welfare and Management of Demographic Uncertainty

Richard M. Smith

INTRODUCTION

Some demographers are inclined to observe the irony in two themes that are proceeding concurrently and have come to occupy a prime position in their discipline. One research theme has marshalled a good deal of evidence to suggest that an increase of welfare and social insurance by governments or politically constituted agencies not organised around kin-groups has effects that are both demographically and economically advantageous in Third World situations. Such wealth transfers are supposed to reduce both mortality and morbidity and are believed to be especially important in undermining the security value offered to parents in old age by their children (Cain 1983; Potter 1983). However, another focus of research, much of it policy oriented in Developed Economies, and influenced greatly by ideas emanating in North America tends to emphasise the drain upon economic growth and the increasing sense of 'inter-generational injustice' that follow from recent age-structural changes. The ageing of the population in such economies is shown to have been caused demographically by increasing longevity and near or sub-replacement rate fertility. These improvements in life expectancy, especially at advanced ages and the falls in family size norms are in their turn viewed as partially attributable to an increasingly pervasive state welfare system which is furthermore, believed to be largely responsible for the demographic developments that increase the numbers of those recipients from, but reduce the contributors to the welfare funds (Ermisch 1983; Lee and Rogers 1987).

It is not my intention in this chapter to review what has come to be an enormous body of literature. Rather, I wish to focus upon one of its characteristics; that is, the categorical tone identifiable in much of the causal modelling employed, often of an overtly uni-directional kind. In particular, at the risk of sketching with brush strokes no doubt too broad for all tastes, I will try to consider the tendency, albeit implicit, in much of this work that treats demographic phenomena as fundamentally induced in their relationship with welfare, either in its incidence or organisation. I wish furthermore, to question this latter trait and to point towards the value to be gained from an awareness of comparative and historical approaches to these issues, especially in the field of policy making.

In using the phrase 'demographic uncertainty' in this discussion I will be referring to demographic processes and their probabilities of occurrence that threaten the capacity of individuals to be self sufficient and families to be collectively sufficient. Furthermore, since this is a discussion concerned with rather general themes, a somewhat loose definition of what is implied by 'welfare' will be used. In employing it I will not be concerned with all the actions that may be supposed to improve the well-being of members of society but with those more obvious measures that may be supposed to lessen privation and poverty.

Much of the research interesting us has occurred against a paradigmatic background that entails an implicit acceptance of Demographic Transition Theory. This explicitly portrays population growth whether in nineteenth-century Europe or the post-war underdeveloped world as being initiated by a fall in mortality that was in one sense or another believed to be attributable to rising real incomes and, in particular, to governmental measures to improve sanitary conditions and to intervene actively in the field of health care and health education (Heer and Smith 1968; Scrimshaw 1978; Heer 1983). Loosely, although unquestionably, attached to this descriptive model of demographic change is the idea of 'modernisation' with its unspoken acceptance of the teleological position that regards change over time as having been part of a pre-ordained shift towards the present higher, indeed superior order of social organisation (Easterlin 1983).

An inevitable assumption in all of this work is that in pre-industrial or pre-modern societies the family was principally, indeed wholly, responsible for the well-being of its members. Those in need of assistance for any number of reasons would look initially for aid to their immediate families, to more distant kin if that first recourse was impracticable and only towards charitably inclined neighbours as a last resort. Looking towards the wider community was not really an option, as society outside the kin-group is portrayed as bereft of organisations capable of handling the frail and the victims of various demographic uncertainties such as widowhood, orphanhood and bastardy and without ideologies well disposed towards such actions. The corollary of this view is that 'modern' society is distinguished from 'traditional' society by the availability of predictable bureaucratic support of a non-familial kind for the weak and vulnerable. As a consequence of the primacy of the state in the area of welfare the family has been downgraded to occupy a minor role very largely restricted to providing an emotional retreat, a 'haven in a heartless world' to use the expression of one American scholar (Lasch 1977).

THE FAMILY'S IMPLIED INTER-GENERATIONAL CONTRACT AND ITS DISSOLUTION

The economic premise underlying our assumption that families supported their disadvantaged members is that as social groupings they effected redistributions of resources between their productive and unproductive members. Certain social demographers are therefore disposed to see the extended family as a co-residential arrangement that yields an overlapping of individual life-cycles, thereby providing a means by which a flow of resources is achieved from those who have more to those who require more (Caldwell 1981). Such a domestic group is presented as being inherently more effective in dealing with the problems biologically unavoidable within an individual's life-cycle which begins and ends with quite extensive phases of dependency, than the restricted two-generational nuclear family struggling under a 'disproportionate burden of pre-mature dependents in its early stages and a disproportionate burden of post-mature dependents in its later stages' (Ryder 1984). The nuclear family would seem also to be structurally ill-suited to balancing the resources available with those needed over time.

Consequently, the extended family is often portrayed as a social arrangement capable of maintaining a flow of transactions over time by ensuring that the junior generation does not leave the family of orientation when it becomes productive (Ben-Porath 1980; Kotlikoff and Spivak 1981; Pollak 1985). If the argument is pursued further along these lines it is also easy to see why the descent group might be thought to provide a still more complete or risk-free supply of replacements available for the care of others when its members die. Such conclusions are derived from the elementary principle of spreading risk, and as such the descent group might be thought to possess greater viability than even the extended family.

Whether considered from the point of view of the extended family or the descent group an inter-generational contract is tacitly assumed to achieve resource transfers from those who are net producers to those who are net consumers (Caldwell 1982). Some theorists conceptualise each individual's life time as if it were encompassed by two such contracts, one with the senior generation in the family of orientation and the other with the junior generation in the family of procreation. Of particular significance from the focus of our interests in this discussion is the treatment of this matter by Norman Ryder (1984) who with characteristic perceptiveness suggests that long-term justice from the standpoint of the individual is obtained by writing the contract he initiates in the same terms as the contract written for him by his father. Provided that there is the same relationship between expectation and fulfilment in the two cases, the latter conditional on the success of efforts at socialisation and the former facilitated by social control of the junior by the senior generation, the system may be thought as existing in a state of dynamic equilibrium. As is the case with dynamic equilibrium models it is frequently found difficult to generate internal means of transformation so that inevitably a search is made for an exogenous force that can perform this role.

For many commentators the continuity or predictability in the nature of the inter-generational debt is seen to be disturbed by exogenously determined mortality decline which brings about a stirring of inter-generational discord (David and Sundstrom 1984). When the Net Reproduction Rate is equal to one it is believed that there is an assurance that on average each role in the present generation will be filled in turn by a member of the succeeding generation; a father's age at death is in close correspondence with his sons age at marriage; more formally, the average age of marriage is approximately equal to the expectation of life of the preceeding generation in the middle of its reproductive period (Ohlin 1961; Schofield 1976).

For families in the earlier marital durations, mortality decline means a higher ratio of net consumers to net producers and thus the incurring of a larger debt to the older generation and because there are more families in the earlier than the later marital durations there is available individually to the former a smaller source of borrowing. Similarly, an increase in parental survival defers the time when control of the family property is passed to the junior generation. This may increase the length of the period during which the junior generation contributes to the needs of their family of orientation, meaning that the strain on the system of respective rights and responsibilities caused by these changes is exacerbated. In theory, in these circumstances the contractual obligations of sons to fathers can be met with relative ease because there are more of them available for these tasks. Fathers, however, because there are more surviving sons, find it harder to reciprocate. The possibility therefore arises of an increasingly tenuous hold by fathers over their sons and their economic output or by the older generation more widely defined over the younger.

It is perhaps understandable that demographers, more than other social scientists might be inclined to approach the problem of social change with a particular emphasis upon the implications of reduced mortality. Indeed such a process has taken on a central, in fact pivotal position in classical Transition Theory. Perhaps it is also understandable, given the remarkable depth to which this idea has become embedded in the concepts of social science, that these demographers should employ an evolutionary model of family development that points to a transition from the extended to the nuclear form. For such scholars this transition is an essential element in the beginnings of a socio-cultural transformation away from familism in the direction of individualism with its demographic counterpart of fertility decline. It is nonetheless worth pondering whether the increasing possibility of overlap between successive generations as a consequence of lower mortality might at first seem to favour greater emphasis on lineage affiliation in a society. The forces working against any such trend are, however, far greater it would seem. Routine expected survival to old age certainly permits orderly individual planning of life but is thought by some observers to erode the important mutual insurance basis for close lateral kin ties. Paradoxically, as the task of managing one's family to ensure generational continuity becomes demographically more feasible, it also becomes, if we adopt the argument we have considered above, socially more problematic (McNicoll 1984).

Complementing the approach that sees the decline in the viability of the extended family as a self-contained 'welfare republic' contingent upon rising life expectancy is that which posits a sweep of socio-economic change to which demographic variables respond. But like the former this latter notion tends to regard the family as an entity apart from or largely independent of other institutions in society. Indeed it is frequently presented as if it existed *in vacuo*.

Consequently the growth of alternative outlets for the labour of the young or for their minds through the provision of state organised education are seen to constitute crucial influences that alter the terms of the inter-generational contract (Mendels 1978). State-provided social welfare, whether seen as a part of this process whereby familial functions are stripped away by outside agencies or viewed as a service developed by the State on account of the erosion of familial cohesion and mutual allegiance, is perceived as in fundamental opposition to familial solidarity and morality rather than an integral part of it (Caldwell 1980)

Of course, it should be obvious, but still worth stressing, that much thinking along these lines has developed in the context of a view of a 'traditional family' where allocational norms are held to provide fathers with no incentive to curtail fertility. Therefore, a transition to lower fertility becomes thinkable only when generational confrontations are created by exogenous demographic and socio-economic changes and the emergence of competing institutional structures strains the loyalty of children to their parents. As such, this style of argument utilises a set of conventional sociological principles that associate conflict with institutional transformation and social change (Coser 1957) rather than with equilibria established by the resolution of opposing forces (Homans 1958). It implicitly accepts the notion of the traditional family as a monolithic social entity from which internal conflicts have been exiled (David and Sundstrom 1984). Furthermore, by explicitly recognising the inadequacy of the nuclear two-generational family as a viable structure for welfare purposes, it presumes the overriding significance of the extended family. One might nonetheless view this paradigm at least as one with any claim to being generalisable in all pre-transitional societies with some suspicion; for north-west European evidence bearing upon behaviour over many centuries belies this stereotype (Laslett 1972).

TRANSFER INCOMES, THE 'DEMOGRAPHIC LOTTERY' AND FAMILY FORMATION PATTERNS IN PRE-TRANSITIONAL NORTH-WEST EUROPE.

Once we consider the evidence from the European past a difficulty might be quickly seen to arise in accepting the relevance of the inter-generational contract model we have discussed above or of debates surrounding the adequacy, indeed the *raison d'être*, of the extended family as a small-scale welfare agency. Changes predicted by the model elaborated for example by Ryder (1984) are less likely to have been encountered in societies in which extended kinship as a social and political organising principle is of limited significance. We can possibly go further and suggest that once the validity of any evolutionary model of the shift from extended to nuclear family forms is questioned then other widely-held beliefs about the relationship of family to non-family based welfare will require more careful attention than they generally receive. For instance, in looking broadly at the social history of Western societies we find that families have only rarely functioned in ways such as those proposed in Ryder's model. Consequently it would be hard to accept the evolutionary certainty displayed by some authors. We would be obliged to question, for instance, the view that *'loss of solidarity* [my emphasis] in the family helped impel social security programs in the first place' (Keyfitz 1985).

If, for the moment, we focus our attention on the demographic viability of the inter-generational relationships restricted to those of parents (or more specifically to fathers) and their offspring we will find that in a two-generational nuclear family we can identify certain obvious features that expose its fragility. Under stationary demographic conditions which are associated with life expectancies comparable to those found in pre-transitional societies, the problem of social replacement and social support of one generation by the other are profound. Simple deterministic modelling relying on the use of the binomial expansion reveals that whether the stationarity is maintained by high or low pressure equilibria (i.e. whether, for instance, an individual had a 33 per cent or 50 per cent chance of surviving to father's death) roughly similar proportions of families will be found with zero direct male heirs, zero male heirs but at least one direct female heiress and one or more male heir. In the low pressure regime (see Table 6.1) 19.8 per cent of men die with no surviving children, 20.9 per cent with no sons but at least one daughter available to inherit or provide care in the last days and months of life and only 59.3 per cent of fathers are able to have a son as their successor. In the high pressure circumstances (see Table 6.2) the comparable proportions were 21.3, 18.2 and 60.5 (Wrigley 1978; Smith 1984a; Goody 1976).

More sophisticated modelling using Monte Carlo methods reveals patterns that are basically similar although not directly comparable. For instance, highly revealing simulations of kin sets have been

Table 6.1 Son survivorship in a stationary pre-industrial demographic regime: 'low pressure' equilibrium

Population 1
Number of sons surviving to father's death (p = 0.50)

Family size	Frequency per 1000	0	1	2	3	4	5	6	7	8	9	10	11	12	Total born
0	85	85	–	–	–	–	–	–	–	–	–	–	–	–	0
1	125	93.7	31.1	–	–	–	–	–	–	–	–	–	–	–	125
2	125	70.3	46.9	7.8	–	–	–	–	–	–	–	–	–	–	250
3	125	52.7	52.8	17.6	1.9	–	–	–	–	–	–	–	–	–	375
4	125	39.6	52.7	26.4	5.9	0.4	–	–	–	–	–	–	–	–	500
5	125	29.7	49.4	33.0	11.0	1.8	0.1	–	–	–	–	–	–	–	625
6	90	16.0	32.0	26.7	11.9	3.0	0.4	–	–	–	–	–	–	–	540
7	75	10.0	23.3	23.3	12.9	4.3	1.1	0.1	–	–	–	–	–	–	525
8	60	6.0	16.0	18.7	12.5	5.2	1.4	0.2	–	–	–	–	–	–	480
9	25	1.9	5.7	7.5	5.8	2.9	1.0	0.2	–	–	–	–	–	–	225
10	20	1.1	3.8	5.6	5.0	2.9	1.2	0.3	0.1	–	–	–	–	–	200
11	10	0.4	1.5	2.6	2.6	1.7	0.8	0.3	0.1	–	–	–	–	–	110
12	10	0.3	1.3	2.3	2.6	1.9	1.1	0.4	0.1	–	–	–	–	–	120
Total	1000	406.7	316.7	171.5	72.1	24.1	7.2	1.5	0.3						4075

No male heir, but at least 1 female = 208.5
No heir (male or female) = 198.2
Source: Smith (1984a).

116

Table 6.2 Son survivorship in a stationary pre-industrial demographic regime: 'high pressure' equilibrium

Family size	Frequency per 1000	Number of sons surviving to father's death (p = 0.33)													Total born
		0	1	2	3	4	5	6	7	8	9	10	11	12	
0	70	70	–	–	–	–	–	–	–	–	–	–	–	–	0
1	70	58.4	11.6	–	–	–	–	–	–	–	–	–	–	–	70
2	70	48.6	19.5	1.9	–	–	–	–	–	–	–	–	–	–	140
3	70	40.5	24.3	4.9	0.3	–	–	–	–	–	–	–	–	–	210
4	70	33.8	27.0	8.1	1.1	–	–	–	–	–	–	–	–	–	280
5	70	28.2	28.1	11.3	2.3	0.1	–	–	–	–	–	–	–	–	350
6	70	23.4	28.1	14.1	3.8	0.6	–	–	–	–	–	–	–	–	420
7	70	19.5	27.4	16.4	5.5	1.1	0.1	–	–	–	–	–	–	–	490
8	70	16.3	26.1	18.2	7.3	1.8	0.3	–	–	–	–	–	–	–	560
9	90	17.5	31.4	25.1	11.7	3.5	0.7	0.1	–	–	–	–	–	–	810
10	100	16.2	32.3	29.1	15.5	5.4	1.3	0.2	–	–	–	–	–	–	1000
11	90	12.1	26.7	26.7	16.0	6.4	1.8	0.3	–	–	–	–	–	–	990
12	90	10.1	24.2	26.6	17.8	8.0	2.6	0.6	0.1	–	–	–	–	–	1080
Total	1000	394.6	306.7	182.4	81.3	26.9	6.8	1.1	0.1						6400

No male heir but at least 1 female = 182.1
No heir (male or female) = 212.5
Source: Smith (1984a).

Table 6.3 Some types of descendant and lateral kin under pre-industrial
English demographic conditions

		Late 17th century		18th century	
	Age of ego	Mean value	Proportion without	Mean value	Proportion without
Sons	33	0.78	.54	1.02	.44
	55	1.25	.41	1.48	.32
	66	1.12	.43	1.29	.37
	88	0.88	.56	0.89	.48
Daughters	33	0.66	.58	1.03	.45
	55	1.10	.44	1.49	.31
	66	0.97	.46	1.31	.35
	88	0.68	.54	0.94	.46
Children	33	1.45	.47	2.05	.28
	55	2.35	.30	2.97	.16
	66	2.09	.31	2.60	.19
	88	1.36	.39	1.82	.27
Nephews	33	0.91	.64	2.13	.35
	55	1.56	.50	3.64	.22
	66	1.45	.52	3.22	.24
	88	0.94	.60	2.10	.30
First Cousins	0	3.84	.27	8.46	.12
	22	6.73	.13	14.24	.04
	44	6.08	.18	11.35	.04
	66	2.50	.28	6.12	.09
	88	0.51	.66	3.27	.25

Source: based on data in Laslett (1984) and J. Smith (1987).

carried out by James Smith (1987) under demographic conditions applicable to the English pre-transitional past. When two quite different situations are compared, namely one of low nuptiality and moderately severe mortality such as distinguished the late seventeenth century (an era of stationary or slightly falling numbers), and another of relatively intense nuptiality and moderate mortality of the kind that was associated with relatively rapid growth in the eighteenth century, it is strikingly apparent that the survivorship outcomes are highly susceptible to the influences of the intrinsic growth rates (see Table 6.3). Males in the later seventeenth century dying at the ages of 55 and 66 years would in 41 and 43 per cent respectively of occurrences have had no surviving sons and in the demographically relatively more favourable conditions of the eighteenth century men of the same ages would have been without male offspring in 32 and 37 per cent of instances (Laslett 1984). Nonetheless, even under the demographically buoyant conditions which yield above-average growth rates for pre-transitional populations one third of men are without sons when they enter their sixties.

Obviously, if social replacement or 'support' for whatever purpose is carried out in a lateral direction there is no theoretical difficulty about finding heirs or substitutes for children to sustain an aid network. You search sideways until you find a candidate that fills the vacant cell. For instance, under the relatively favourable demography of the eighteenth century 76 per cent of men would have had nephews who could succeed them and even in the more difficult later seventeenth century 72 per cent of men would have had cousins upon whom they could call in their later years.

With vertical inheritance or obligations that are assumed to be fulfilled via vertical linkages the problem is both more complex and more profound. If welfare obligations are assumed to fall primarily upon the children it is obvious that complications arise from the simple fact that not every couple produces children, and even when they do, their offspring may consist only of daughters and, if the latter are married, their sons-in-law who may have obligations towards their own parents.

Further difficulties are evident when it is realised that these fundamental attributes of the demographic background co-existed with certain other characteristics of the social structure. It is far from evident whether those children that were available as a potential source of assistance were capable of offering the material support that is taken for granted in the models that we have considered earlier in our discussion. When marriage was late for both sexes, neo-local and based upon an assumed economic independence for the newly formed household, as it was in north-west Europe, the parents of married couples began to lose their children's earnings or labour power and to lose each other in widowhood at the point in the life course where those children in their turn may have been severely pressed because of an unfavourable balance of consumers (in the form of unproductive children) in their still relatively 'youthful' household (Smith 1984a; 1986a).

A familiarity with these behavioural norms and their implications for potential flows of resources between the generations of a nuclear family might assist us greatly in explaining why so many of the regular recipients of relief identifiable in the account books of the parochial overseers of the poor in seventeenth, eighteenth and early nineteenth century England were elderly persons (especially widows) and young couples over-burdened in their early marital durations with children (Smith 1984a). The elderly can be observed in such evidence receiving weekly pensions or 'collections' in amounts that compare favourably with wages paid to labourers and appeared in such a state of 'structured dependency', even though the individuals involved might have had children resident in the parish or indeed may have resided with them. Weekly pensions were a feature of wealth redistribution organised on a communal basis deeply embedded in pre-transitional English society (Smith 1984b). Apart from the flows of support from the community, widows were able to exercise other options in Western Europe that have frequently been noted as unavailable to women in many other societies. The relative freedom they possessed in the management of resources they acquired in marriage, the ability to engage in labour outside the strictly domestic arena and to employ non-familial labour to maintain the former husband's business, workshop or farm gave them a security or capacity for existing without the assistance of children or of more distant kin in their widowhood (Prior 1985; Hufton 1983; Smith 1986b).

In the vast majority of societies widows appear either to have been supported by natal kin or through some form of remarriage such as the levirate – the latter found widely over the Middle East and South Asia. Under the intense forms of this latter institution a man was obliged to marry the widow of a brother who had died without issue, his duty being to produce offspring on behalf of the dead man (Goody 1983; Bhat and Kanbargi 1984). Although remarriage was clearly a feature of West European societies it certainly seems never to have involved any such severely prescriptive practices.

Furthermore, research on contemporary non-European populations seems to be confirming that there are many societies which also have strict prohibitions on widow re-marriage – a characteristic that often coincides with a marriage regime in which wives are considerably younger than their husbands. This latter feature, it would seem, based on the historical demographic research of the last two decades, has never been generally identifiable as an element in first marriages outside the elites of Western Europe. The wider the age gap, *ceteris paribus*, the greater the likelihood of the wife being pitched into widowhood. In general, large differences in age of spouses (males being older than females at marriage) are associated with patrilineal kinship structures and patrilocal residence, while a small age difference is consistent with bilateral kinship and greater flexibility in the residence patterns of newly married couples (Casterline and MacDonald 1983). The notable correlation between wide age gaps, greater likelihoods of and indeed greater risks in widowhood and fertility have suggested to some commentators that this structural feature of marriage remains a major factor explaining why women are inclined in certain parts of the Third World to desire large numbers of offspring, and especially sons as a hedge against the possibilities of widowhood and the uncertainties that would accompany old age in that condition without the presence of direct lineal kin (see Figure 6.1) (Cain 1981,1984; Nugent 1985).

Other potential victims of a dissolved conjugal union are of course the children and certainly in the mortality regimes of pre-transitional societies the risks of orphanhood were considerably higher than those with which we are currently familiar (Le Bras 1973). What remains a striking feature of Western societies is the extent to which the parentally deprived were cared for by the community, whether in orphanages, or put out at parish expense into the homes of others to whom they were frequently unrelated as apprentices (Laslett 1977a and b; Snell 1985) or placed under the wardship of persons appointed by politically constituted bodies outside the family (Clarke 1985).

What is more, any conceptualisation of pre-transitional society that is predisposed to treat the family as a unit capable of indefinitely absorbing labour from adolescents and young adults must confront the implications of the institution of 'life-cycle service' (Hajnal 1982). In so far as it involved substantial proportions (most likely a majority) of those aged 15–25 or 15–30, it was an institution that drew labour away from households most likely overburdened with children and redistributed them towards households in which their labour could be utilised more effectively in terms of its marginal productivity. Exploitative it certainly was in so far as a system it was largely based upon a drift of young persons from the households of the poor to those more wealthy (Kussmaul 1981). But it was another aspect of north-west European society that served to limit the flow of wealth from child to parent, given that it seems to have been an integral part of a system of adolescent geographical mobility that ensured a high proportion of children would meet and eventually reside with spouses in parishes other than that of their birth or their parent's home (Smith 1981).

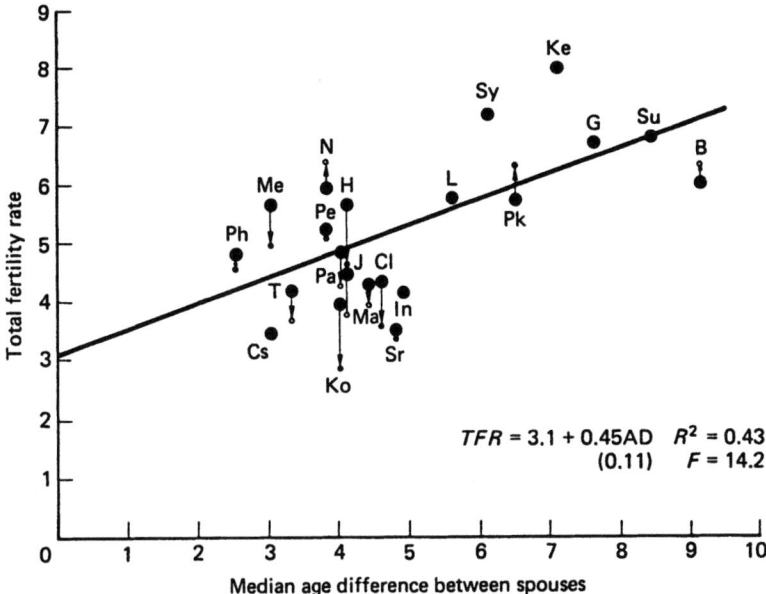

Figure 6.1   The relationship between fertility rate and age difference
between spouses

Source: Cain (1984)
Key: Ghana (G), Kenya (Ke), Lesotho (L), Sudan (Su), Syria (Sy), Ban-
gladesh (B), Nepal (N), Pakistan (Pk), Sri Lanka (Sr), Indonesia (In), Korea
S. (Ko), Malaysia (Ma), Philippines (Ph), Thailand (T), Colombia (Cl),
Paraguay (Pa), Peru (Pe), Costa Rica (Cs), Mexico (Me), Haiti (H), Jamaica
(J).

A case might be made, furthermore, to suggest that service was a
vital factor providing a *raison d'être* for a significant amount of
personal saving on the part of households that had, because of this
system, rather longer periods when families were composed of more
adult producers than child consumers. Because women were as much
a part of this phenomenon as males, service helped to ensure that
women were economically productive longer than had they com-
menced child bearing at, or close, to puberty. Household resources
so enhanced by this institution were a critical source for the
community-based systems of rating used to fund the welfare needs
which had a distinctive age-specific character (Smith 1984a). Indeed
recent research suggests that one's liability to contribute to the parish

rate varied considerably in response to the consumer – worker ratios of the household, compatible with a pattern of wealth flows in which those with few family dependents who were economically active gave to those with costly dependents or those who were economically inactive (Newman Brown 1984). It is doubtful whether such a system can be regarded as having contributed to pro-natalist values in north-west European society, for there was most likely a major divergence between the private or familial and the social or communal rate of return to investments in children.

Service remained an important feature of West European rural society well into the nineteenth century and gave that region a highly distinctive pattern of young adult mobility that was an integral part of its household formation system. Its implications can be more readily appreciated when it is compared with joint-family systems in which male offspring tend generally to be immobile, staying in or residing close to the parental home when young adults or newly married. Their sisters would be likely to marry out at or close to puberty and to be replaced in the patrivirilocal household by their wives, who remained for very long time periods in a subservient position to their husbands' kin and, in particular, their mothers-in-law (Hajnal 1982). Such a system is far more likely to be successful in inculcating familistic values than one in which young adults of both sexes are transported into a context of what has been termed 'extra-familial secondary socialisation' such as was true of the servant-keeping societies of Western Europe.

When we do encounter a system of child relocation in a non-European area such as that quite widespread practice of fosterage in West Africa, we discover that it seems to be distinguished by highly specific age patterns and is pursued predominantly within the wider kin group (Goody 1978, 1982; Isiugo-Abanihe 1985). Fosterage tends to involve for the most part, young children under the age of 10 and often under 5 and most frequently involved grand parents, uncles and aunts as foster-parents. It is also thought by many observers to be pro-natalist in its effects, in so far as it reduces the perceived costs of child bearing to the natural mother and serves to reallocate resources within the extended family or kin group, possibly ensuring maximum survival for that unit and helping to strengthen kinship over space in societies where that is politically vital, indeed a *sine qua non*. A foster child is however likely to return to its natal hearth ultimately. He or she may be away from a few weeks to a number of years. But on returning, his or her parents are ensured of support in their old age and may in the fostering period have forged links with their wider kin group or lineage that may prove to be a source of security or a route for upward social mobility in the future.

We might in these institutions of European service and West African fosterage perceive means by which young persons are redistributed in the case of the latter to enhance the viability of the wider kin group. In the former we see an institution that served to ameliorate possibly damaging effects from unfavourable consumer–worker ratios in rather vulnerable nuclear family households. Service also provided young adults with some means for undertaking the savings that were needed to set up their own independent households, especially as their stipends were paid annually rather than by the day or week. Indeed with service we can observe that socio-economic transactions involved flows between unrelated households over geographical areas and political units that transcended kin groups and served as another means by which the problems produced by the 'demographic lottery' with their obvious implications for personal and family welfare to which I referred earlier were solved without resort to the kin network.

FAMILISM, INDIVIDUALISM, AND THE STATE AND WELFARE

In referring to this far from complete set of contrasts between family systems I have addressed my remarks to certain difficulties that arise from encapsulating within one general model divergent social structures. For instance, those societies conventionally seen as Western in which the relatively restricted nuclear family has had a structurally dependent relationship with the collectivity cannot justifiably be subsumed with others which, although highly varied, have been characterised, I would submit, by considerably fewer external dependencies on the part of the family which has itself been of central significance to the welfare needs of its members. Such an enduring contrast between cultures or social systems requires us to reassess much of the questionable treatment of individualism, familism, collectivism, the state and welfare that pervades the literature.

In entering this area we inevitably confront in no uncertain terms the vigorous debate concerning the definition of the community within which is found responsibility for welfare provision and the necessary solidarity or sense of reciprocity underpinning the transfers involved. The more sociologically sensitive demographic writers on these issues, particularly those working in North America, are apt to place considerable stress upon what they see as a contradiction between government provision of certain welfare services and what might be termed 'inappropriate behaviour' on the part of those who are recipients of transfer incomes that flow from these services (Becker 1981). Once more, Ryder (1985) has perhaps been the most elegant exponent of demographically structured social theories. He has extended the argument he developed, concerning the discrepancies between socialised expectations and actual receipts of differing age cohorts in an inter-generational model under differing intrinsic growth rates, to those same relations considered at the level of a whole society rather than that of the family. In approaching this matter at a societal scale the argument is therefore premised upon the view that each cohort is socialised by the experience of its predecessors into expecting and accepting the fixed life-cycle patterns of dependency and support. With that conceptual underpinning he proceeds to contrast the experience of the growing population with that which is stationary or slowly shrinking in size. We should therefore recall from his intra-familial model (Ryder 1984) that his thesis posits that in the move from demographic stationarity to growth, the relationship between parents and children becomes strained and the disquiet so produced is regarded as an essential element in the beginning of the move from familistic to individualistic values, with an attendant fertility fall as parents become disenchanted with the tensions surrounding the difficulties of meeting obligations to children who are increasingly disposed to default on their particular side of the bargain.

However, an eventual concomitant of this shift in behaviour is a transformation in the age distribution resulting from the conditions of demographic stagnation or decline which in turn leads to a strain in the relationship between adult workers and their senior rather than junior dependents. The root of the problem in the earlier 'crisis', when assessed at the level of the functionally extended family, was attributable to the demographic growth caused by the fertility of the younger sections of the working age population, and was therefore susceptible to amelioration by a fertility reduction. But the nub of the problem in the second 'crisis' is the low or 'lost' fertility of those senior dependants in the past, and as such is not capable of *post hoc* rectification. As such the junior generation is portrayed as being asked to assume a kind of demographic debt for which they had not been socialised; in that such demanding obligations had not been part of the experience of their predecessors the young had in no way been consulted as to their willingness to be parties to such an agreement. Therefore, so this argument suggests, they experience a sense of inequity which is exacerbated by the fact that in the shift between the growth phase and that of demographic decline there is an interim phase (which, incidentally, happens to be the one in which most developed nations are now to be found) during which there is a temporary favourable relationship between the work force and its junior and senior dependents.

If we accept the implications of the break-down in the inter-generational contract that Ryder developed in his earlier model, then obviously the problems of sustaining the growing welfare demands of the older generations cannot be managed within the family because of the incessant march 'from familism to individualism' which erodes any familial basis for assuming responsibility for their elderly members. The ultimate effect therefore of this lower fertility involves a further transformation of the support system inexorably away from inter-generational and inter-cohort transfers towards a system which is based upon self-financing. There is in this evolutionary treatment of the changing welfare 'communities' more than a hint of the following sequence: a change firstly away from pre-transitional demographic stationarity to transitional growth and eventually to post-transitional stationarity and decline; the stages are accompanied respectively by the family, the State and then the individual as the principal 'contexts' within which welfare is organised and funded. Nathan Keyfitz (1985) has recently given further emphasis to certain of these developmental arguments but begins from a position never openly stated by Ryder that the loss of family solidarity actually impelled moves towards social security. However, very much as Ryder (1985) and, like John Ermisch (1985) in his recent evaluation of the implications of changing age structures for British pension costs in the second quarter of the twenty-first century, Keyfitz asks whether the generations working *c*. 2015 will stand for the high pension costs that will then start. He does, however, seem sure that people will reflect that by each person saving for his or her self that the premiums would be smaller than they are under a pay-as-you-earn, ostensibly collectivist system. Inevitably, so this argument goes, rationality will dictate that people opt for a system of self-financed old age support.

Many of the same preoccupations concerning a break-down of older forms either of intra-familial or inter-generational contract are evident in the thoughts that Sam Preston (1984) revealed in his remarkable presidential address given recently to the Population Association of America. On that occasion he presented what he believed to be convincing evidence charting divergent paths in recent years for the young and the old in terms of their economic well-being in the United States. The elderly, so Preston believes, are increasingly claiming a larger share of the public purse and on the basis of a number of attitudinal indicators are displaying a growing satisfaction with their lot. In contrast, behavioural patterns of young adults, particularly those connected with rising divorce levels, greater extramarital fertility and a retreat from marriage altogether, expose an American preoccupied with a self-fulfillment achieved very largely at the expense of the youngest generation which, according to a range of measures of both economic and psychological well-being, appears to have become increasingly disadvantaged. Preston's diagnosis of these shifts primarily revolves around an evaluation of two major influences: firstly, he emphasises the social and economic forces leading to greater marital instability which includes the well-known influence of higher earnings for both spouses, their greater exposure to alternative partners in the less sex-segmented working environment and, in particular, for lower income groups expanded welfare nets, such as the Aid to Families with Dependent Children that is regarded as penalising couples for staying together. Secondly, the rapidly increasing uncertainties surrounding marriage are constrasted with the relative demographic certainty of reaching old age. Furthermore some stress is placed upon the fact that children can be shown to live with mature adults with increasing rarity. Barely more than a third of American households contain a child under 18 and the orientation towards the ascendant, rather than descendant generations is confirmed by the fact that at no stage in the life-cycle does an American couple expect to have more children below 20 than it does surviving parents. Self-interest, therefore is interpreted by Preston as ensuring that the elderly themselves, the older working population who vote on behalf of the elderly who might otherwise have needed support from their families and those of working age whose only concern is in securing in old age a living standard that will not entail a major reduction in income, consort through the ballot-box to effect a redistribution of resources away from younger sections of society. For these sections their economic well-being is largely secured by families whose own self-sufficiency was being made increasingly precarious by the greater likelihood of the principal bread-winner being absent.

It is possible that a similar case could be made for more recent developments in Britain and other developed countries. On the demographic side of the equation we may be able to identify evidence that is at least suggestively supportive. We should nonetheless note that the political economy of welfare varies considerably between societies and therefore makes comparisons somewhat hazardous. In fact, we should in considering some of these questions from a British vantage point place Preston's approach within a longer-term perspective than he adopted in assessing developments in the United States. On doing this we would find that in the first two-thirds of the twentieth century the British witnessed an increasing predictability and homogenisation of experience in the matter of their family demography. There is no space here to treat these developments with the elaboration they so obviously deserve but mention can be made of certain noteworthy changes that have been discussed very recently by Michael Anderson (1983; 1985; 1986).

For instance, at the beginning of the century almost six per cent of children would have lost both parents by their twenty-fifth birthday. Among the 1946 birth cohort only one per cent would have been so deprived. Almost one quarter of marriages would at the end of the nineteenth century have been broken by the death of a spouse in their first 25 years. Today, other things being equal the average duration would be 45 years. By the early 1970s almost 95 per cent of women married and the vast majority (80 per cent) did so within a remarkably constrained seven-year period between their seventeenth and twenty-fifth birthday (Kiernan and Eldridge 1985). In 1911, by contrast, proportionately many more life-time spinsters were to be found in the population than in the two decades since World War II and the sense of a right time to marry was in the earlier period far less evident. Then, the central 80 per cent of marriages were spread out over a 17-year age range. A similar narrowing in experience can be observed in completed family sizes. In the 1870s no one family size from 0 to 11 and over had more than ten per cent of the population. By the 1970s three-quarters of all families were under four in size. A less striking but important shift affected the early part of the adult life cycle. For instance in 1851 by age 25 although three-quarters of all males had left home, only 50 per cent were by that age heading their own households. By 1979 almost all 17 year olds were still living with one or other of their parents compared with the 15 per cent who were by that age separated from their parents in the 1851 census. Entry into what might be termed full adult status was in the early part of this century far more protracted and was done from a previous experience that was not so restricted to the parental residence as it is today. A similar sluggishness was to be found in the pace at which males departed from the labour force, with almost 50 per cent of 80 year olds still returned as employed in the 1851 census. Today 80 per cent of 65 year olds are no longer in work and that departure has until recently been very largely concentrated in one rather than a span of years.

Social historians are only just beginning to document the true scale of what Michael Anderson, the principal researcher into these developments, has termed this 'homogenization of experience' with all of its attendant predictability. The respective place in the determinants of this narrowing variance of social experience to be allocated to full employment, rising real incomes and a particularly benevolent welfare state will no doubt be the subject of frantic enquiry by present and future historians. However, that 'modern life cycle' as identified in its fully-fledged condition was very largely a phenomenon of the 20 to 30 years after World War II. Already there are signs, and we must obviously tread cautiously here, that it may prove to have been a relatively short-lived affair, in that currently the range of experiences may be becoming far greater than we had been conditioned to expect from our familiarity with the relatively recent past. The most striking development has been the decline in the incidence of marriage (Kiernan and Eldridge 1985), the rise in its age, the increase in remarriage (Coleman 1984), the rise in first marriage age, the increasingly protracted period of cohabitation that precedes its eventual formalisation (Brown and Kiernan 1981) and the greater willingness to terminate it once entered (Haskey 1982). Indeed it is sobering to contemplate as Michael Anderson (1985) reminds us, that the rate of dissolution in the early 1980s by divorce and death combined reached the same level as death alone achieved in the 1820s. At the two ends of the working life-cycle, long-term unemployment (and this varies tremendously over space) is lengthening the process of withdrawal from work while youth unemployment stretches its commencement.

It is not my desire to pursue the question of whether the shifts or the increasing uncertainty surrounding the earlier phases of the family cycle that so much exercised the President of the Population Association of America are having similar effects in Britain on the patterns of age-specific well-being as they appear to do in the United States. What I would like to consider by way of a conclusion is the interpretation to be placed upon US trends in the matter of the relative well-being of what may be termed the dependent cohorts at the early and later ends of the life-course. Preston (1984) is struck by what he treats as self-evident facts, namely that public resistance to higher levels of taxation and state expenditure and a re-orienting of them in such a way that sizeable gains accrue to one dependent group at the expense of the other. He goes on to propose the simple rule that transfers to a cohort whether private or public are related to that cohort's size when the cohorts in question are *out of the labour force*. Furthermore, he adds the caveat that the larger the role of transfers relative to earnings and in particular, the larger the role of government in the economy, the more advantageous it may be to live in a large cohort. It is not clear from his argument whether he regards this principle as applying only to the relatively recent past or whether these principles have relevance over a longer sweep of human history. In mentioning the State Preston seems in dealing with the USA to suggest a time frame that is most likely post-New Deal in its dimensions.

In considering these principles in an English context I would prefer to relate them to a longer time frame. I have earlier in this discussion suggested that the pattern of family organisation in pre-transitional England (and also more generally in north-west Europe) implied that in practice, many, indeed the majority of, families relied on wealth flows in which those with few family dependents who were economically active gave to those with costly dependents or those who were economically inactive, regardless of their kin resources. Such a system was in its functioning therefore highly susceptible to changes in age structures and associated real incomes within society as a whole. In fact, it implied potential competition between generations for funds raised by the transfers, not so much at the familial but at the broader societal level – a factor, incidentally, pointing, I believe, to the dubious relevance of the inter-generational, intra-familial contract that I considered at such length earlier in this discussion.

For England, we are fortunately, thanks to the magnificent demographic data created for us by Wrigley and Schofield (1981), much better informed about the long-term character of age structures over time than is the case with any other society. A familiarity with the history of English welfare legislation and practice and the political debate surrounding it will reveal that the fact of human survival from infancy to old age and its profound implications for the predictability of human relationships, have figured prominently in what Peter Laslett (1979) has called the 'conversation between the generations'. Reflections on such matters as the uncertainty surrounding debility, parental deprivation, a superfluity of children, senility and death, have all been recurring themes of this long-running political economic discourse. Indeed, the more individualistic or more specifically familistic solutions to the problems of caring for the older generations were advocated (embodied as they were in the 1601 Act which stated that 'the children of every poor, old blind, lame and impotent person . . . shall at their own charge relieve and maintain such poor persons') during the sixteenth and early seventeenth century, and again in the more strident tones of the New Poor Law in the nineteenth century when the welfare claims on the communal funds were very pressing as a consequence of the rapid growth of youthful dependents (see Figure 6.2). In these conditions we can possibly observe some justification for Preston's claim concerning the relative advantages to be gained from being in the larger and, perhaps more relevant, swiftly expanding cohorts of youths and children. Such episodes spawned much reflective writing on the ill-effects upon incentives and the potential for seeking self-fulfillment at the expense of a commitment to the 'commonwealth' that flowed from welfare provided by sources outside the family (Laslett 1985). Of course it is very well known that Malthus was one such commentator upon the unfortunate outcomes for their own and their peer group's economic well-being that he believed resulted from subsidising labourer's family incomes in the matter of the latter's marital propensities. It is interesting to speculate whether when confronted by present-day debates he would be predisposed to remark just as Nathan Keyfitz (1985) that 'by telling people that they do not need children to look after them in their old age, we help the birth rate to go down and then find that there are too few workers to support the old.' But let us not forget that Malthus' diagnosis of the relationship between the Poor Law and demographic behaviour increasingly looks as if it misspecified the direction of the causal relations, so ill-informed was he about the character of the family system and its relationship to politically constituted agencies outside the family (Smith 1986a). I think it is unclear whether Keyfitz is equally in error although history of a specifically north-west European kind is not on his side.

In juxtaposing Malthus and Keyfitz I do not, however, wish to suggest that some of the commentators whose views I have discussed

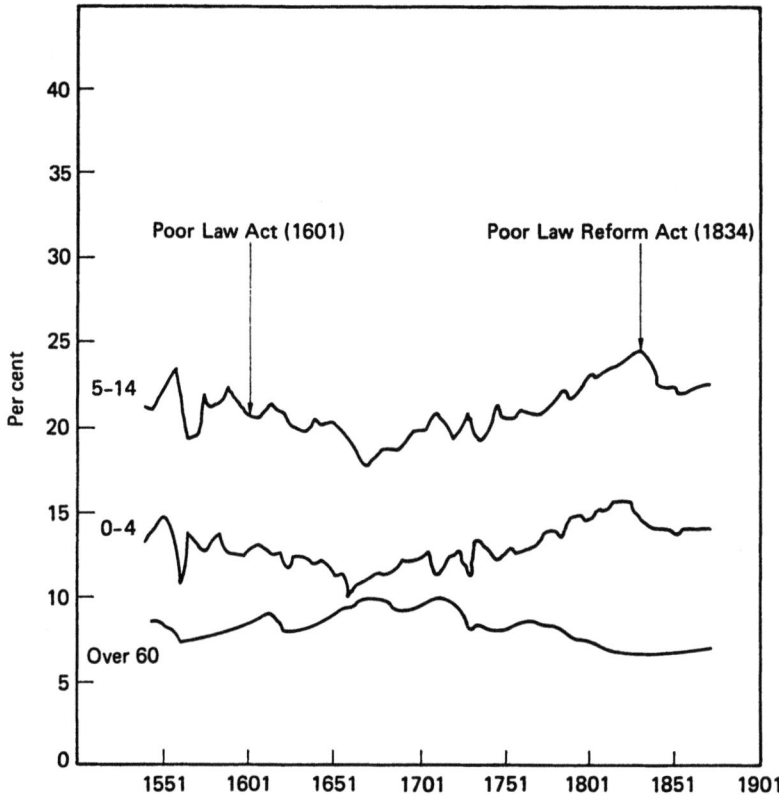

Figure 6.2   The changing age structure of the English population
1541–1871 (percentages in certain five-year age groups)

Source: Wrigley and Schofield (1981).

are, in this data-rich era in which we currently operate, likely to be so poorly informed as was an eighteenth century parson, but an awareness of our demographic heritage requires us to give greater significance in our analysis to the past and in our policy recommendations for the future to what has been polemically called 'the subversive family' (Mount 1982). In returning to the principle specified by Preston I would prefer when considering the transfers, whether public or private, to dependent cohorts very largely located outside of the labour force to suggest that the larger the role of transfers relative to earnings, and in particular the larger the role of the collectivity (which in the English past until the early twentieth century was the parish or Poor Law Union) relative to the restricted nuclear family, the more advantageous it *may have been* in the battle for welfare funds to have been in the larger cohorts. My adoption of the past tense is a cautious historical device and should not necessarily be interpreted as a predictive statement.

References

Anderson, M. (1983) 'What is new about the modern family: an historical perspective', *Occasional Paper No. 31* (London: Office of Population Censuses and Surveys).

Anderson, M. (1985) 'The emergence of the modern life cycle in Britain', *Social History*, 10, 69–88.

Anderson, M. (1988) 'The significance of demographic change in Britain, 1750–1950', in *The Cambridge Social History of Britain* (Cambridge: Cambridge University Press).

Becker, G. S. (1981) *A Treatise on the Family* (Cambridge, Mass.: Harvard University Press.

Ben-Porath, Y. (1980) 'The F-connection: families, friends and firms and the organization of exchange', *Population and Development Review*, 6, 1–30.

Bhat, M. and R. Kanbargi (1984) 'Estimating the incidence of widow and widower re-marriage in India from census data', *Population Studies*, 38, 89–104.

Brown, A. and K. E. Kiernan (1981) 'Cohabitation in Great Britain: evidence from the General Household Survey', *Population Trends*, 25, 4–10.

Cain, M. (1981) 'Risk and insurance: perspectives on fertility and agrarian change in India and Bangladesh', *Population and Development Review*, 7, 435–74.

Cain, M. (1983) 'Fertility as an adjustment to risk', *Population and Development Review*, 9, 688–702.

Cain, M. (1984) 'Women's status and fertility in developing countries: son preference and economic security', *Centre for Policy Studies Working Paper No. 110* (New York: The Population Council).

Caldwell, J. C. (1980) 'Mass education as a determinant of the timing of fertility decline', *Population and Development Review*, 6, 225–55.

Caldwell, J. C. (1981) 'The mechanisms of demographic change in historical perspective', *Population Studies*, 35, 5–27.

Caldwell, J. C. (1982) *Theory of Fertility Decline* (London: Academic Press).

Casterline, J. B. and McDonald, P. F. (1983) 'The age difference between union partners', *World Fertility Survey*, WFS/TECH 2070 (also presented at the Population Association of America Annual Meeting, Pittsburgh, May 1983).

Clarke, E. (1985) 'The custody of children in English manor courts', *Law and History Review*, 3, 333–48.

Coleman, D. A. (1984). *The Contemporary Pattern of Remarriage in England and Wales*, Paper presented to IUSSP seminar on the later phases of the family life-cycle, Berlin, 3–7 September.

Coser, L. (1957) 'Social conflict and the theory of social change', *British Journal of Sociology*, 8, 158–70.

David, P. and Sundstrom W. A. (1984) 'Bargains, bequests and births: an essay on intergenerational conflict, reciprocity, and the demand for children in agricultural societies', *Stanford Project on the History of Fertility Control Working Paper No. 12* (Palo Alto, Calif.: Department of Economics, Stanford University).

Easterlin, R. A. (1983) 'Modernization and fertility: a critical essay', in *Determinants of Fertility in Developing Countries*, vol. 2, ed. R. A. Bulatao and R. D. Lee (London: Academic Press).

Ermisch, J. (1983) *The Political Economy of Demographic Change* (London: Heineman).

Ermisch, J. (1985) 'Economic implications of demographic change', *Discussion Paper No. 44* (London: Centre for Economic Policy Research).

Goody, J. (1976) *Production and Reproduction: A Comparative Study of the Domestic Domain* (Cambridge: Cambridge University Press).

Goody, E. N. (1978) 'Some theoretical and empirical aspects of parenthood in West Africa', in *Marriage, Fertility and Parenthood in West Africa*, ed. C. Oppong (Canberra: Australian National University Press).

Goody, E. N. (1983) *Parenthood and Social Reproduction: Fostering and Occupational Roles in West Africa* (Cambridge: Cambridge University Press).

Goody, J. (1983) *The Development of the Family and Marriage in Europe* (Cambridge: Cambridge University Press).

Hajnal, J. (1982) 'Two kinds of pre-industrial household formation system', *Population and Development Review*, 8, 449–94.

Haskey, J. (1982) 'The proportion of marriages ending in divorce', *Population Trends*, 27, 4–8.

Heer, D. M. (1983) 'Infant and child mortality and the demand for children', in *Determinants of Fertility in Developing Countries*, vol. 1, ed. R. A. Bulatao and R. D. Lee (London: Academic Press).

Heer, D. M., and Smith, D. O. (1968) 'Mortality level, desired family size, and population increase', *Demography*, 3, 423–44.

Homans, G. C. (1958) 'Social behaviour as exchange', *American Journal of Sociology*, 63, 597–606.

Hufton, O. (1983) 'Women in history I: Early Modern Europe', Survey Articles, *Past and Present*, 101, 125–141.

Isiugo-Abanihe, U. C. (1985) 'Child fosterage in West Africa', *Population and Development Review*, 11, 53–74.

Keyfitz, N. (1985) 'Demographic ageing and pressures on the welfare state', in *Population and Societal Outlook*, ed. S. Feld and R. Lesthaeghe (Brussels: Fondation Roi Baudouin).

Kiernan, K. E. and Eldridge, S. M. (1985) 'A demographic analysis of first marriages in England and Wales: 1950–1980', *Centre for Population Studies Research Paper 85–1* (London: London School of Hygiene and Tropical Medicine).

Kotlikoff, L. J. and Spivak, A. (1981) 'The family as an incomplete annuities market', *Journal of Political Economy*, 89, 372–91.

Kussmaul, A. (1981) *Servants in Husbandry in Early Modern England* (Cambridge: Cambridge University Press).

Lasch, C. (1977) *Haven in a Heartless World* (New York: Basic Books).

Laslett, P. (Editor) (1982) *Household and Family in Past Time* (Cambridge: Cambridge University Press).

Laslett, P. (1977a) 'Characteristics of the Western family considered over time', in *Family Life and Illicit Love in Earlier Generations*, ed. P. Laslett (Cambridge: Cambridge University Press).

Laslett, P. (1977b) 'Parental deprivation in the past: a note on orphans and steparenthood in English history', in *Family Life and Illicit Love in Earlier Generations*, ed. P. Laslett (Cambridge: Cambridge University Press).

Laslett, P. (1979) 'The conversation between the generations', in *Philosophy, Politics and Society*, fifth series, ed. P. Laslett and J. Fishkin (Oxford: Basil Blackwell).

Laslett, P. (1984) 'The significance of the past in the study of ageing', *Ageing and Society*, 4, 379–89.

Laslett, P. (1985) 'Gregory King, Robert Malthus and the origins of English social realism', *Population Studies*, 39, 351–62.

Le Bras, H. (1973) 'Parents, grands-parents, bisaieur', *Population*, 28, 9–38.

Lee, R. D. and Rogers, G. (eds) (1986) *The Economics of Changing Age Distributions in Developed Countries* (Oxford: Oxford University Press).

McNicoll, G. (1984) 'Adaptation of social systems to changing mortality regimes', *Centre for Policy Studies Working Paper No. 108* (New York: The Population Council).

Mendels, F. (1978) 'La composition du menage paysan en France au XIXe siècle: une analyse économique du mode de production domestique', *Annales, Economies, Sociétés, Civilisations*, 4, 780–802.

Mount, F. (1982) *The Subversive Family: An Alternative History of Love and Marriage* (London: Cape).

Newman Brown, W. (1984) 'The receipt of poor relief and family situation: Aldenham, Hertfordshire 1630–90', in *Land, Kinship and Life-cycle*, ed. R. M. Smith (Cambridge: Cambridge University Press).

Nugent, J. B. (1985) 'The old-age security motive for having children', *Population and Development Review*, 11, 75–98.

Ohlin, P. G. (1961) 'Marriage, mortality and growth in pre-industrial populations', *Population Studies*, 14, 190–7.

Pollak, R. A. (1985) 'A transactions costs approach to families and households', *Journal of Economic Literature*, 23, 581–608.

Potter, J. E. (1983) 'Effects of societal and community institutions on fertility', in *Determinants of Fertility in Developing Countries*, vol. 2, ed. R. A. Bulatao and R. D. Lee (London: Academic Press).

Preston, S. H. (1984) 'Children and the elderly: divergent paths for America's dependents', *Demography*, 21, 435–57.

Prior, M. (ed.) (1985) *Women in English Society 1500–1800* (London: Methuen).

Ryder, N. B. (1984) 'Fertility and family structure', in *Fertility and Family: Proceedings of the Expert Group on Fertility and Family, New Delhi, 5–11 January 1983* (New York: United Nations).

Ryder, N. B. (1985) 'Some views on the demographic future', in *Population and Societal Outlook*, ed. S. Feld and R. Lesthaeghe (Brussels: Fondation Roi Baudouin).

Schofield, R. (1976) 'The relationship between demographic structure and environment in pre-industrial Western Europe', in *Sozialgeschichte der Familie in der Neuzeit Europas*, ed. W. Conze (Stuttgart: Ernst Klett).

Scrimshaw, S. C. M. (1978) 'Infant mortality and behaviour in the regulation of family size', *Population and Development Review*, 4, 383–403.

Smith, J. (1987) 'The computer simulation of kin sets and kin counts', in *Family Demography: Methods and Their Applications*, ed. J. Bongaarts, T. Burch and K. Wachter (Oxford: Oxford University Press).

Smith, R. M. (1981) 'Fertility, economy and household formation in England over three centuries', *Population and Development Review*, 7, 595–622.

Smith, R. M. (1984a) 'Some issues concerning families and their property in rural England 1250–1800', in *Land, Kinship and Life-cycle*, ed. R. M. Smith (Cambridge: Cambridge University Press).

Smith, R. M. (1984b) 'The structured dependence of the elderly as a recent development: some sceptical historical thoughts', *Ageing and Society*, 4, 409–28.

Smith, R. M. (1986a) 'Transfer incomes, risk and security: the roles of the family and the collectivity in recent theories of fertility change', in *The State of Population Theory*, ed. D. Coleman and R. Schofield (Oxford: Basil Blackwell).

Smith, R. M. (1986b) 'Women's property rights under customary law: some developments in the thirteenth and fourteenth centuries', *Transactions of the Royal Historical Society*, 36, 165–94.

Snell, K. D. M. (1985) *Annals of the Labouring Poor: Social and Agrarian England, 1660–1900* (Cambridge: Cambridge University Press).

Wrigley, E. A. (1978) 'Fertility strategy for the individual and the group', in *Historical Studies of Changing Fertility*, ed. C. Tilly (Princeton: Princeton University Press).

Wrigley, E. A. and Schofield, R. S. (1981) *The Population History of England and Wales: A Reconstruction* (London: Edward Arnold).

7 The Welfare Crisis in an Ageing Population

John A. Kay

The benefit reviews published in 1985 were proclaimed by their authors as the most fundamental reassessment of the welfare state since Beveridge. These claims were exaggerated; but not as exaggerated as suggested by many critics, who mostly concentrated on identifying particular groups whose interests might be adversely affected. These reviews signal two major changes in direction. Although neither is taken far in the present proposals, if pursued they could lead to very radical changes in the structure of welfare in Britain. One of these changes is recognition of the need to achieve greater integration of tax and social security. The other change is that retirement benefits no longer command priority within the welfare budget. What I shall call 'the age of retirement' is over. Each of these topics would justify an extensive paper in itself.

What brought about 'the age of retirement', and what is bringing it to an end? First, look at the numbers of the elderly (Figure 7.1). We see that the numbers of people over retirement age doubled between World War II and now. In the context of little change in overall population level, this implied a marked decline in the support level – the number of people of working age needed to support each person of retirement age.

At the same time, the relative incomes of the elderly increase. In Table 1, we see that the basic state pension for a married couple increased from 30 per cent of average net earnings to 50 per cent of average net earnings over the period, and the single pension rose by a similar amount in relative terms. It is important that this comparison is based on net earnings. The change in the ratio of the pension to gross earnings has actually been rather small, and the principal factor driving this change has been that the tax burden on earnings has increased – principally as a result of the increased national insurance contributions required by increased expenditure on a larger number of pensioners. The mechanism is thus a slightly convoluted one, but the effect – a rise in the living standards of pensioners relative to the working population – is indisputable. The result, as we see in Table

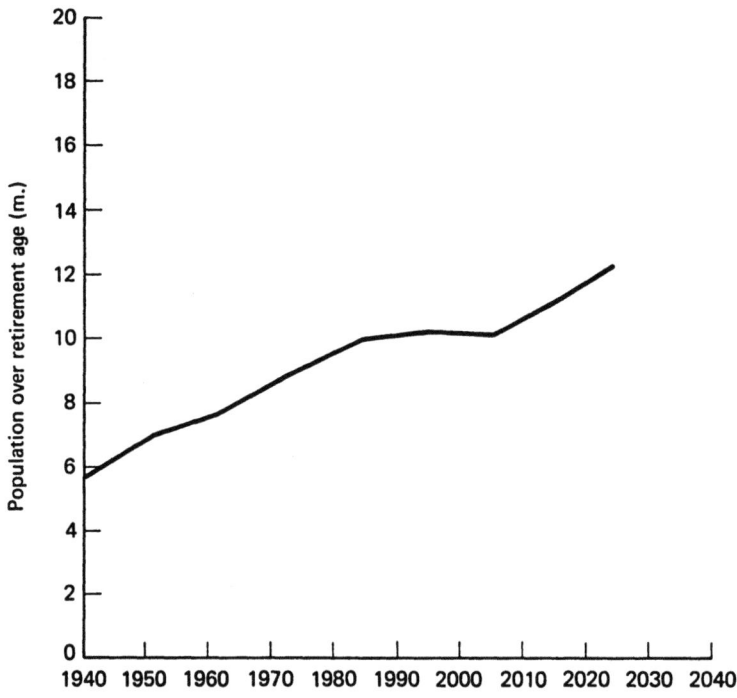

Figure 7.1   Population over retirement age, 1940–2025

7.1, is that pensioners' share of total personal disposable income has more than doubled.

It is still true, of course, that their share of income is less than their share of population numbers – pensioners incomes are on average lower than those of the rest of the population. And indeed the rise in income share is less than one might have expected, looking at the combined effect of the rise in number and the rise in the level of state benefits. The reason for this is that pensioners have become increasingly dependent on state benefits. Table 7.2 shows how pensioner incomes are derived. The majority of pensioners are in the lowest income range, and derive virtually all their income from the state. In aggregate almost 70 per cent of the income of people of pensionable age is derived from benefits. This proportion is about 15 per cent higher than immediately after the war.

This seems surprising, since occupational pensions have expanded greatly. But the growth of occupational pensions has been almost

Table 7.1   Pensioners' share of income

	Basic pension as % of average net earnings		Pensioner's share as % of personal disposable income
	Single	Married	
1951	20	30	7.0
1961	23	35	8.5
1971	24	37	11.5
1981	33	50	14.5

Table 7.2   Composition of pensioner couples by source

Percentages in each category	Income range (£ per week) (1982)				All
	Up to 75	75–100	100–150	150+	
State pension	75	58	40	23	62
Other pensions	8	21	34	35	17
Earnings	1	10	14	21	6
Other benefits	12	2	1	1	7
Investments	4	9	11	21	8
% of all pensioner couples in range	58	18	15	9	

Source: estimates based on 1982 Family Expenditure Survey.

exactly offset, for pensioners taken as a whole, by a decline in their investment income. Perhaps this equivalence is coincidental, perhaps not: the impact of pension provision on personal saving is another subject for another lecture. There has been a substantial fall in the contribution of earnings to the incomes of those of pensionable age, as retirement at retirement age has become possible, customary, or compulsory. Here too there is probably substitution between pensions and earnings. As benefits become more generous – either from public or from private schemes – more people are able to retire earlier from fulltime work.

Thus expenditure on pensions now accounts for around three-quarters of spending on national insurance benefits, even at current levels of unemployment, and over half of all social security spending is for the benefit of the elderly. If we go back to Beveridge, however, we do not find that provision for the elderly is a dominant theme. The Beveridge report (1942) is predominantly a report on unemployment and how to deal with it.

That should not surprise us. For most of the inter-war period, the number of people who were unemployed or were in families where the head of the household was unemployed was greater than the number of people over retirement age. In the immediate post-war period, unemployment was far below even Beveridge's optimistic projections, while the decline in mortality before retirement age implied the inexorable increase in pensioner numbers shown in Figure 7.1. The number of victims of old age, if one may call them that, far exceeded the number of victims of unemployment. For the first twenty years after the war, the former groups was between five and ten times as large as the latter.

Political attention is, of course, a matter of numbers; and it is not surprising that pensions became a focus of interest for politicians in the 1950s. The real level of pension benefits was increased, and this, combined with the growth in pensioner numbers, wrecked the planned financing of the national insurance scheme and broke any-thing but the pretence of a financial link or contractual relationship between contributions and benefits. Occupational pension provision grew rapidly and so did the size of the associated funds. The Labour party devised an elaborate scheme of national superannuation and both parties went into the 1959 election with competing versions of the same basic concept; an offer to finance higher pensions now by the promise of even higher pensions in future.

This was the underlying principle, if one may call it that, of state pension provision in Britain for the next twenty-five years. The device of paying yesterday's claims from tomorrow's premiums, or satisfying the old depositors with the money raised from the new ones, is one that has been familiar to fraudulent or foolish financiers for centuries. Reality breaks in eventually, of course, and – to jump ahead a little – much of the current complaint by industry about the increased costs on them which might result from the abolition of the state earnings-related scheme mirrors the complaints of those who discover that soundly managed banks and insurance companies offer lower interest and charge higher premiums.

Labour lost the 1959 election, and hence it was the Conservatives' modest scheme of graduated pensions rather than Labour's extensive scheme of National Superannuation which was implemented. National Superannuation was not dead, however, and when its architect

Richard Crossman became Secretary of State for Social Services later in the decade the concept was reviewed and, in a modified form, passed into law. With Labour's defeat in 1970, however, the scheme was never implemented; and the Conservatives proposed a new scheme of their own with a much more substantial role for the private sector. This too passed through Parliament but never became effective because of the electoral defeat of its sponsoring government.

Thus when the next round of pension discussions began after 1974, it is hardly surprising that finding a set of proposals to which all interested parties would agree was the dominant objective; and, in particular, a more important objective than finding a scheme which was good, understandable or affordable. This is reflected in the design of SERPS, the State Earnings-Related Pension Scheme, which was the product of the 1975 Act and which came into operation from 1978. It is a scheme of astonishing complexity, as well as substantial cost.

In brief, it provided for pensions based on one quarter of average revalued earnings in the best twenty years of a working lifetime after 1978. Members of good occupational schemes could 'contract-out'. This does not mean that they receive no state earnings-related pension: rather that their earnings-related pension is reduced by an amount – the 'guaranteed minimum pension' – which must be at least made up by their occupational scheme.

Figure 7.2 shows how the costs of earnings related pensions would have increased if SERPS had continued unchanged. As you can see, the costs rise very rapidly from the 1990s, as an increasing proportion of pensioners have rights in SERPS and as the rights which they do have reach their upper limit. The most serious burden, however, occurs between 2010 and 2030.

We noted that the number of pensioners increased steadily until 1980. For the next two decades, however, it is static: the effects of the low inter-war birth rate, which caused so much concern at the time, pass into the retired population. Thereafter, the demographic factors underlying pension provision reverse rapidly – from being exceptionally favourable to being exceptionally adverse. The reason is that the particularly large cohort born in the twenty years after World War II fail to be supported by the particularly small cohorts born subsequently. This is the basic cause of the funding crisis in pension provision. It is a worldwide problem, because these demographic trends are a worldwide phenomenon: indeed the British variant of it

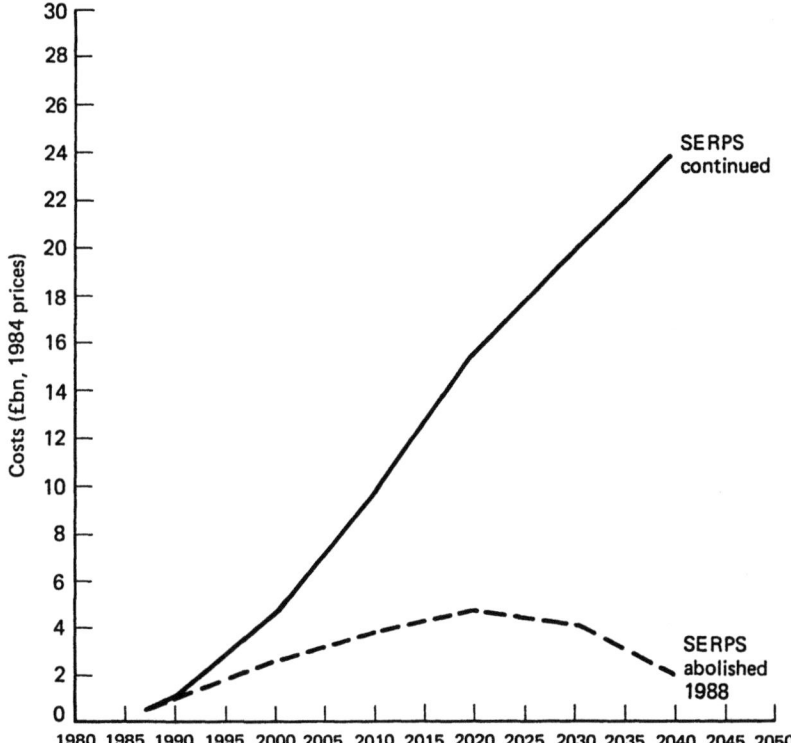

Figure 7.2   The costs of SERPS

is comparatively mild and certainly slight in relation to equivalent difficulties in North America, or, particularly, Japan.

But it is a problem which we compounded for ourselves by committing ourselves to substantially increased rates of pension provision due to mature more or less simultaneously with demographic problems. There were two parts to this. One – which remains – is the introduction of provisions which ensure that next century most married women will qualify for flat rate state pensions in their own right. But the other, and much more substantial, is SERPS which, if it had continued unmodified, would in the long run have added around 70 per cent to the total state pensions bill.

But SERPS is not to continue unmodified. In its initial Green Paper proposals, the government proposed its abolition, with extensive

Table 7.3   The position in 2010

	£ Billion 1985 prices
SERPS cost	9.6
Green paper	7.7
SERPS retained for over 50s	6.6
Full abolition	3.8

transitional provisions. (Table 7.3). Following pressure from the pensions and insurance industry, and elsewhere, it retreated from these proposals and instead intends a series of provisions which will eventually reduce the costs of SERPS by around half. As with the earlier proposals, those retiring this century will be largely unaffected by the changes. Thereafter, pensions will now be based on average lifetime earnings, rather than best twenty years; the pension fraction is reduced in stages from 25 per cent to 20 per cent; occupational pension schemes will be obliged to revalue guaranteed minimum pensions at 3 per cent; and survivors will inherit half, rather than the whole, of their spouse's earnings-related pension.

Full members of SERPS will obtain lower pensions and the government also proposes to allow individuals to contract-out of the scheme on their own behalf and not only through their membership of a contracted-out occupational scheme. Because the ultimate pension from this will depend on investment returns, those who do this will no longer be guaranteed pensions at least as good as they would have derived from the State scheme. The calculations involved are very complex ones and the information made available will require careful scrutiny and regulation.

Widows' pensions will be reduced from the possible over-generous levels provided for by the initial design of SERPS. The State pensions payable to the contracted-out will be reduced very considerably. Under the 1975 scheme, contracted-out workers still received substantial benefits from SERPS because the State scheme paid the difference between their best twenty years and average earnings and accepted responsibility for revaluation after retirement (up to the level of the earnings-related pension which would otherwise have been received). The new proposals terminate the first of these payments and restrict the second to inflation above 3 per cent.

This greatly increased concern for the cost of pensions is the product of several factors. Firstly, welfare spending is now under pressure. After three decades in which it has taken a growing share of a growing total of public expenditure, it now faces a more hostile political climate. And it is obvious that this is not simply the product of this particular administration in this particular country. Similar trends seem evident in many different countries with governments of varying political persuasions.

At the same time, the relative importance of retirement provision within the social security budget is diminishing. In part, this is the effect of numbers. We saw right at the beginning that the numbers of the elderly were no longer increasing. I noted that, in contrast to the inter-war period, the numbers directly affected by unemployment in the 1950s and 1960s had been far smaller than the numbers directly affected by old age. This gap has narrowed and is now very small. Hence it is unemployment which has – again – become the primary social welfare issue.

The controversy over SERPS raises again a number of fundamental issues in pension policy; I shall only attempt to sketch the principal ones. The most basic question of all concerns the appropriate role of the state in pension policy. After all, old age is a predictable contingency and one for which well developed private insurance markets exist. Why then should the government be involved?

One rationale comes from a problem which lay beneath the surface of Professor Shorrocks' discussion. When he talked about inequality of incomes, what exactly was he talking about inequality of? In particular, was he taking a life-cycle view – which treats earnings as accruing over the whole lifetime of an individual – or a snapshot view, in which I at 40 and I at 70 are regarded as two different people, and inequality between these two different versions of one is of as much concern as inequality between two entirely different people. Although Shorrocks' data related to a snapshot, I suspect he would prefer to subscribe to the life-cycle view, and that it is data availability, rather than preference, which governed his choice. A decision as to which of these views is appropriate is partly an empirical, partly a philosophical, question. But if, as I do, you feel that the life-cycle stance is a more appropriate one, then the further issue arises of why the government should concern itself with the distribution of resources over the life-cycle when it does not, in the main, concern itself with the distribution of resources between commodities and any particular point in time.

One reason may be that individuals are myopic in making these decisions; they will, in old age, regret the inadequate provision made during their lifetimes. True though this may be, the case that collective decisions are made by governments less myopic than the individuals they represent requires some arguing. Or private markets for insurance against old age may fail, because individuals are sold inappropriate or costly policies. Another issue is that it is obvious that even if individuals make no personal provision for retirement, we are not prepared to allow them to accept the consequences. Given that the state will ensure some minimum level of pension provision in any case, it may reasonably require them to achieve that level for themselves. While myopia might point to earnings related pensions, this argument would not take one beyond the provision of – possibly generous – state flat-rate provision.

Reliance on the private market as the primary source of pension provision has two primary advantages. One is flexibility – it can easily permit individuals to choose their own time, and degree, of retirement, the extent of provision they make for it, and so on. The second, and to my mind the more important, is the discipline imposed by funding. It is immediately obvious that SERPS, for example, includes many provisions which would not be there if anyone had been obliged to cost them, far less set aside the funds which such costings would have implied. Without funding, there is no mechanism for preventing current politicians from satisfying today's electorate with pension promises which future generations must either finance or repudiate. If you doubt this, note that today there are quite serious and responsible people who suggest that we should wait and see whether the costs of SERPS do indeed pose a funding problem or not before deciding whether to take action on it. By then, of course, the only way in which any problem that did emerge could be dealt with is by reneging on existing commitments.

Against this, however, a predominantly private sector route has two disadvantages. One is that its flexibility is bought at the expense of substantially higher administrative costs. The second is that – at least as presently constructed – private sector provision involves considerable uncertainty about what it is that the prospective pensioner will eventually get.

The alternative option – and the dominant one in Europe – relies more heavily on the public sector. Many of the weaknesses of private provision – its lack of effective transferability, or of indexation, or solvency guarantees – are overcome by public provision. If flexibility is reduced, so is freedom to be foolish. What you get out of a private sector scheme depends, ultimately, on market conditions; what you get from the public sector depends, ultimately, on political conditions. My personal preference would be to avoid too great dependence on either.

Yet the story of SERPS gives us a combination that offers most of the worst of both worlds – inflexibility, uncertainty, complexity. By seeking to privatise pensions, the government has now put down a challenge to the private pension industry. It is a challenge which I believe that industry could meet; but it would be unwise to have any great confidence that it will do so. If it does not, then the inevitable result will be a return to a more European pension system in which the state has the dominant role.

Reference

Beveridge, Sir William (1942) *Social Insurance and Allied Services*, Report, Cmd 6404 (London: HMSO).

Part III

Economics and the Improvement of Health

8 The Performance of Health Services

Walter W. Holland and Ellie Breeze

INTRODUCTION

Concern about the performance of the National Health Service (NHS) is a recent but logical development, given the apparently inexhaustible demand for health care, the ever-increasing costs of providing services and the finite amount of resources available. The greater involvement of government and the public at large in the organisation of health services has brought further pressure for more accountability within the NHS.

The founders of the NHS believed that its introduction in 1948 would eventually lead to less demand for health services following an initial increase owing to untreated illness. Regrettably, no attempt was made to determine systematically what was being achieved by this change of social policy. This can be contrasted with the introduction of a compulsory universal public insurance programme in Quebec in November 1970. Comprehensive measures, including population surveys twelve months before and after implementation of the programme, were made to obtain baseline population data against which to monitor short and longer term achievements (Enterline *et al.* 1973; McDonald *et al.* 1974; Siemietyoki *et al.* 1980).

Few figures exist for the NHS, but initial assumptions about future demand were grossly incorrect. Only in areas such as demand for spectacles and dental care has unmet demand been satisfied. Frequency of edentulous individuals (Todd and Walker 1980) and of carious teeth in young children (Todd and Dodd 1985) has fallen dramatically with time resulting in a major change in the focus and demand for dental services.

Although it was recognised quite early on that demand for and costs of care were continually rising, the open-ended system for allocating further resources meant that the problem was not confronted. Doctors were concerned primarily with providing the best treatment to individual patients and dealing with immediate problems secure, as Doll (1974) has commented, in the knowledge that

149

each year would bring improved methods of treatment. The cost of providing care was not considered a responsibility or concern of doctors. On their side government and the public as a whole assumed that doctors were providing the best possible service and that the necessary funds should be found from somewhere to finance them.

By the 1970s this situation was changing. Rising inflation rates meant substantial increases in expenditure in all public sectors. There was concern that public expenditure was out of control and a growing call for greater accountability to confirm that the health service was giving value for the money invested in it. This was compounded by the introduction in the mid-1970s of cash limits on expenditure which are likely to continue for the foreseeable future.

The growing elderly population and further technological developments will continue to impose new demands on the health service. Health planners are faced with the dual problem of maintaining existing services and providing for new ones within rigid constraints on expenditure. As Klein commented in 1982, it is easy to fall into the trap of assuming that extra resources will improve the service provided and cuts automatically lead to deteriorating services and standards. The challenge to planners and health service professionals is to examine not only the efficiency of the services they provide but also their quality and appropriateness.

The white paper introducing the 1974 reorganisation of the NHS (Department of Health and Social Security 1972) recommended that health authorities should become involved in monitoring their achievements and the DHSS has subsequently become more actively involved in this process. To this end, performance reviews are now undertaken once a year with each Authority in turn to assess shortcomings and to rectify the situation as appropriate.

To improve this process the DHSS has been developing performance indicators which have been used as the starting point for more recent Authority performance reviews (Barnes 1984; Jefferies 1984). 1985 has seen a further refinement of these indicators and of their presentation following the work of the Joint Group on Performance Indicators (1985). These indicators have been welcomed as an important step forward in providing authorities with a meaningful and timely system for identifying areas where there may be shortfalls in the service provided. However, they have been criticised (Pollit 1985) as providing an incomplete view of performance focusing on how resources are being deployed but not on the quality and outcome of the services provided. This reflects the fact that outcome is much more difficult to measure and most routinely collected data are on the process of care.

The following section reviews briefly the different components of health service provision that need to be considered to provide a comprehensive review of performance. After briefly outlining the performance indicators currently in use, we will discuss some of the work being conducted at St. Thomas's which attempts to develop outcome indicators that would be practical for routine use by health authorities. The discussion is directed specifically at how to determine and compare the performance of health services in different areas of Britain and does not consider the problems of making international comparisons. What follows is not intended as a comprehensive review as, for example, Doll (1974) and Donabedian (1980; 1982; 1985) have presented. Hopefully, it will set in context some of the approaches to monitoring health service performance currently being explored.

PERFORMANCE OF HEALTH SERVICES

Donabedian (1980; 1982; 1985), who has discussed the evaluation of health services extensively, identifies three components to health care – its structure or organisation, its process and the outcome – about which it is necessary to obtain information in an assessment of quality of care. Similarly recent guidelines from the World Health Organisation (1985) on quality assurance recommend that this include the monitoring of professional performance, resource use, risk management, and patient satisfaction. We do not intend to discuss in depth the complexities and ramifications of different approaches to evaluation. Much has been written on the subject. A recent critique of current thinking, for example, is presented by Carr-Hill (1985).

We wish to focus on strategies for the monitoring of the performance of the NHS. For this purpose we will take the aspects of service provision identified by Doll (1974) as our starting point. He recognises three major components to evaluation:

- Economic efficiency
- Social acceptability
- Medical efficacy

Each requires a different approach and data set, each is essential to monitoring performance, and individually each will give only an incomplete view of how successful health services are in providing for the needs of the population they serve.

Most routinely-collected data relate to the efficiency and process of providing care – i.e. to how money is spent and the amount and range of services provided. A health care system cannot be performing well if it is inefficient or fails to provide items of service at all. However, if the services provided are inappropriate or unacceptable to the population, fail to achieve their objectives, or efficiency is improved at the expense of quality then something is wrong with the system. Efficiency must be linked to some assessment of quality of care.

The acceptability of services to patients, their relatives and friends, and the outcome of care, i.e. improvement of the health status of individual patients and population as a whole now and in the future are the two dimensions of quality that need to be considered.

Indicators for Routine Monitoring of Performance

Health care systems cannot be looked at as individual items of care but as a complex network of services and while an enormous amount of data is collected on a routine basis it is impossible to monitor each component in detail on a regular basis. Much effort has been focused on how to provide managers and planners on a regular basis with a manageable set of data that will be meaningful and provide a comprehensive view of how the various components of the system are operating. In addition to a complete overhaul of the NHS system of data collection undertaken by the Korner Steering Group, attention has been directed to identifying health care performance indicators. These are sentinel events and key aspects of service provision about which data can be collected on a routine basis. Indicators are not absolute measures of performance but their routine monitoring is intended to serve as a means of identifying areas of service provision which may not be performing as expected and require detailed investigation. The challenge has been to compile a comprehensive set of indicators to cover every aspect of service provision.

DHSS Performance Indicators: Rationalisation of Input and Process Data

The remit of the Joint Group was to identify performance indicators from routinely collected data and devise a system for presenting these data to assist managerial decisions.

A series of performance indicators has been established for hospital and community services covering the five care groups, elderly, children, mentally ill, mentally handicapped and acutely ill, and for manpower, hospital support services and estate management. These are grouped hierarchically and can be explored in greater depth as necessary. The published indicators, linked to a computer program to assist accessibility, give values for each District Health Authority (DHA). It is possible to identify whether an Authority falls outside the range occupied by 80 per cent of Districts or, in some cases, hospitals and also where the indicator lies within the range of values. New sets of the indicators are to be published every year to allow a review of change over time in a District's performance indicators and in their ranking against other Districts and against regional and national averages.

The indicators are based on routine statistical returns and mainly relate to inputs and processes within the health system. This includes information such as length of waiting lists, expenditures on domestic staff compared to area of floor cleaned, length of stay in hospital, time taken to perform an operation, etc. The 1985 revisions of the indicators include some measures of access but as with the Resource Allocation Working Party (1976) recommendations, these are mainly measures of equity based on levels of service provision in relation to population size and composition. Check lists of items about acceptability have been included for hospital care. These cover only hotel aspects of stay and are directed to hospital personnel not to patients. While perinatal, neonatal and maternal mortality have long been recognised as indicators of the outcome and performance of maternal services, the DHSS indicators have made little progress in providing outcome indicators for other health services.

Thus, despite the major advance that these performance indicators represent as a tool of health service managers, they provide an incomplete view of service performance. How can the quality of care be measured? Do routine statistical returns provide any potential for generating more comprehensive indicators of acceptability and outcome to complement currently available indicators?

Acceptability

Many attempts have been made to measure satisfaction with particular services. All depend on specific and often voluminous questionnaires to individuals receiving the service. There have been *ad hoc* surveys of satisfaction with hospital care in the UK (Raphael 1969; Barr 1975) and these have indicated a fairly high (80–90 per cent) level of satisfaction with the service.

Hospitals in the USA have been more interested in the routine collection of data on patient satisfaction with services provided. Teetsel (1975) outlines a system which allows the generation of quarterly and annual statistics which provide the hospital administration and its various departments with indicators of the acceptability of both care and hotel facilities to patients. On discharge, patients are given a short form on which they are asked to rate various aspects of services with space at the end for any specific comments. The comment form is on one sheet and folds into a self-mailing envelope with postage paid. The hospital generates quarterly and annual statistics circulated to all department heads. An example is shown in Table 8.1. Such a system might equally be applied to NHS hospitals but at present such statistics are not available.

Some GPs have attempted to look at satisfaction with the service they provide (Cartwright and Anderson 1981) but again no national or routine system for monitoring this has been put forward.

One UK statistic which has not been used in a routine way and which covers the whole spectrum of services is complaints submissions. The NHS Ombudsman deals with specific complaints and reports to Parliament each year on numbers of complaints upheld and rejected. These will not give a comprehensive view of how health services are received. However, routine analysis of complaints against different parts of the services in relation to number of patients treated in a District or Region, might prove a useful indicator of aspects of service where there is patient dissatisfaction.

The limitation with these approaches is that they sample only those patients who have accepted a service. They do not include individuals eligible for a service but who choose not to make use of it. A more universal canvassing of potential NHS customers on a routine basis might be achieved through adaptation of the General Household Survey (Home Office 1971) which collects information on a range of subjects from a random sample of households on an annual basis.

Clearly, there is scope for further work on the development of indicators of acceptability and a present limitation is the absence of a system for collecting data on individuals' opinions about health services.

Table 8.1 Quarterly tabulation of patient comments based on 1088 responses

1.	Admissions department	492 Excellent	358 Good	64 Fair	17 Poor	157 Blank
	Reasonable time	935 Yes		68 No		85 Blank
	Personnel courteous	888 Yes		10 No		190 Blank
2.	Room accommodation	458 Excellent	316 Good	78 Fair	28 Poor	208 Blank
	Kept clean	782 Always		178 Usually	25 Seldom	103 Blank
	Quiet	375 Always		423 Usually	65 Seldom	225 Blank
3.	Nursing care	639 Excellent	180 Good	33 Fair	10 Poor	226 Blank
	Nurses show concern	822 Always		142 Usually	23 Seldom	101 Blank
	Were they prompt	595 Always		263 Usually	30 Seldom	200 Blank
	Available to talk	600 Always		306 Usually	53 Seldom	129 Blank
4.	Food service	393 Excellent	386 Good	69 Fair	29 Poor	211 Blank
	Menus well planned	667 Always		279 Usually	20 Seldom	122 Blank
	Food well prepared	576 Always		270 Usually	25 Seldom	217 Blank
	Proper temperature	510 Always		374 Usually	58 Seldom	146 Blank

continued on page 156

Table 8.1 *continued*

Table 8.1   Quarterly tabulation of patient comments based on 1088 responses

5. Patient account service	358 Excellent	346 Good	23 Fair	6 Poor	355 Blank
Interviewer courteous		785 Yes	13 No		290 Blank
Cashiers courteous		663 Yes	11 No		414 Blank
6. Visiting hours	967 Convenient	40 Too long	15 Too short		66 Blank
7. Rating of hospital	710 Excellent	299 Good	22 Fair	7 Poor	50 Blank
8. Comments	342 Favourable	74 Unfavourable	77 Mixed		595 Blank

Source: adapted from Teetsel (1975).

Outcome Indicators

To monitor the effectiveness of a service, it must have a defined objective against which to measure the outcome of care. Ultimately this would be to improve the current and future health of the population. But how can the impact of the complex mix of services that constitute the NHS on health be monitored? The difficulty arises in translating this general statement into specific objectives about which data may be generated.

A simple, routinely available measure that has been in use for many years is examination of mortality rates and trends over time. Overall mortality is not very informative. However mortality rates from specific conditions by age and/or sex have been used as indicators for the outcome of particular services or groups of services.

Rates for maternal, perinatal and neonatal mortality are accepted as indicators of the outcome of maternal services. Mortality from other conditions is also avoidable given timely and appropriate medical intervention, but until recently their application as routine indicators has not been explored. Rutstein *et al.* (1976; 1980) have drawn up sets of conditions where mortality is avoidable. We have selected a series of these conditions appropriate for curative services in Britain. Investigations of their potential as outcome indicators are described below.

While careful examination of mortality from specific causes can provide information on the outcome and effectiveness of health services, mortality is not always an appropriate indicator. It cannot in all circumstances serve as a proxy for morbidity and is irrelevant where services, e.g. for the elderly, are focused mainly on relieving pain and improving quality of life.

A major difficulty encountered in identifying outcome indicators is the lack of clarity as to the objectives of many services. The objectives of maternity services – to prevent maternal death and ensure the birth of a healthy baby – are clear. So too are the objectives of many acute services: e.g. services for cases of acute appendicitis aim to relieve pain and prevent death, and for hernia patients to provide curative surgery. In other cases objectives have not been defined satisfactorily. What are the objectives of, for example, psychiatric services or those for elderly hip fracture cases? Can they be expressed in such a way as to allow routine data collection to assess the extent to which services are achieving their stated aims? In collaboration with the Community Physicians of the South East Thames

Regional Health Authority (1984) we have made a start in defining objectives for services for the different health care groups. This has provided some measurable routine indicators but as discussed below much work is still required.

Despite recognition of the problems and limitations of measures of the outcome of services, progress in generating routinely available indicators has been slow. It was in this climate that the Unit at St Thomas's launched a programme to attempt to define outcome indicators which would complement the currently available DHSS performance indicators. We followed two lines of research, one to explore the use of statistics on apparently avoidable deaths as indicators of curative services and the second to establish objectives and outcome indicators to cover the whole spectrum of services for which a District is responsible.

Approaches to Monitoring Outcome

Avoidable deaths – outcome indicators for curative services

As a means of monitoring the quality of curative services based on routinely collected statistics we selected 14 disease groups for which mortality should be wholly or substantially avoidable if appropriate medical attention is sought and provided in good time. Age standardised mortality ratios (SMRs) were calculated for age ranges in which medical care is most likely to be effective. The causes were chosen to reflect different aspects of health care including primary care, GP referrals to hospital, and hospital care. Table 8.2 lists the conditions, the health care providers concerned and aspects of intervention the performance of which might influence the outcome.

A high SMR for any of these indicators is intended to serve as warning of potential shortcomings in the health care services and a starting point for initiating detailed enquiry at a local level to determine the reasons behind apparent excess mortality.

We looked at SMRs for these conditions in the then 98 Area Health Authorities in England and Wales for 1974–9. There was considerable variation between Areas, for both individual conditions and for the summary score for all avoidable mortality (Table 8.3). A further analysis of data for 1979–84 for the conditions for which data were most readily available has shown that while mortality has fallen overall for most conditions (asthma mortality has not changed with time), the ranking of AHAs in terms of scores for individual avoid-

Table 8.2   Causes of mortality suggested as outcome indicators

Disease group	Age	Health care providers*	Aspect of health service potentially influencing mortality
Hypertension	5–64	Primary care*, hospital	Case detection, anti-hypertensive medication
Cancer of cervix uteri	5–64	Primary care, hospital, community health services*, pathology services	Screening, surgery, radiation therapy
Pneumonia and bronchitis	5–49	Primary care, hospital	Antibiotics, early detection of complications
Tuberculosis	5–64	Public health programme*, primary care, hospital	Immunisation, contacts tracing, antibiotics
Asthma	5–49	Primary care*, hospital	Therapy, casualty department care
Chronic rheumatic heart disease	5–44	Primary care, hospital*	Case detection of streptococci, antibiotics, prophylaxis
Acute respiratory disease	5–49	Primary care*, hospital	Early detection of complications, antibiotics
Bacterial infections	5–64	Primary care*, public health programmes, hospital	Early detection of complications, antibiotics
Hodgkin's disease	5–34	Primary care, hospital*, pathology services	Case detection, chemotherapy and radiation therapy
Abdominal hernias	5–64	Primary care, hospital*	Case detection, surgery prior to complications
Acute and chronic cholecystitis	5–64	Primary care, hospital*	Case detection, surgery prior to complications
Appendicitis	5–64	Primary care, hospital*	Case detection, surgery prior to complications
Deficiency anaemias	5–64	Primary care, hospital, pathology services	Case detection, laboratory services

Source: adapted from Charlton et al. (1984).
* Most important provider.

Table 8.3 Distribution of 5-year SMRs among Area Health Authorities of England and Wales

Cause of death	Total deaths (5 years)	Standardised mortality ratios		
		Median	Minimum	Maximum
Hypertension	7700	96	29	213
Cancer of cervix uteri	6026	99	43	162
Pneumonia and bronchitis	4650	96	39	294
Tuberculosis (exc. silico)	2305	92	19	250
Asthma	1308	97	31	249
Chronic rheumatic heart disease	1200	105	0	263
Acute respiratory disease	934	90	0	374
Bacterial infections	772	101	16	257
Hodgkin's disease	744	98	0	288
Abdominal hernias	694	94	18	279
Acute and chronic cholecystitis	649	99	0	323
Appendicitis	485	106	0	228
Maternal deaths	363	0.6*	0.0*	1.8*
Deficiency anaemias	212	87	0	508
Perinatal	10472**	18.0*	10.0*	24.0*
All causes	596662**	101	64	118
All "non-preventable"	494030**	101	63	119

*   Deaths per 1000 births

** 1976 only

Source: adapted from Charlton *et al.* (1983).

able conditions and summary scores has not changed substantially (Charlton *et al.* 1986). That is, Areas performing poorly in the first time period continue to do so in the second. The indicators appear to be stable over time and identify significant variation between Areas and, as shown for 1979–84, also between DHAs.

It must then be asked whether these indicators provide managers with any meaningful information. As stressed earlier, these are not absolute measures of outcome and do not provide definitive evidence that a particular service is wrong. There are, as indicated in Table 8.2, various stages in the process where the system may have broken down. Furthermore, various factors other than service provision, e.g. disease incidence, social factors, failure to make use of service, or data inaccuracies, which may also contribute to the observed mortality ratios. A high SMR or summary score must be treated as a starting point for local enquiry to ascertain which factor or combination of factors are involved and what further measures should be undertaken.

To explore the value of these indicators, two Districts with high SMRs for certain avoidable deaths agreed to conduct local enquiries to look in depth at the reasons behind this apparent poor performance. One District examined all deaths from cancer of the cervix and hypertension and the other only deaths from cancer of the cervix. Each District scrutinised available case records from general practice and hospitals between 1979 and 1984 to identify all individuals who had died from the conditions concerned.

Analysis of deaths from cancer of the cervix in one District indicated that women were coming forward for screening. However, owing to shortcomings in the screening system, in more than half the deaths studied there was a delay in follow up and rescreening after an abnormality not definitive of cancer had been detected. The gap between first report of an abnormality and rescreening ranged from 1 to 10 years. In the second District the method of recall for rescreening was adequate but very few women identified as having died of carcinoma of the cervix appeared to have come forward for screening. This suggests that in this case the failure was in educating and motivating women to make use of the service. Further scrutiny would determine if and why some women found the service inaccessible or unacceptable.

The District that analysed premature deaths due to hypertension found that although individuals were correctly identified, treatment was inadequate when compared with preset criteria.

There is a major problem with using avoidable mortality rates in this way in that variation in disease incidence will also affect the number of observed deaths. Unfortunately, there are few accurate sources of information on disease incidence. Cancer registries are relatively complete. For these and other conditions for which appropriate indices of incidences exist, we have shown that variation in mortality between areas is not explained entirely by differences in morbidity. Thus, it is possible that the differences are due to variations in case-fatality rate. Only in the case of asthma have we found variation of prevalence to have a major influence on mortality rates. Deaths from asthma in young people have long been considered avoidable, and a number of studies have cited inadequate treatment as associated with asthma deaths. We have shown wide variation in asthma mortality, and set up a pilot study to determine the prevalence of asthma in two adjoining areas of southern England – one with a high and the other a low mortality rate from asthma. The area with high mortality also appears to have higher prevalence of asthma but there was no difference in type or levels of treatment in the two areas. Although only a small study, this suggests that for this condition at least, prevalence rather than ineffective services seems to explain higher mortality rates.

Accurate morbidity data will not be available until the introduction of record linkage to allow episodes of illness and hospitalisation, etc., to be linked to individual patients. In the absence of such a data collection system, the use of mortality data as outlined above provides a relatively simple tool for monitoring outcome of curative services. We have explored the potential of adjusting for social factors such as social class, housing tenure and car ownership, as a proxy for disease incidence. However, these also influence the use of services. Thus we have recommended that Districts should look at these indicators both with and without adjustment for social factors.

Following our analysis of data for 1979–84, during which the tenth revision of the International Classification of Disease (ICD) was in operation, we have recommended that deaths from stroke and hypertension be combined to reduce the problems of diagnostic variation and inaccuracies. Our analyses of national data and the local enquiries that have been conducted suggest that annual review of SMRs for these avoidable conditions would provide DHAs with a useful additional tool for the routine monitoring of health service performance.

Objectives for Services to Health Care Groups

Following on from work on the use of avoidable deaths as outcome indicators, we have attempted to draw up outcome indicators for the full range of services for which a DHA is responsible. The first stage of this project, conducted in collaboration within the South East Thames Regional Health Authority was to identify objectives for the various services about which data might be collected routinely. To this end, services were grouped according to the particular care group in the community that they served. The following care groups were recognised:

- Mental handicap
- Mental illness
- Paediatric
- Maternity
- Youth disabled
- Acutely ill (general medicine, general surgery)
- Elderly

Consensus was reached about certain service objectives for each care group with a view to developing indicators of their performance that could be analysed simply and routinely at the District level. Where data were available indicators were based on measures of outcome. However this was not felt to be feasible for some services and in these cases measures of good practice (i.e. measures of the process of care) were identified.

These indicators are not perfect and further refinement is necessary. However, the following brief description demonstrates the important elements of this attempt at comprehensive monitoring of service outcome. Table 8.4 presents the agreed policy objectives for each care group and the proposed indicators. Data for these indicators have been examined for the 15 DHAs in the South East Thames RHA for the years 1978–81 and compared with regional averages. Considerable variation was detected between Districts and the indicators appear to have potential for monitoring the quality and effectiveness of District services.

In the next stage of assessing the value of these indicators as management tools, data are to be collected on a routine basis in certain Districts in the Region and analysed at the District level. Further work to refine the indicators will include more detailed

Table 8.4   Objectives for health care services for different care groups

---

1.   Mental handicap

Objectives in prevention	*Indicator*
To prevent cases of Down's Syndrome in mothers over 38 years, by offering referral to Paediatric Research Unit, Guy's Hospital	No. and proportion of referrals and abortions carried out following amniocentesis in women over 38 years
To prevent cases of congenital hypothyroidism and PKU	No. and proportion of all births who are diagnosed
Good practice	
To encourage those with handicap to remain outside large institutions	No. of children by medical diagnosis/disabilities who live at home, in foster homes, hostels etc. No. who are employed

2.   Mental Illness

Good practice	
To prevent new long stay patients	No. and proportion of new patients whose admission lasts over 1 year
To prevent deaths from attempted suicide	No. and proportion of patients admitted as attempted suicides who die within 7 days

3.   Paediatric

Objective in prevention	
To prevent cases of measles, diphtheria, polio, pertussis and rubella	No. and proportion of all vaccinations at specific ages No. of notified diseases
Good practice	Perinatal mortality rate, neonatal mortality rate
To reduce perinatal and neonatal deaths	

4.   Maternity

Good practice	
To encourage natural delivery	No. and rates of induced deliveries No. and rate of forceps deliveries No. and rate of caesarian section by different age groups
To encourage breast feeding	No. of women breast feeding on discharge
To prevent cases of cerebral palsy	No. of cases of cerebral palsy per year

5.   Youth Disabled

Prevention	
To reduce the number of head injuries	No. and rates of deaths and discharges of head injuries for 15 year olds, by sex

Table *8.4 continued*

To reduce cases of paraplegia	No. and rates of deaths and discharges for cases of paraplegia aged 15–34 years/35–44 years, by sex

6. Acutely Ill
A. General Medicine

Objectives in preventable deaths

Hodgkin's disease	No. and rates of discharges and deaths for those under 35 years
Asthma	No. and rates of deaths for those under 35 years.
Hypertensive disease	No. and rates of discharges and deaths for those under 45 years No. of deaths in community
Acute myocardial infarction	No. and rates of discharges and deaths for those under 45 years No. of deaths in community

Good practice

To reduce admissions for diabetic ketoacidosis or coma	No. and rates of admission under 35 years and 35–46 years

B. General Surgery

Number of tonsillectomy/adenoidectomy	No. and rates for those under 15 years
Radical mastectomy	No. and rates for different age groups
Hysterectomy in young women	No. and rates for those under 35 years

7. Elderly

Prevention of loss of function	No. and rates for total hip replacement No. and rates of cataract removal

analysis to determine, particularly for indicators of good practice, whether a regional average score is appropriate as the norm against which to rate individual District performance. It is not clear, for example, whether the regional mean rate of caesarian section should be taken as the expected level. Analysis of data on admissions for cases of diabetes showed that the District with the highest admission rate had on the other hand a lower rate of mortality from the condition in young people and lower occurrence of ketosis and coma compared to other Districts. This suggests that the policy of this

District to admit diabetic patients more frequently than in other Districts may be a more appropriate approach. Thus, further investigation will be needed before establishing an admission rate against which to judge good practice. Because of the limitations of the currently available data and difficulties encountered in identifying appropriate sentinel events, the indicators for the young disabled, the mentally ill and the elderly were less satisfactory than other indicators. It is hoped to develop new and more appropriate indicators for these groups.

Conclusion

It should be evident from the discussions above that a major problem with attempting to monitor the performance of health services is the availability and accuracy of information. Mortality rates are probably the only information source at this time that covers the country as a whole and is readily available, relatively complete and easily analysable. The Hospital Activity Analysis, while national in coverage, deals with events rather than with individuals. To try to use this as a method of measurement of performance is fraught with difficulty in view of the incompleteness of the data and the inadequacies of the system. Other measures of morbidity are equally flawed. The Korner Steering Group has suggested ways of improving data collection and as these are implemented our power to measure the performance of health services within individual Districts and Regions may be increased.

Information is only useful if it is analysed and presented in a way that is meaningful to the health planners. It is illusory to expect to provide a system of data collection and analysis comprehensive enough to cover all aspects of health services to the same depth on a routine basis. However, surveillance of health services must move away from concern solely with the amount of services provided. The work described here represents one step towards a more complete assessment of what services are achieving and emphasises the need for a comprehensive examination of the objectives and value of the NHS.

To succeed in monitoring health service activities, objectives must be clearly defined in such a way as to allow the development of indicators based on data that can be collected and analysed routinely. Mortality data can be manipulated, as demonstrated here, to provide health service managers with indicators of the outcome of health service. However, dissatisfaction, pain and discomfort are much

Table 8.5   Outcome – mortality rates (per 100 000, age-standardised).

Cause of death	UK 1956	(%)	1978	US 1956	(%)	1978
Infant Mortality (per 1000 live births)	25.8	–48	13.3	26.4	–48	13.6
Tuberculosis	10.0	–90	1.0	7.5	–90	0.74
Cancer of Cervix	10.6	–20	8.5	13.9	–63	5.2
Appendicitis	1.2	–84	0.19	0.9	–79	0.19
Maternal Mortality (per 100 000 live and still births)	41	–76	10	40	–75	10

more difficult to assess, and in many areas there may be no alternative to indicators of process. However, much work is required to define what many services aim to achieve. If agreement can be reached on even simple medical objectives – such as, is treatment to be provided for all hypertensives? Are all elderly hip fracture cases to be provided with replacement surgery? – then the service would be in a stronger position when negotiating with those concerned with the funding of health care services.

We have deliberately not complicated the discussion by introducing international comparisons. However, it is encouraging to find as shown in Table 8.5 that with the exception of carcinoma of the cervix, the UK has achieved similar reductions in mortality from specific, avoidable causes of mortality as has the US. Thus, despite very different expenditures on services the NHS may still be providing value for money.

Acknowledgements

The paper was prepared in part while one of us (WWH) was a Fogarty Scholar-in-Residence at NIH, Bethesda, Maryland, USA. Our work is supported by the UK Department of Health and Social Security.

References

Barnes, K. S. (1984) 'Health authority performance indicators', *Hospital and Health Services Review*, May, 118–19.

Barr, A. (1975) *Total Patient Care Study: Patient Comments on Hospital Care, Treatment, and After Care* (unpublished report), (Oxford: Oxford Regional Health Authority).

Carr-Hill, R. A. (1985) 'The evaluation of health care', *Social Science and Medicine*, 21, 367–75.

Cartwright, A. and Anderson, R. (1981) *General Practice Revisited* (London: Tavistock).

Charlton, J. R. H., Bauer, R. and Lakhani, A. (1984) 'Outcome measures for district and regional health care planners', *Community Medicine*, 6, 306–15.

Charlton, J. R. H., Lakhani, A. and Aristidou, M. (1986) 'How Have "Avoidable Death" Indicies for England and Wales changed? 1974–78 compared with 1979–83', *Community Medicine*, 8, 304–14.

Charlton, J. R. H., Hartley, R., Silver, R. and Holland, W. W. (1983) 'Geographical variation in mortality from conditions amenable to medical intervention in England and Wales', *Lancet*, i, 691–6.

Department of Health and Social Security (1972) *National Health Service. Reorganisation England*, Cmnd. 5055, (London: HMSO).

Department of Health and Social Security (1985) *Performance Indicators for the NHS. Guidance for Users* (London: DHSS).

Doll, R. (1974) 'Surveillance and monitoring', *International Journal of Epidemiology*, 3, 305–14.

Donabedian, A. (1980) *Explorations in Quality Assessment and Monitoring. Vol. 1. The Definition of Quality and Approaches to its Assessment* (Ann Arbor: Health Administration Press).

Donabedian, A. (1982) *Explorations in Quality Assessment and Monitoring. Vol. II: The Criteria and Standards of Quality* (Ann Arbor: Health Administration Press).

Donabedian, A. (1985) *Explorations in Quality Assessment and Monitoring. Vol. III: The Methods and Findings of Quality Assessment and Monitoring – An Illustrated Analysis* (Ann Arbor: Health Administration Press).

Enterline, P. E., Salter, V., McDonald, A. D. and McDonald, J. C. (1973) 'The distribution of medical services before and after "free" medical care – the Quebec experience', *New England Journal of Medicine*, 289, 1174–8.

Home Office (1971) *General Household Survey. Introductory Report* (London: HMSO).

Jefferies, M. (1984) 'The manpower performance indicators', *Health Services Manpower Review*, 80, 9–12.

Joint Group on Performance Indicators (1985) *Report to the Secretary of State for Social Services* (London: DHSS).

Klein, R. (1982) 'Auditing the NHS' [Editorial], *British Medical Journal*, 285, 672–3.

Pollit, C. (1985) 'Can practice be made perfect?', *Health and Social Services Journal*, June 6, 706–7.

McDonald, A. D., McDonald, J. C., Salter, V., Enterline, P. E. (1974)

'Effects of Quebec Medicine on physician consultations for selected symptoms', *New England Journal of Medicine*, 291, 649–52.

Raphael, W. (1969) *Patients and Their Hospitals. A King's Fund Report* (London: King Edward's Hospital Fund for London).

Resource Allocation Working Party (1976) *Report* (London: DHSS).

Rutstein, D. D., Berenberg, W., Chalmers, T. C. *et al.* (1976) 'Measuring the quality of medical care', *New England Journal of Medicine*, 294, 582–8.

Rutstein, D. D., Berenberg, W., Chalmers, T. C. *et al.* (1980) 'Measuring the quality of medical care: second revision of tables of indexes', *New England Journal of Medicine*, 302, 1146.

Siemietyoki, J., Richardson, B. A. and Pless, I. B. (1980) 'Equality in medical care under national health insurance in Montreal', *New England Journal of Medicine*, 303, 10–15.

South East Thames Regional Health Authority (1984) *Outcome Indicators in S. E. Thames RHA* (unpublished report)(Bexhill on Sea: E. Thames RHA).

Teetsel, R. F. (1975) 'The comment form is a hospital performance indicator', *Hospitals*, 49, 38–41.

Todd, J. E. and Dodd, T. (1985) *Children's Dental Health in the United Kingdom*, 1983 (London: HMSO).

Todd, J. E. and Walker A. M. (1980) *Adult Dental Health. Vol. 1: England and Wales 1968–78* (London: HMSO).

World Health Organisation (1985) *The Principles of Quality Assurance. Report on a WHO meeting*, Copenhagen: WHO Euro Reports and Studies, 94.

9 Prevention Versus Cure: Use of Resources in the National Health Service

Roy M. Acheson

INTRODUCTION

One way of addressing this subject would be, like Freymann (1974), to assume that any 'versus' between prevention and cure stems from a fundamental discordance between curative medicine and public health, and proceed to analyse, as he did in the USA the reasons for such a discordance. Another approach would be to attempt to weigh the advantages brought by high technology clinical medicine against those that would be gained if the same resources were invested in a preventive programme. I am not properly qualified to attempt this even were suitable data available, and I am reluctant simply to dismiss 'high tech' anyway. The only procedure based upon it I have studied at first hand (with colleagues) is cardiac transplantation (Buxton *et al.* 1985). This operation is only offered to patients who have been considered unsuitable for coronary artery by-pass graft and all other forms of therapy and who are not expected to live for more than six months. Our analysis showed that the expectation of life for 94 per cent of a comparison group of 70 for whom no organ was available, was six months or less as anticipated, but 50 per cent of those receiving a new heart could expect to live for at least five years. Whereas at the time they were put on the waiting list for the operation only 11 per cent were employed, subsequently 57 per cent had jobs and a further 23 per cent were actively seeking them. On the basis of these facts it is reasonable to consider it to be an outstandingly successful operation.

Although there may be ways of slowing technological research and its applications, it is as unrealistic to expect to stop it as it would have been to try to stop mankind from exploring first his own planet and then space – and as we shall see 'high tech' can play an important role in prevention any way. It is fashionable but perhaps facile to condemn it out of hand, but it is also foolish to invest heavily in it without being prepared to evaluate the benefits it provides.

I believe that treatment, even though it does not cure, will be the chief concern of the National Health Service (NHS) for the foreseeable future, and properly so. Two of several reasons for this are that it is a natural and humane thing to do, and that some of the great infectious diseases apart, changes in morbidity patterns from the most important degenerative diseases will be slow, no matter how hard we try, so that treatment on a large scale will continue to be badly needed.

'PREVENTION IS BETTER THAN CURE'

That 'prevention is better than cure' is a widely stated aphorism and unlike my title proposes values. Its validity is worth looking at nevertheless, with a view:

- To deciding the relevance of comparing (or does 'versus' connote a contest?) prevention and cure.

- To examining some of the problems underlying the establishment of really satisfactory and successful preventive procedures.

- And, finally, to considering how the NHS might contribute to these.

At face value the statement seems incontrovertible. Who wants to suffer an illness they do not have to have? Surely nobody does? But then doubts arise. Is prevention painful? Costly? Does it always work? Does the cure always work? Is it painful? What would happen if nature were allowed to run its course? For every disease the answers are different. For instance, for smallpox, one of the eradicable scourges, prevention by vaccination is virtually painless and without complication, whereas the disease itself has common consequences ranging from hideous scarring to death; in another with a closely similar epidemiology, namely measles, inoculation is marginally less pleasant and the complications of the disease itself depend largely upon the level of nutrition of the sufferer. Among the deprived they can be frequent and serious and death can be common.

But for neither is there a cure, nor, apart from palliation, a treatment. The alternative to prevention is therefore not cure but inaction. In the case of smallpox, as is well known, through energetic programmes in areas where it was endemic, the disease appears to have been eradicated.

Cholera is another somewhat different world scourge. In Bengal, where it probably originated, its management is not readily in accord with the view that prevention is better than cure. As this audience well knows, this vicious disease is caused by what Robert Koch, its discoverer, called the comma bacillus, and this is a normal inhabitant of the Ganges where it uses its flagellum to get around. Passage through the human gut is not essential for its reproduction and survival. It has shown itself to be equally at home in many of the other great rivers of the world, including the Thames and the Hudson, provided that the temperature of the water remains comfortably warm.

As we like to think every schoolboy should know, it was to protect the poor of England that first Chadwick (a lawyer) and later Snow, by systematic observation and logical reasoning, saw the need for the legal reforms which made drinking water clean and the sewage flow separately from it. Cholera was prevented, and prevented so effectively that no individual had to modify his behaviour to protect himself. Protection, perhaps for the first time knowingly and deliberately, was wrought in a primary form by changing man's environment. Thus, a group of diseases which included typhoid and some dysenteries was prevented. Again, there was at that time no cure, but the benefit was incontrovertible even on the grounds of preventing cholera alone. (I shall return to what I mean by protection in a minute.)

Yet, cholera continues to ravage Bangladesh and Indian Bengal. There are two reasons for this. First, the Ganges Delta consists of vast areas of rice paddies tended by villagers who live on humps of ground, similar to those which rise with their mediaeval churches above the Anglian Fens. During the spring floods the paddies are inundated, and the water table is a matter of a few centimetres below the houses. Within the limits of available technology, and of national resources (taking its huge population and its economy together, Bangladesh is probably the poorest large country in the world), Chadwickian sewage and water supply systems are quite simply impossible to introduce.

What then of protection, which can be attained by making demands on every Bengali to modify his health behaviour in his own interests? He may for instance do this by ensuring that he gets inoculated. Antigens against *Vibrio cholerae* have been developed, but unfortunately the proportion of people they protect from the outset has been under 50 per cent and the certainty of protection in that small proportion starts to fall off in a matter of months. In other words, it simply is not a proposition for an impoverished government – nor even for international bankers and donors – to use inoculation as a means of preventing people from getting cholera in Bengal. A second, but complementary approach is to teach this population of tens of millions of people, who are more or less isolated for some months each year, the principles of hygiene – to boil drinking water, to sterilise excrement, to wash their hands, etc. – another daunting prospect but possibly one which will be achieved (perhaps by the year 2000?). However, the real point is that motivation towards the distribution of a satisfactory vaccine on a large scale or of conducting crash health education programmes is undermined by the availability of a highly effective and inexpensive electrolyte solution which keeps a patient with cholera alive until his own body defences cope with the bacillus. In one study, (Moseley *et al.* 1972), 80 per cent of the cases coming for treatment reported that they had received the vaccine during the previous three months. In this case cure is 'better' than prevention.

So far we can draw two conclusions as follows:

1. When effective prevention and cure are both available for a disease, prevention is not, as the axiom would have us believe, necessarily the best choice, although it usually is.
2. Curable diseases for which the question of whether to prevent is real are rare, and as an alternative, in policy formulation, cure is of little relevance. The real choice is usually between prevention and treatment, but, often enough between prevention and simply allowing the disease to follow its own course aided by symptomatic relief.

THE CONCEPT OF PROTECTION

To return to the concept of protection; from the point of view of policy formulation it is helpful to subdivide the various procedures used in prevention into two chief categories (Acheson and Hagard

1985; Acheson 1986): those which provide *primary protection* and those which provide *secondary protection* – so called to differentiate them from Hugh Leavell's three categories of prevention. The latter are chiefly clinical in conceptualisation (Leavell 1953), and based on the natural history of disease; the third of them is not prevention at all but treatment. To provide primary protection is to provide an environment where the disease cannot occur because the necessary cause is no longer part of it. This has been achieved for smallpox (to be followed perhaps by measles) by biomedical means: for cholera and the other graver gastroenteric diseases in the developed world, by sanitary engineers; and for diseases associated with an unhealthy workplace or polluted air, by the law and by chemical and civil engineers among others. Secondary protection is less effective because it must always involve active co-operation and participation; this amounts to behavioural change and has to be provided by the individual members of society themselves. Not only need they for instance modify their own eating, drinking and smoking habits, but they must co-operate on behalf of themselves and their families in screening and inoculation programmes. The NHS may not contribute much to the provision of primary protection, but as we shall see, it must be prepared to co-operate extensively with other public and private agencies in working towards the provision of secondary protection. The most effective form of prevention, but one which is frequently impossible, is therefore derived by providing primary protection. Even so, for a given disease this may effectively be achieved in one ecosystem, yet it may not be feasible in another.

DEGENERATIVE AND NEOPLASTIC DISEASES

These arguments have been based on three important diseases of relatively simple aetiology, each of which is 'caused' by a micro-organism, and each in an unprotected population may have an attack rate approaching 100 per cent – justification in its own right for prevention.

In the degenerative and neoplastic diseases which have more complex aetiologies, as a rule only secondary protection which, as we have just seen, requires behavioural modification can be offered so that the probability of benefit becomes less certain and costs generally higher (Wright *et al.* 1983). In one of the most logical and thoughtful papers on the prevention of non-infectious disease, Shapiro

(1977) writes that before we can accept a preventive measure against any of them we should attempt to answer several questions of which I paraphrase five:

1. Is the aetiology of the condition satisfactorily elucidated (or are there differing views about it)?
2. Does an effective preventive measure involve risk to anyone in the population concerned?
3. What is the scope of the medical, social or economic changes that would be needed to implement the preventive measure?
4. Does the preventive measure involve the introduction of something new or the withdrawal of something already present? In either case what are the overall consequences?
5. What is the total range of potential outcomes? For instance does a sharp decrease in mortality bring with it in some subjects a protracted increase in morbidity?

Each of these is worthy of consideration in more depth.

1. Preventing a Disease of Complex Aetiology

The following have been some research findings over the years in respect of ischaemic heart disease, which probably has the most complex aetiology of all diseases.

a. Hypertension is the most important *single* risk factor for ischaemic heart disease.
b. Hypertension can satisfactorily, without untoward side-effects, be controlled with drugs.
c. Some reduction in the incidence of ischaemic heart disease has been brought about by using those drugs in people with *severe* hypertension.

This has led quite naturally to the hypothesis that if such drugs are given to those with *moderate* or *mild* hypertension the incidence of ischaemic heart disease (IHD) should be reduced in them also. The hypothesis has not been sustained, or perhaps it is more appropriate to say that the null hypothesis has not been satisfactorily rejected, even though in several trials blood pressure has fallen convincingly, and this in turn has been associated with a sharp decrease in the incidence of cerebrovascular disease (CVD). In CVD the relative risk for hypertension has generally been found to be much higher than for IHD. No doubt the lack of a clear difference between case and control groups for IHD can in part be attributed to a Hawthorn Effect during the research – nevertheless this cannot be assumed wholly to explain why the reduction of mild hypertension has such a disappointing influence on the incidence of IHD (Oliver 1982; *Lancet* 1982).

A parallel example is to be found in the case of Clofibrate, a drug which reduces the serum cholesterol – a slightly less potent risk factor for IHD than hypertension. A controlled trial was therefore undertaken by the World Health Organisation to determine whether the drug reduced mortality from IHD (Oliver *et al.* 1980); it did but its use was associated with an increased death rate from everything else!

The Multiple Risk Factor Intervention Trial of Primary Prevention of Coronary Heart Disease (1982) in the USA met with similar results to the hypertension trials; blood pressure and other individual risk factors were reduced; but there was again no clear relative reduction of incidence of or mortality from IHD. We must conclude also that, despite the thousands of millions of pounds (most of them in dollars!) that have been spent on studying the epidemiology of IHD we have not learned enough, with any confidence, to invest heavily in a preventive programme on research findings (Hypertension Detection and Follow-Up Program 1977, 1979; Acheson 1973; Veterans Administration Co-Operative Study Group 1967; 1970). For IHD therefore the answer to Shapiro's (1977) first question is "No, we do not understand the aetiology as adequately as we might". Nevertheless, presumably because of changes in the *modus vivendi* brought about by biomedical findings and epidemiological research, morbidity rates from IHD in highly developed countries are falling and many epidemiologists and cardiologists attribute this to direct moderate modification of behaviour and I would not disagree with them. In contrast population trials have satisfactorily shown that CVD with its relatively simple aetiology can, like measles and smallpox, at least in part be prevented by controlling hypertension which for it is a dominant risk factor. And the cost to the NHS of CVD is much higher than IHD.

2. Risk to Subjects

It is widely accepted that oral contraceptives, one of the most effective modern preventive measures, carry a risk for several conditions which though manifest to a negligible extent during the early reproductive years, magnifies with age, and is aggravated in some circumstances such as existing peripheral vascular disease or hypertension (as well as by smoking).

Less widely discussed are the side-effects of fashions of a shapely figure and of diet (Ryle, 1936). Nobody knows, and it is to be hoped that nobody will again have a chance of determining, what the true range and gravity of the complications of the laced-in wasp-waist of the young women of the turn of the century were. 'Chlorosis' was one, but it is very probable that had they been available, modern epidemiological techniques would have identified others. The craze for slimness which has again been fashionable for a couple of decades is closely associated with medical and public reactions to epidemiological work which indicates the protean ill-effects of obesity. No doubt much good has been done, but it has brought with it an increase in the incidence of anorexia nervosa, a condition of the intelligent middle class girl in some of whom a desire to be pretty and healthy has slipped dangerously out of control (Crisp 1980; 1983).

Another issue is that of dietary salt. We have been advised that it is - what? It is bad for us? It may be bad for us? That we should eat a salt-free diet or perhaps a no added salt diet? We do know that withdrawal of salt (sodium chloride) from the diet of hypertensives reduces their blood pressure, yet have had the greatest difficulty in demonstrating a relationship in members of unbiased samples of the general populations between dietary salt and blood pressure. A valid reason commonly given for this is that dietary salt is so difficult to measure. Another, less frequently aired, is that while some members of the population have indeed blood pressures sensitive to salt, others do not. My blood pressure is 118/77 and my mother was normotensive till she died at 89, both of us happy salt eaters. It is widely agreed that to some extent blood pressure is a heritable trait and it is not unreasonable to suggest that this may, in part at least, be due to genetic determination of salt sensitivity. A percentile analysis of blood pressure taken in a cross-sectional national probability sample in the United States indicated that there is no change with age between ages 20 to 80 years in the 3 per cent of males with the lowest blood pressures (McGregor *et al.* 1982). In the lowest quintile of black males there was a rise in systolic pressure of about 10 mm of mercury. In white females the rise was about 10 mm of mercury compared with nearly 40 mm among black females. This implies that I am not the only white male to go through life with constant low blood pressure, but that Blacks and females are less likely to share the experience. Beard (1982) has shown that several thousand healthy Australians are capable of living, evidently contentedly, free of salt over a period of a few years, without evident ill-effect and doubtless some benefit but no-one really knows that no-one will be spared untoward consequences in the long run (see also National Heart Foundation of Australia, 1980). Again, the possibility of the few suffering for the many has been put forward. Is it either reasonable or wise to bully the salt tolerant into doing without? So to Shapiro's (1977) second question, the answer is that we know less than we should.

3. The Scope of Necessary Changes

The issue of ascertaining the magnitude of demand on resources, should a measure be considered a serious candidate for implementation in terms of the benefit it can be expected to provide, is of course critically important. Firm proponents of nationally funded programmes ask themselves what reasonably can be done to allow vigorous, effective screening programmes for breast and cervical cancer to be universally introduced. Beral and Booth (1985) have undertaken a cohort analysis of the incidence of invasive cancer of the cervix, which shows that should current trends continue, in women below the age of fifty years incidence may more than double between 1981 and 2001; incidence of cancer of the breast is rising too, though not so dramatically. Treatment of cancer of the breast has changed little over recent decades, but for cancer of the cervix the laser beam has been found to have all the necessary qualities for large scale treatment and perhaps in a real sense cure, provided lesions are identified before there are symptoms. Because this 'high tech' procedure is non-invasive and very precise and no general anesthetic required, it is effective with minimal discomfort. Once the considerable capital investment has been made it is very inexpensive to use (Evans and Monaghan 1983; Popkin 1983; Wright *et al.* 1983; Hare and Cooper 1985). Electrocoagulation has its proponents (Shurmans and Carmichael 1984), but some authorities consider anaesthesia to be necessary (Chanen and Rome 1983) and this raises revenue costs. Because the high risk groups for this condition are poor and ill-informed and therefore less amenable to co-operating in screening programmes, the demand on resources required to obtain really wide coverage will be very much greater (no herd immunity here) than those required for cancer of the breast. But because of the effectiveness of early treatment, the potential benefit to society compared with the very unfavourable prognosis of women treated after symptoms develop, there is an excellent case for giving it priority. So the programme which makes the larger demand on society and its resources can be looked upon as a preferable investment for the NHS than the less costly breast screening. But this is not to say that breast screening in the NHS supplemented perhaps on a private or semi-private basis should not be officially encouraged.

4. Withdrawal of An Old Practice or Introduction of a New One?

Some of the most pressing aspects of a programme for prevention involve withdrawing noxious substances, such for instance, tobacco and addictive drugs. Years of study have shown that the willing co-operation of the subject is required – but also more recently that people can be helped to decide to be willing to co-operate. In the past few years attention has been turned towards the selection and rejection of various foodstuffs, but policy and advice have been developed on very uncertain grounds. The arguments I advanced in the case of salt, namely, first, that because something is bad for some people, it is not necessarily bad for everyone; second, that even though excess may be harmful this does not mean that moderation is not beneficial and third, that for some at least, total withdrawal may have unforeseen consequences, can, for all we know, be applied to many other foodstuffs (perhaps even butterfats?) The reason, as we have seen, is that the only question that is generally asked has been 'Is this substance harmful to some people?'. In short, although we can confidently point to some harmfully constituted diets, the way we seem to have gone about putting together a 'good' one has been to describe one which does not have too many of any of the constituents which evidently are bad for some people. We have some idea about what to withdraw, but have little basis for recommending what to substitute. The extent to which the new way is an improvement on our old ways we cannot really say with confidence.

5. Balancing Reduced Mortality Against Increased Morbidity

If Leavell's (1953) concept of tertiary prevention is classed as treatment (for instance the use of surgery in the management of spina bifida), as I have already suggested it should be, then the delicate

ethical issues which emerge with the postponement of death, becomes in Leavell's terms a matter for primary and secondary prevention only. The balance between them and permanent disability or
death are confined chiefly to infectious diseases and the rare complications of inoculation, such as encephalitis. The issues involved have
recently been well argued by Miller and his colleagues in their report
to the DHSS on the benefits of inoculation against whooping cough
(Alderslade *et al.* 1981). This with my caveat is, perhaps, of Shapiro's
five questions, the least important in the prevention of degenerative
and non-infectious disease.

CONCLUSION

As I see them the issues are:

1. Attempting to suppress the development of 'high technology'
   procedures out of hand is no more in the best interests of preventive medicine than it is in those of medicine in general.
2. Primary protection can only be provided for diseases of simple
   aetiology, and only then when research has satisfactorily answered
   the basic questions. When this has been done the box-watching
   man on the Clapham bus would expect it to be provided. Such
   provision will rarely be a matter of using NHS resources (e.g. the
   implementation of the Clean Air Act) although it could be (e.g.
   eradication of measles). Just because primary protection can be
   offered in one ecosystem, it cannot necessarily be provided in
   others, however. Nevertheless, and this is important, primary
   protection in its nature will, if it is successful, free NHS resources
   by obviating the need for treatment.
3. We must rely on *secondary protection* for controlling most disease
   both infectious and non-infectious. Depending as it does upon
   modifications of human behaviour it is complex and difficult to
   execute. The co-ordinated support of a wide range of government
   and private agencies, of which the NHS is just one is necessary.
4. The planning of services for prevention which is based only on
   inductive reasoning is undesirable and is especially true in diseases
   of complex aetiology, because:
   a. Anticipated consequences have a nasty habit of not being
      consequent.

b. Unanticipated consequences may prove to be unfortunate consequences.

5. NHS resources should of course, be used for prevention, and it is appropriate that budgeting for them should be initiated at district, and processed upwards in the usual way. If for no other reason (and clearly there are other reasons), this approach should allow maximum opportunity for joint budgeting to be based on joint planning with Health Education Officers, and Local Authority Departments of Education and Social Services as well as joint planning between Community and Hospital sections within the NHS itself in this respect. It is regrettable that because Family Practitioner Committees are no longer funded through the Regional Health Authorities, the General Practitioners are funded and administered by a system which is functionally separate from the rest of the National Health Service.

6. Treatment and cure are long established and appropriately the central component of health care; prevention in a broad sense is not well established and we just do not know enough about it yet to recommend any large scale switch of NHS resources to it from services which provide treatment. Clearly, we should advocate procedures in which we have a genuine and well founded confidence; these might be financed in part by funds released by preventive successes, and in part by those diverted from other sectors of the economy. But the first priority for investment should be a lot more imaginative research into prevention.

References

Acheson, R. M. (1973) 'Blood pressure in a national sample of US adults: percentile distribution by age, sex and race', *International Journal of Epidemiology*, 3, 293–301.
Acheson, R. M. (1986) 'An ecological approach to preventive medicine', *Journal of the Royal Society of Medicine*, 79, 636–8.
Acheson, R. M. and Hagard, S. (1985) *Health, Society and Medicine: An Introduction to Community Medicine* (Oxford: Blackwell Scientific).
Alderslade, M. H., Bellman, N. S., Rawson, E. M., Ross, E. M. and Miller, D. L. (1981) *The National Childhood Encephalopathy Study in Whooping Cough*, ch V, DHSS (London: HMSO).
Beard, T. C., Cooke, H. M., Gray, W. R. and Barge, R. (1982) 'Randomised controlled trial of a no-added-sodium diet for mild hypertension', *Lancet*, ii, 455–60.
Beral, V. and Booth, M. (1985) 'Projections of incidence of, and mortality

from, carcinoma of the cervic uteri in England and Wales', *Personal communication*.

Buxton, M., Acheson, R. M., Caine, N., Gibson, S. and O'Brien, B. (1985) *Costs and Benefits of Heart Transplant Programmes at Harefield and Papworth Hospitals*, DHSS Report 12. (London: HMSO).

Chanen, W. and Rome, R. M. (1983) 'Electrocoagulation diathermy for cervical dysplasia and carcinoma in situ: a fifteen year survey', *Obstetrics and Gynaecology*, 61, 673–9.

Crisp, A. H. (1980) *Anorexia Nervosa: Let Me Be* (London: Academic Press).

Crisp, A. H. (1983) 'Anorexia nervosa', *British Medical Journal*, 287, 855–8.

Evans, A. S. and Monaghan, J. M. (1983) 'Treatment of cervical intra-epithelial neoplasia using the carbon dioxide laser', *British Journal of Obstetrics and Gynaecology*, 90, 553–60.

Freymann, J. G. (1974). *Medicine's Great Schism; Prevention Versus Cure: An Historical Interpretation* (New York: Medical Communications).

Hare, M. J. and Cooper, P. (1985) Personal communication on a series of 2000 cases of cervical dysplasia treated by laser.

Hypertension Detection and Follow-up Program Co-operative Group (1977) 'Five-year findings of the hypertension detection and follow-up program: 1. Reduction in mortality of persons with high blood pressure, including mild hypertension: Results of a ten-year intervention trial, Hypertension XXV Supplement, *Circulation Research*, 40, (I)98 – (I)105.

Hypertension Detection and Follow-up Program Co-operative Group (1979) 1. Reduction in mortality of persons with high blood pressure, including mild hypertension, *Journal of the American Medical Association*, 242, 2562–77.

Lancet editorial (1982) 'Trials of coronary disease prevention', *Lancet*, ii, 803–4.

Leavell, H. R. (1953) 'Levels of application of preventive medicine', in *Preventive Medicine For the Doctor and His Community*, ed. H. K. Leavell and E. G. Clark, ch. 2, 3rd edn (New York: McGraw Hill).

MacGregor, G., Best, F., Cam, J. M., Squires, M., Sagnella, G. A., Elder, D. and Markandu, N. (1982) 'Double blind randomised crossover trial of moderate sodium restriction in essential hypertension, *Lancet*, i, 351–5.

Moseley, W. H., Bart, K. J. and Sommer, A. (1972) 'An epidemiological assessment of cholera control programs in rural East Pakistan', *International Journal of Epidemiology*, 1, 5–11.

National Heart Foundation of Australia (1980) 'The Australian therapeutic trial in mild hypertension', *Lancet*, i, 1261–7.

Oliver, M. F. (1982) 'Does control of risk factors prevent coronary heart disease?', *British Medical Journal*, 285, 1065–6.

Oliver, M. F., Heady, J. A., Morris, J. N. and Cooper, J. (1980) 'WHO co-operative trial on primary prevention of ischaemic heart disease using Clofibrate to lower serum cholesterol: mortality follow-up', *Lancet*, ii, 379–86.

Popkin, D. R. (1983) 'Treatment of cervical intraepithelial neoplasia with the carbon dioxide laser', *American Journal of Obstetrics and Gynaecology*, 145, 177–80.

Ryle, J. A. (1936) 'Anorexia nervosa', in *Natural History of Disease*, ed. J. A. Ryle, pp. 118–29 (London: Oxford University Press).

Schurmans, S. N. and Carmichael, J. A. (1984) 'Treatment of intraepithelial neoplasia with electrocautery: report of 426 cases', *American Journal of Obstetrics and Gynaecology*, 148, 544–6.

Shapiro, S. (1977) 'Measuring the effectiveness of prevention, II', *Milbank Memorial Fund Quarterly*, V, 291–301.

Veterans Administration Co-operative Study Group on Antihypertensive Agents (1967) 'Effects of treatment on morbidity in hypertension: Results in patients with diastolic blood pressures averaging from 115 through 129 mm Hg', *Journal of the American Medical Association*, 202, 116–22.

Veterans Administration Co-Operative Study on Antihypertensive Agents (1970) 'Effects of treatment on morbidity in hypertension, II: Results in patients with diastolic blood pressure averaging 90 through 114 mm Hg', *Journal of the American Medical Association*, 213, 1143–52.

Wright, V. C., Davies, E., Riopelle, M. A. (1983) 'Laser surgery for cervical intraepithelial neoplasia: principles and results', *American Journal of Obstetrics and Gynaecology* 145, 181–4.

10 Public Health and the Extension of Life Expectancy in England and Wales, 1901–60

J. M. Winter

The debate about the causes of the extension of life expectancy in this century is a contentious one, and rightly so, since it touches on an issue of central social and political importance. One indicator of the success of states in promoting the well-being of their populations is the increase over time in the average length of life, and when progress slackens or is even reversed as may have been the case in the Soviet Union in recent years (Feshbach 1982), the political dimensions of this question surface rapidly.

Even when progress is steady, or at least less mercurial, discussions of this subject take place in a charged atmosphere. Investment in health is a controversial political issue, and it is in this context that we must place arguments about the claims that medical care, health administration, and standards of living were primarily or centrally responsible for recent increases in life expectancy. In a period of economic retrenchment and soaring health costs, this issue is bound to be more than an academic one.

The question this chapter addresses is, therefore, what light can historical evidence throw on the question of the character and causes of the increase in life expectancy in England and Wales in this century? To provide the beginnings of an answer to this question, we first examine data on the age-structure and cause-structure of mortality over the period 1901–60. After having established when the greatest gains in life expectancy were registered, we consider which causes of death were primarily responsible for them. Against this background, we then turn to the question of how public policy affected these developments.

1. RISING LIFE EXPECTANCY: DIMENSIONS, TIMING, AGE-STRUCTURE, AND CAUSE-STRUCTURE

It is only in recent years that demographers have begun to investigate the cause-structure of mortality with the precision already devoted to the age-structure of mortality. Inaccuracies in cause-of-death diagnosis and substantial variations in degrees of completeness and in modes of classification undoubtedly exist and ensure that any statistical analysis using cause-of-death data must allow for a wide margin of error. What we must identify is clear and unambiguous evidence concerning specific mortality trends; marginal cases must be discounted due to the high proportion of unspecified causes of death in all official returns.

The most ambitious and searching attempt to overcome these difficulties and to develop a model of causes of mortality is that of Preston, who accumulated and analysed data on mortality in 162 populations over the period 1860 to the present. In work done jointly with Keyfitz and Schoen, he adopted a twelve-part classification of causes of death based on aetiological rather than anatomical criteria and then distributed within this scheme all causes of death enumerated in the successive international classifications of causes of death produced and revised between 1909 and 1955 (Preston *et al.* 1972). He then calculated age-specific and cause-specific death rates for each country at regular intervals. This permitted an analysis of the contribution of different causes of death to overall mortality decline over time, on the assumption that each cause of death was independent of all other causes. This premise is questionable, since some infectious diseases produce increases in mortality due to their sequelae. Some distortion is inevitably introduced, but it is probably small enough to permit us to use this framework for an analysis of English and Welsh data over the period 1901–60.

The abridged life tables which Preston constructed for England and Wales differ in two respects from those published in successive decennial supplements to the Registrar-General's reports. First, Preston examined data for single years, whereas the series of English Life Tables is based on triennia. The resulting differences in figures for life expectancy are small. Life expectancy at birth in English Life Table 12, for the years 1960–2, is half a year lower than that in Preston's table for 1960; life expectancy in English Life Table 11, for 1950–2, is half a year higher than Preston's figure for 1951. But since we are

Table 10.1   Life expectancy at age (x), male population, England and Wales, 1901–60

Age (x)	1901	1911	1921	1931	1940	1951	1960
0	45.319	49.382	55.936	58.204	59.387	65.846	68.242
1	53.834	56.752	60.632	61.905	62.361	67.143	69.019
5	54.481	56.866	59.252	59.873	59.628	63.523	65.275
10	50.538	52.815	55.055	55.529	55.237	58.725	60.441
15	46.091	48.331	50.520	50.921	50.627	53.885	55.552
20	41.847	44.031	46.208	46.547	46.238	49.112	50.792
25	37.779	39.839	41.955	42.285	44.739	44.427	46.065
30	33.760	35.679	37.767	37.950	37.326	39.736	41.285
35	29.889	31.606	33.578	33.607	32.950	35.064	36.520
40	26.181	27.659	29.493	29.372	28.667	30.438	31.843
45	22.670	23.851	25.491	25.284	24.507	25.940	27.279
50	19.289	20.226	21.615	21.402	20.569	21.692	22.919
55	16.167	16.838	17.961	17.711	16.970	17.805	18.875
60	13.215	13.712	14.602	14.266	13.734	14.290	15.299
65	10.623	10.932	11.556	11.136	10.826	11.260	12.186
70	8.249	8.455	8.888	8.477	8.215	8.628	9.492
75	6.406	6.489	6.715	6.275	5.974	6.366	7.245
80	4.617	4.936	5.015	4.596	4.383	4.580	5.460
85	3.611	3.698	3.529	3.294	3.132	3.242	4.309

Source: Preston *et al.* (1972).

mainly interested in trends over time rather than in absolute levels, this disparity between sources is not especially worrying.

The second distinction concerns the year 1940. The upheaval of the Second World War is responsible for the fact that no English Life Table exists for the interval between 1930–2 and 1950–2. For an historian this is a serious difficulty, not only intrinsically, but also because major developments in medical care and chemotherapy took place in the 1930s and 1940s, and it is essential to try to measure their impact. For this reason, Preston's data for England and Wales in 1940, if handled with care, can serve to complete the time series and to provide further clues as to the processes underlying the increase in life expectancy in this century.

The general outline of rising life expectancy at birth is straightforward. In 1901, men could expect to live approximately 45 years; women, nearly 50. By 1921, men and women had both added a decade to the average length of their lives. It took another 30 years to add yet another decade, and by 1960, life expectancy at birth had reached over 68 for men and over 74 for women. In Tables 10.1 and

Table 10.2   Life expectancy at age (x), female population, England and
Wales, 1901–60

Age (x)	1901	1911	1921	1931	1940	1951	1960
0	49.433	53.398	59.920	62.362	63.901	70.947	74.127
1	56.534	59.625	63.533	65.087	66.113	71.816	74.612
5	57.174	59.742	62.070	62.896	63.279	68.170	70.841
10	53.300	55.716	57.881	58.497	58.830	63.318	65.958
15	48.910	51.270	53.389	53.912	54.199	58.432	61.040
20	44.662	46.939	49.077	49.525	49.800	53.611	56.146
25	40.475	42.656	44.837	45.207	45.482	48.838	51.265
30	36.381	38.412	40.596	40.887	41.104	44.104	46.413
35	32.418	34.240	36.336	36.541	36.688	39.409	41.600
40	28.594	30.191	32.140	32.229	32.315	34.763	36.862
45	24.921	26.236	28.000	27.988	28.018	30.198	32.234
50	21.283	22.435	23.963	23.875	23.873	25.794	27.745
55	17.878	18.799	20.102	19.938	19.917	21.554	23.416
60	14.643	15.431	16.457	16.222	16.162	17.541	19.268
65	11.761	12.355	13.102	12.816	12.745	13.817	15.425
70	9.153	9.505	10.104	9.775	9.719	10.504	11.949
75	7.069	7.314	7.601	7.226	7.184	7.683	8.930
80	5.161	5.532	5.646	5.276	5.234	5.498	6.544
85+	4.021	4.300	4.101	3.907	3.892	3.931	4.752

Source: Preston *et al.* (1972).

10.2 we present data on life expectancy for men and women at regular intervals between ages 0 and 85.

The first question that emerges immediately is which were the periods of greatest improvement in life expectancy in this century? As a glance at Tables 10.3 and 10.4 will show, the answer is the two war decades, 1911–21 and 1940–51.

We must treat this finding cautiously, since unusual conditions in the two initial years 1911 and 1940 were responsible for particularly high mortality levels in those years, thus exaggerating the pace of decline in the subsequent decade. The summer of 1911 was exceptionally hot, thereby increasing the spread of infectious disease, particularly among children, and (to state the obvious) 1940 was the year when the Blitz began and a Coalition Government just started to mobilize the nation for total war. But the gains registered in these decades are so striking that, even if we allow for some degree of distortion attributable to the opening dates of our intervals, we can still conclude that for men aged 0–50 and for women aged 0–45, the two war decades were the periods of greatest improvement in life

Table 10.3   Extension of life expectancy for men, England and Wales, 1901–60, by decade, and at certain ages

Additional years life expectancy at age (x)

Age	1901–11	1911–21	1921–31	1931–40	1940–51	1951–60
0	4.063	6.554	2.268	1.183	6.459	2.396
1	2.878	3.880	1.273	0.456	4.782	1.876
5	2.385	2.386	0.621	–0.245	3.895	1.752
10	2.277	2.240	0.474	–0.292	3.488	1.716
15	2.240	2.189	0.401	–0.284	3.258	1.667
20	2.184	2.177	0.339	–0.309	2.874	1.680
25	2.060	2.116	0.330	–0.546	2.688	1.638
30	1.919	2.088	0.183	–0.624	2.410	1.549
35	1.717	1.972	0.029	–0.657	2.114	1.456
40	1.428	1.834	–0.127	–0.705	1.771	1.405
45	1.181	1.640	–0.207	–0.777	1.433	1.339
50	0.937	1.389	–0.213	–0.833	1.123	1.227
55	0.671	1.123	–0.250	–0.741	0.835	1.070
60	0.497	0.890	–0.336	–0.532	0.556	1.009
65	0.309	0.624	–0.420	–0.310	0.434	0.926
70	0.206	0.433	–0.417	–0.262	0.413	0.864
75	0.083	0.226	–0.440	–0.301	0.392	0.879
80	0.319	0.079	–0.419	–0.213	0.197	0.880
85+	0.087	–0.169	–0.235	–0.162	0.110	1.067

Source: Preston, *et al.* (1972).

expectancy in this century. At later ages, the greatest gains were registered in the 1950s. For all age groups, though, relatively little progress was made in the interwar years.

The rapid progress of the two war decades was most marked at early ages. For example, over seven years were added to female life expectancy at birth between 1940 and 1951, and over six years were added to male life expectancy in both war decades. Similarly impressive gains were registered at ages one, five and ten, but progress tapers off in later age groups. And while some gains were registered at more advanced ages, life expectancy for the elderly did not rise substantially in the two war decades.

Now that we have established some features of the age-structure of mortality decline, we can begin to sketch the cause-structure of mortality decline. Tables 10.5 and 10.6 present standardised death rates for males and females in twelve categories of causes of death in the period 1901–60. Taking 1901 levels as a standard of comparison,

Table 10.4 Extension of life expectancy for women, England and Wales, 1901–60, by decade, and at certain ages

Additional years life expectancy at age (x)

Age	1901–11	1911–21	1921–31	1931–40	1940–51	1951–60
0	3.962	6.520	2.442	1.539	7.046	3.180
1	3.091	3.908	1.554	1.026	5.703	2.796
5	2.568	2.328	0.826	0.383	4.891	2.671
10	2.416	2.165	0.616	0.333	4.488	2.640
15	2.360	2.119	0.523	0.287	4.233	2.608
20	2.277	2.138	0.448	0.275	3.811	2.535
25	2.181	2.181	0.337	0.275	3.811	2.535
30	2.031	2.184	0.291	0.217	3.000	2.309
35	1.822	2.096	0.205	0.147	2.721	2.191
40	1.597	1.949	0.089	0.086	2.448	2.099
45	1.315	1.764	−0.012	0.030	2.180	2.036
50	1.152	1.528	−0.088	−0.002	1.921	1.951
55	0.921	1.303	−0.164	−0.021	1.637	1.862
60	0.788	1.026	−0.235	−0.060	1.379	1.727
65	0.594	0.747	−0.286	−0.071	1.072	1.608
70	0.352	0.599	−0.329	−0.056	0.785	1.445
75	0.245	0.287	−0.375	−0.042	0.499	1.247
80	0.371	0.114	−0.370	−0.042	0.264	1.046
85+	0.279	−0.199	−0.194	−0.015	0.039	0.821

Source: Preston *et al.* (1972).

indices of these data (Tables 10.7 and 10.8) show which causes declined, at what pace and at which points in this century.

First let us consider aggregate mortality rates. Taking all causes of death, the most substantial decline occurred in the years 1911–21: total death rates for men dropped by 16 per cent over those years. For women, 17 per cent gains were registered both during 1911–21 and during 1940–51; at no other interval was progress so rapid for either sex.

Now let us turn to individual categories of cause of death. The prominence of the period 1911–21 in overall mortality decline is clearly attributable to major improvements in death rates due to most infectious diseases, as well as to steep declines in certain non-infectious diseases of infancy and certain degenerative diseases, such as diabetes, kidney disease, and cirrhosis of the liver. Many of these conditions are nutrition-related, a point to which we shall return below.

Table 10.5   Standardised death rates by cause or combination of causes, male population of England and Wales, 1901–60

Cause of death	1901	1911	1921	1931	1940	1951	1960
All causes	.02348	.02072	.01698	.01662	.01688	.01363	.01157
Respiratory TB[1]	.00160	.00121	.00099	.00082	.00061	.00033	.00009
Other infectious and parasitic diseases[2]	.00204	.00172	.00095	.00082	.00052	.00017	.00006
Neoplasms	.00117	.00143	.00162	.00185	.00184	.00206	.00219
Cardio-vascular diseases	.00426	.00397	.00406	.00531	.00589	.00623	.00562
Influenza, bronchitis, pneumonia[5]	.00389	.00321	.00299	.00257	.00276	.02020	.00136
Diarrhoeal diseases [6]	.00123	.00144	.00054	.00019	.00015	.00006	.00005
Certain degenerative diseases	.00106	.00099	.00079	.00090	.00079	.00042	.00030
Maternity [8]	–	–	–	–	–	–	–
Certain diseases of infancy	.00116	.00102	.00077	.00066	.00057	.00039	.00031
Accidents and violence	.00108	.00094	.00072	.00081	.00140	.00059	.00060
Other and unknown	.00600	.00481	.00355	.00269	.00234	.00134	.00099
Infectious diseases (1,2,5,6,8)	.00876	.00758	.00547	.00440	.00404	.00258	.00156

Source: Preston *et al.* (1972).

In Tables 10.7 and 10.8 we find abundant evidence of the prominence of infectious diseases in the process of mortality decline in the 1911–21 decade. Taking 1901 data as the standard of comparison, we note that while overall male and female mortality dropped by 16 and 17 per cent respectively, mortality due to infectious diseases fell by fully 25 per cent for both men and women. At the same time, mortality due to certain degenerative diseases fell by 22 per cent and 23 per cent for men and women respectively. Among all infectious diseases, non-respiratory causes fell particularly sharply. Even allowing for some distortion due to special conditions in 1911, it is still remarkable that the polyglot group of 'other infectious and parasitic diseases', which cover most childhood diseases, fell by approximately 40 per cent in these years.

Progress over the years 1940–51 was similarly based on important, though less precipitate, declines in death rates for most infectious diseases. In this decade standardised death rates dropped by 14 per cent for men and 17 per cent for women. The decline of all infectious diseases was of roughly the same order.

Table 10.6   Standardised death rates, by cause or combination of causes, female population of England and Wales, 1901–60

Cause of death	1901	1911	1921	1931	1940	1951	1960
All causes	.01971	.01715	.01375	.01313	.01264	.00932	.00732
Respiratory TB[1]	.00106	.00082	.00073	.00058	.00042	.00017	.00003
Other infectious and parasitic diseases[2]	.00169	.00148	.00080	.00062	.00040	.00012	.00004
Neoplasms	.00150	.00154	.00160	.00168	.00155	.00145	.00139
Cardiovascular diseases	.00393	.00353	.00346	.00440	.00472	.00461	.00381
Influenza, bronchitis, pneumonia[5]	.00320	.00256	.00230	.00199	.00182	.00117	.00058
Diarrhoeal diseases[6]	.00107	.00124	.00043	.00015	.00013	.00006	.00005
Certain degenerative diseases	.00077	.00075	.00055	.00065	.00053	.00026	.00018
Maternity[8]	.00024	.00016	.00015	.00011	.00007	.00002	.00001
Certain diseases of infancy	.00090	.00080	.00059	.00049	.00043	.00028	.00022
Accidents and violence	.00044	.00038	.00029	.00037	.00087	.00028	.00031
Other and unknown	.00493	.00389	.00286	.00209	.00172	.00091	.00071
Infectious diseases (1,2,5,6,8)	.00726	.00626	.00441	.00345	.00284	.00154	.00071

Source: Preston *et al*. (1972).

The most striking feature of the data for the period 1940–51, though, is the steep decline in respiratory disease mortality. For example, between 1940 and 1951, female death rates for respiratory tuberculosis fell by 24 per cent, and those for the collective category of influenza, bronchitis and pneumonia fell by fully 20 per cent, far outstripping the 8 per cent gain registered for both categories of respiratory disease mortality in 1911–21.

Other features of the cause-structure of mortality may be noted in Tables 10.7 and 10.8. The well-known increase in mortality due to neoplasms and to cardiovascular diseases over the century is clearly visible. Partly this reflects the transfer of deaths from infectious diseases of early life to chronic diseases of later life, inevitable in an ageing population. Partly this reflects environmental and behavioural changes, for example, in diet or smoking.

Finally, let us examine the question of the contribution of different causes or combinations of causes to aggregate mortality decline over

The Extension of Life Expectancy

Table 10.7   An index of standardised death rates by cause or combination of causes, male population of England and Wales, 1901–60 (1901 = 100)

Cause of death	1911	1921	1931	1940	1951	1960	Greatest gain during
All causes	88	72	71	72	58	49	1911–21
Respiratory TB[1]	76	62	51	38	21	6	1901–11
Other infectious and parasitic diseases[2]	84	47	40	25	8	3	1911–21
Neoplasms	122	138	158	157	176	187	–
Cardiovascular diseases	93	95	125	138	146	132	1901–11
Influenza, bronchitis, pneumonia[5]	83	77	66	71	52	35	1940–51
Diarrhoeal diseases[6]	117	44	15	12	5	4	1911–21
Certain degenerative diseases	88	66	57	49	34	27	1911–21
Maternity[8]	–	–	–	–	–	–	–
Certain diseases of infancy	88	66	57	49	34	27	1911–21
Accidents and violence	87	67	75	130	73	74	1940–51
Other and unknown	80	59	45	39	22	17	1911–21
Infectious diseases (1,2,5,6,8)	87	62	50	46	29	18	1911–21

Source: Preston *et al*. (1972).

time. In Table 10.9, we present data on the cause-structure of female mortality decline in England and Wales in the intervals 1901–11, 1912–21, 1940–51, and 1951–60.

Five comments are necessary before we discuss these data. First, we limit our discussion to female mortality levels to avoid problems related to an unrepresentative civilian male age-structure in populations facing compulsory military service. Secondly, data for 1921–31 and 1931–40 have been omitted, since relatively small total changes exaggerate the percentage contribution of individual causes to total mortality decline. Thirdly, we have used data on 1912–21 for the

Table 10.8   An index of standardised death rates by cause or combination of causes, female population of England and Wales, 1901–60 (1901 = 100)

Cause of death	1911	1921	1931	1940	1951	1960	Greatest gain during
All causes	87	70	67	64	47	37	1911–21/ 1940–51
Respiratory TB[1]	77	69	55	40	16	3	1940–51
Other infectious and parasitic diseases[2]	88	47	37	24	7	2	1911–21
Neoplasms	103	107	112	103	97	93	1931–40
Cardiovascular diseases	90	88	112	120	117	97	1951–60
Influenza, bronchitis, pneumonia[5]	80	72	62	57	37	18	1901–11/ 1940–51
Diarrhoeal diseases[6]	116	40	14	12	6	4	1911–21
Certain degenerative diseases	89	66	54	48	31	24	1911–21
Maternity[8]	67	63	46	29	8	4	1901–11
Certain diseases of infancy	89	66	54	48	31	24	1911–21
Accidents and violence	86	66	84	198	64	70	1940–51
Other and unknown	79	58	42	35	18	14	1901–11
Infectious diseases (1,2,5,6,8)	86	61	48	39	21	10	1911–21

Source: Preston *et al.* (1972).

years surrounding the First World War to take advantage of a more complete analysis of this issue we have published elsewhere (Winter 1985). Fourthly, we have included a column to reflect the general experience of all 162 populations Preston examined in his study. This may be taken to be a 'model' of mortality decline, useful for comparative purposes.

Finally, we must note the limitations of a system of classification which retains such a sizeable residual category of 'other and unknown' causes. Preston believes that most of these are deaths due to

Table 10.9   Percentage contribution of causes of death to decline in
female mortality in England and Wales, 1901–60

Cause of death .	Preston estimates for 162 populations	1901–11	1912–21	1940–51	1951–60
Respiratory TB	10.6	9.4	3.5	7.5	7.0
Other infectious and parasitic diseases	14.0	8.2	24.8	8.4	4.0
Neoplasms	–	–	–	3.0	3.0
Cardiovascular diseases	1.8	15.6	22.8	3.3	40.0
Influenza, bronchitis, pneumonia	24.3	25.0	–	19.6	29.5
Diarrhoeal diseases	10.4	–	14.5	2.1	0.5
Certain degenerative diseases	1.7	0.8	13.8	8.1	4.0
Maternity	2.0	3.1	0.4	1.5	0.5
Certain diseases of infancy	4.2	3.9	13.6	4.5	3.0
Accidents and violence	0.4	2.3	3.5	17.2	–
Other and unknown	33.1	40.6	27.9	24.4	10.0

Sources: Preston (1976) Table 2.2; Winter (1985) Table 4.7; Winter (1986) Table 1.

cardiovascular diseases. This inference arises from the clear parallelism between the rise of this category and the decline of the residual category over time (Preston and Nelson 1974, p. 25). This may contain a grain of truth, but it is even more likely that both more accurate reporting and changes in diagnostic fashion account for this development.

With these qualifications in mind, the data in Table 10.9 provide further confirmation of our earlier findings. Over half of total female mortality decline in the decade of the 1914–18 war was due to the general category of non-respiratory infectious diseases, diarrhoeal diseases, and certain diseases of infancy. A further 20 per cent was due to a decline in cardiovascular diseases, and 13 per cent was attributable to a drop in deaths due to certain degenerative diseases.

In contrast, mortality decline for women in the period of the Second World War had more to do with the trajectory of respiratory infections than with other categories of cause of death. Together respiratory tuberculosis and influenza, bronchitis and pneumonia accounted for over 27 per cent of total mortality decline. The category of other infectious and parasitic diseases accounted for a further eight per cent of overall decline, but this was only one-third of its contribution to mortality decline in the 1912–21 period. The surprisingly large part played by accidents and violence in the post-1940 decline may be set aside as reflecting special war conditions rather than long-term trends.

We may conclude, therefore, that the two salient periods of progress in life expectancy in this century, 1911–21 and 1940–51, clearly differ in significant ways. In the period 1940–51 respiratory diseases led the way in the process of mortality decline, followed by other infectious disorders. In contrast, the earlier (and greater) decline in 1911–21 was attributable not to respiratory diseases but to other infectious and certain chronic diseases. The contrast with the pattern derived from Preston's aggregate analysis is clear; so is that with both the 1901–11 and 1951–60 decades. Evidently, the two war decades present two sides of the story of the extension of life expectancy in England and Wales in this century. We shall return to this point below.

2. RISING LIFE EXPECTANCY: ALTERNATIVE EXPLANATIONS

Now that we have surveyed some of the available demographic evidence concerning rising life expectancy, we may turn to the interpretive literature to try to account for our findings. The relevant literature on the subject of the causes of mortality decline is vast, but it may be useful to examine two alternative explanatory models which have been constructed in recent years. The first is that of McKeown, a physician and Professor (now Emeritus) of Social Medicine. The second is that of Preston, whose demographic research we have already discussed above. We shall first briefly summarise their respective positions and then argue that neither provides a fully adequate framework within which to place the phenomenon of rising life expectancy in Britain in this century. To broaden their approaches, we turn to ideas developed by the economist Amartya Sen, which help locate these questions within a political framework, conspicuously missing in the work of both McKeown and Preston. Our claim is that the only way to account adequately for rising life expectancy in the period of the two world wars is by setting them within the context of the political economy of health and welfare created to win wars but which unintentionally made this country a healthier place in which to live.

McKeown's model of mortality decline reflects his belief in nutritional determinism. It is as if he has taken as his motto Feuerbach's old adage 'You are what you eat'. He argues that population growth in the eighteenth century was a function of mortality decline made possible by the increase in agricultural output associated with the early stages of the industrial revolution. Medical care had either a negative or neutral effect on survival rates from infectious diseases (McKeown and Record 1955; 1962).

Nutritional determinism is also the hallmark of his interpretation of later developments. He shows that mortality due to respiratory tuberculosis and other infections began to decline in the later nineteenth century, decades before any effective medical or chemotherapeutic steps could be taken to control them. He admits that after 1935, antibiotic drugs were of importance in containing or eliminating some infectious diseases. But by then most of the traditional killers of the nineteenth century had lost their former ferocity. The inescapable conclusion is that doctors and health administrators were not responsible for mortality decline. By process of elimination, rising standards of living, yielding rising nutritional standards, McKeown believes, account for rising life expectancy in England since the middle of the nineteenth century (McKeown 1976).

McKeown's assertions about the eighteenth century have come in for some biting criticism in recent years (Wrigley and Schofield 1981). But in this paper we are concerned only with twentieth-century developments. In this context, the most searching challenge to McKeown's interpretation has been offered by Preston. His objections to McKeown's argument may be summarised under three heads. First, Preston claims that it is unwise to base a general model of mortality decline on the English case, the special properties of which make it unrepresentative. Secondly, he suggests that McKeown offers an unnecessarily narrow view of what constituted medical intervention. 'The germ theory of disease', he argues, 'stimulated many innovations other than drugs and vaccines, such as improved antiseptic practices, quarantines, and segregation of infectious patients, and it gave impetus to the movements for cleaner food and water, better personal sanitation, and improved infant feeding' (Preston 1976, p. 82). And thirdly, his statistical analysis of trends in mortality decline and national income throughout the world in the period 1930–60 suggests that 'Factors exogenous to a country's current level of income probably account for 75–90 per cent of the growth in life expectancy for the world as a whole between the 1930s and the 1960s. Income growth *per se* accounts for only 10–25 per cent' (Preston 1976, p. 74).

Preston even goes so far as to claim that 'The logistic curve for the 1960s suggests that, even if England and Wales had experienced no improvement in living standards between 1901–1910 and the present, its life expectancy could be expected to have increased from 50.4 to 69.6 years.' Thus 'economic advance was not an essential prerequisite to a major increase in life expectancy' nor even 'a major factor in that increase' (Preston 1976, p. 82).

It is an oddity of research in this field that it seems to produce extreme or one-dimensional arguments. Preston is on solid ground to argue that the English case is atypical. The vagaries of the climate and the early development and high degree of urbanization are certainly responsible for the prominence of respiratory infections in this country's mortality profile in the past. Equally convincing is his claim that public health is not reducible to what prescriptions a doctor can offer. But just as McKeown goes too far in magisterially dismissing any credit the medical profession might claim for rising life expectancy, Preston goes too far when, with equally magisterial finality, he brushes aside any suggestion that changing nutrition or living standards were key factors in the secular decline in mortality.

There are problems, too with Preston's analysis of the link between economic and demographic change. He chose to study statistically the one generation – from the 1930s to the 1960s – when major medical developments indisputably helped precipitate a rapid decline in death rates in many parts of the world. Leaving aside the question of the inaccuracies and errors embedded in all national income accounts, surely the real test of Preston's argument would be to examine the nature of the statistical relationship between levels or changes in levels of income and mortality *prior* to the chemotherapeutic revolution of the 1930s. Unfortunately, he did not do so, probably because of the absence of adequate economic data on the earlier period.

We seem to have arrived, therefore, at a cul-de-sac, with two seemingly diametrically opposed interpretations of an important demographic phenomenon. It is at this point that our earlier discussion of trends in life expectancy in England between 1900 and 1960 may prove illuminating, by suggesting the need to combine these two interpretive models, and in some respects to go beyond them both.

3. MORTALITY DECLINE IN WARTIME

Both Preston and McKeown are interested in general phenomena over relatively long time intervals. In this paper, we have tried to identify relatively short periods of time in which major gains in life expectancy were registered. In the first parts of this paper we established that the most salient progress in extending the average length of life occurred in the two war decades 1911–21 and 1940–51. We shall argue first that these findings provide greater support for McKeown's view than for Preston's, although it is necessary to recognise as well the significance of medical developments in mortality decline in the latter period. Secondly, we shall claim that both theories are deficient in ignoring the extent to which political factors shaped the conditions leading to mortality decline in the period of the two world wars.

Let us consider the two war decades separately. First, it is necessary to establish whether the gains registered between 1911 and 1921 occurred before, during, or after the outbreak of war. Fortunately, there is substantial evidence of many kinds to support the view that, ironically, wartime was a period of major improvement in the life chances of people lucky enough to stay out of the trenches. The analysis of life tables, occupational mortality data, the cause-structure of mortality, and infant and maternal mortality rates all point in the same direction: towards the view that, unintentionally, war conditions promoted the health of the non-combatant population. The general rule is that the worse off a section of society was in 1914, the greater were the gains registered in life chances in the war years (Winter 1985).

The coincidence of war and the influenza epidemic of 1918–19 has led many scholars to miss this fundamental development in the history of public health. But a close examination of the incidence and age-structure of the 'plague of the Spanish Lady' will show that the toll of lives it took in no meaningful sense can be attributed to the war. It is best to see this epidemic as a *sui generis* development, which fortunately has never recurred (Winter 1985).

There are many reasons to claim that wartime conditions account for the fact that while respiratory-disease mortality remained high in the war period, non-respiratory viral and bacterial disease mortality declined precipitately. We have already presented some evidence to this effect in Tables 10.5 to 10.9. The only convincing explanation of them is in terms of an unanticipated but real improvement in the standard of living of the home population during the war.

How did this country manage to pay for the war and at the same time provide better pay and an improved diet for its home population? The answer is that Britain lived off her capital stock during the conflict. Some of it was invested in the empire, the true economic value of which was proved during the war. But more of it was invested in the form of bricks and mortar, and it is here that we may find one source of the persistence of high respiratory disease mortality. To keep the war effort going required the maintenance of adequate or improved levels of nutrition among munitions workers. But especially under conditions of rent control, it was not possible to avoid a situation where essential repairs and improvements were postponed or abandoned. Given the absence of economic incentives, no one was able to prevent a rundown of the nation's housing stock during the war. Combined with congestion in factories and centres of war production, the result was to exacerbate conditions leading to an increase in death rates for some causes (notably respiratory diseases) virtually as the price that had to be paid for improving conditions leading to a decrease in death rates due to other causes (notably diarrhoeal diseases and other diseases of early life).

Since more than 60 per cent of the medical profession was in the Royal Army Medical Corps during the war, and since initiatives in health policy, such as the provision of child and maternal welfare centres, were too embryonic to have much effect on current mortality trends, it seems that the experience of the First World War supports McKeown's overall view of the causes of mortality decline. It is likely that without adequate or improved levels of nutrition, the gains in life expectancy registered in Tables 10.1 to 10.4 simply could not have been made.

Precisely the same is true for the Second World War. But when we turn to the 1940–51 period, we see the need to find room for both nutritional and medical factors in order to account for the extension of life expectancy noted above. As Richard Titmuss showed 30 years ago, mobilisation of the home population required both a major reorganisation of health provision and the construction of an effective nutritional policy (Titmuss, 1950). Dudley Seers also demonstrated conclusively that there occurred in this decade a shift of income away from the middle class and toward the working class (Seers, 1948). But it would be foolish to ignore the fact that by the later 1940s, penicillin and other antibiotics helped control infectious diseases – such as bronchitis and pneumonia – which had stubbornly remained major killers until then. In part, this may help to explain why severe housing problems in the 1939–45 war did not yield long-term increases in respiratory mortality. Some recrudescence in tuberculosis occurred in 1940–2, as had happened in 1914–16, but this phenomenon was fortunately short-lived, giving way to a precipitate decline in the war years and in the postwar period.

It is unlikely, though, that chemotheraphy was primarily responsible for the gains of the 1940s. This is for three reasons. First, there is reason to doubt whether the relevant drugs were produced in large enough quantities to have made an immediate impact on survival rates. Secondly, during the Second World War itself, when major gains were made for example in infant and maternal mortality, the military had first call on relatively scarce supplies of drugs. And thirdly, the cost of penicillin may have made it difficult in many cases for general practitioners to prescribe it or other drugs, even after the National Health Service was set up in 1948. For these reasons, it seems likely that the full impact of the chemotherapeutic revolution was delayed until the 1950s. Consequently, we must ascribe the major gains to the 1940s first to a rise in nutrition which strengthened resistance to infectious disease, and only secondly to contemporary developments in medical intervention, such as antibiotic treatment and an effective blood transfusion service.

4. MORTALITY DECLINE AND THE POLITICAL
ECONOMY OF WAR: AN ENTITLEMENT APPROACH

We have presented evidence that the major periods of mortality decline in this century were the two war decades 1911–21 and 1940–51. The analysis of cause-of-death data suggests a two-stage interpretation of the extension of life expectancy. In the first stage, which occurred in the decade of the First World War, the most significant contribution to mortality decline was made by non-respiratory infectious diseases. In the second stage, located in the decade of the Second World War, the decline of mortality due to respiratory infections played a salient role in overall trends. In both wars, nutritional standards rose, especially for the poorer sections of the population. And while a deterioration in the nation's housing stock occurred in both world wars, this had clear negative repercussions only in the earlier period. In contrast, by the mid-to-late 1940s, mortality due to respiratory diseases declined substantially, reflecting both improvements in nutrition and to a lesser extent in chemotherapy.

It is one of the ironies of the history of public health in this century that major gains in life expectancy took place in wartime, when both food supplies and medical services were curtailed in significant ways. In conclusion, it may be useful to offer an interpretation of how this happened. To do so, we borrow from the approach of the economist Amartya Sen, in particular that adumbrated in his celebrated study, *Poverty and Famines*. In this work he discusses the problem of poverty not in terms of commodities but in terms of the relation of groups of people to commodities, or of 'the ability of people to command food through the legal means available' in society. Thus the exchange entitlement of all citizens is their right to command access to a bundle of commodities under a given system of law and property. That set of rights is not fixed, but differs markedly across time and space. On occasion the exchange entitlement of labour is insufficient to provide them with sufficient food to avoid starvation. The result is famine, whatever the situation with respect to food supply happens to be. Thus the Bengal famine of 1943 was not a function of food availability decline (or FAD, as he terms it), but arose out of the inability of landless labourers to command an income adequate enough to purchase food at a time of rapid price inflation. What caused the crisis was not a collapse of food supply, but a market failure due to differential inflation and insufficient demand for the goods and services most of the rural population had to offer. Their real incomes therefore dropped below subsistence, and millions starved (Sen 1981).

It may be useful to consider the applicability of this approach to a diametrically opposite situation. We have argued that the improvement in nutrition which took place during both world wars was sufficiently great to underly a major decline in mortality due to infectious diseases. This was because the nation distributed a more limited food supply in wartime more equitably than it had done in peacetime. Why? Because, in Sen's terms, the exchange entitlement of labour changed radically, such that previously poorly nourished people were able, both through the workings of the labour market and the extension of social provision, to command a higher standard of living in general and a higher standard of nutrition in particular.

Sen's approach has the advantage of shifting attention in the study of the economics of health away from Malthusian considerations of scarce food resources to questions of rights over access to resources; that is to say, towards the meaning of citizenship itself. During the two world wars, citizenship entailed the entitlement to command a bundle of commodities, including sufficient food, to enable each adult to contribute effectively to the war effort. That bundle of rights came to include a minimum standard of health. Evidence of this development we see, for example, in the extension of the National Insurance Act to cover all munitions workers during the First World War, and in the erection of the Emergency Medical Service during the Second World War. Both changed the legal basis of entitlement to health care, and formed part of a wider set of measures, including rationing and rent control, to protect the well-being of the home population at war. The results are apparent in the demographic data we presented in the first part of this paper.

The case of mortality decline in Britain in the period of the two world wars, therefore, presents good reasons to argue that the appropriate context in which to place the process of rising life expectancy is that of the political economy of health. This is not to say that questions of food supply and medical provision are of little importance; on the contrary. It is rather to suggest that only by adopting an approach which examines rights as well as resources will we be able to present a full account of this important facet of demographic history.

Of course, to complete this analysis, it is necessary to recognise the significance of longer-term cohort effects in the process of mortality decline. There is a momentum in demographic history, arising from cumulative improvements in conditions of life, which helps account for the relative advantage in life chances of successive generations in this country since the 1870s (Winter 1984). Such progressive changes are mirrored in statistics of rising life expectancy since 1900. But the magnitude of the gains described in this paper, and the clear direct links with contemporary developments, indicate that we are dealing primarily with period effects, or in other words, with the unintended and unplanned impact of war.

In this regard, the achievements of the two war periods are a challenge to anyone interested in current health policy. To paraphrase William James, they suggest that the defence of the nation's health in future may depend in part upon our willingness and ability to build a moral equivalent to the political economy of war, which in Britain in this century had utterly unanticipated beneficial consequences for the health of the civilian population.

References

Feshbach, M. (1982) 'The Soviet Union: population trends and developments', *Population Bulletin*, 37, 1–6.

McKeown, T. (1976) *The Modern Rise of Population* (London: Edward Arnold).

McKeown, T. and Record, R. G. (1955) 'Medical evidence related to English population changes in the eighteenth century', *Population Studies*, 9, 144–55.

McKeown, T. and Record, R. G. (1962) 'Reasons for the decline of mortality in England and Wales during the nineteenth century', *Population Studies*, 16, 94–122.

Preston, S. H. (1976) *Mortality Patterns in National Populations* (New York: Academic Press).

Preston, S. H. Keyfitz, N. and Schoen, R. (1972) *Causes of Death. Life Tables for National Populations* (New York: Academic Press).

Preston, S. H. and Nelson, V. E. (1974) 'Structure and change in causes of death: an international summary', *Population Studies*, 28, 19–51.

Seers, D. (1948) *The Levelling of Incomes since 1938* (Oxford: Basil Blackwell).

Sen, A. (1981) *Poverty and Famines* (Oxford: Oxford University Press).

Titmuss, R. M. (1950) *Problems of Social Policy* (London: HMSO).

Winter, J. M. (1984) 'Unemployment, nutrition and infant mortality in Britain, 1920–50', in *The Working Class in Modern British History*, ed. J. M. Winter (Cambridge: Cambridge University Press).

Winter, J. M. (1985) *The Great War and the British People* (London: Macmillan).

Winter, J. M. (1986) 'The Demographic Consequences of the Second World War' in H. Smith (ed.) *War and Social Change* (Manchester: Manchester University Press).

Wrigley, E. A. and Schofield, R. S. (1981) *The Population History of England, 1541–1871* (London: Edward Arnold).

Part IV

Social and Cultural Barriers to Health

11 Health, Inequality and Social Structure

Richard G. Wilkinson

Class differences in mortality rates are the most widely used measures of the social distribution of health. Though they have many short-comings, they are the best data we have. The last comprehensive figures available for England and Wales centre on 1981 and show differences in age-specific death rates between classes I (professional occupations) and V (unskilled manual occupations), which, if applied throughout the lives of a cohort, would produce a difference of more than seven years in life expectancy at birth (OPCS 1978, p. 190). This amounts to a 10 per cent difference in life-expectancy – the equiv-alent to shortening the unskilled manual worker's day from 24 to about 21 hours or lopping five weeks off every year. (Because of problems in classifying women by occupational class, I refer to male death rates throughout this paper. The differences between the sexes, while important in other contexts, do not affect the argument put forward here.)

The figures of class differences in death rates which have been issued for each census period throughout this century suggest that health inequalities have shown no tendency to narrow. But in the light of the prevailing belief that until recently Britain was becoming a more egalitarian society, the accuracy of the figures of class differ-ences in health has been widely questioned. On the face of it, it seemed unlikely either that the differences were really as large as they appeared or that the gap had failed to diminish during the greater part of this century. However, the research which has taken place since the publication in 1980 of the Black Report on *Inequalities in Health*, gives no reason to think that the picture is substantially incorrect in terms of either the size or the trends in class differences in health (Wilkinson 1986a). Results from the OPCS Longitudinal Survey make it clear that mortality differences have not been signifi-cantly inflated by classification problems, and several studies have shown that the contribution of selective social mobility is likely to be relatively small at most ages, though some would argue that it makes an important contribution to differences in perinatal mortality. (By 'selective social mobility' I mean any tendency for the healthy to move up the social scale while the unhealthy move down.) The effect of changes in the classification of occupations and in the distribution of the population between classes has been examined by Pamuk (1985) who concludes that social inequalities in mortality have increased at least since 1951.

If, however, we are interested in the size of the differences in mortality attributable to overall *socioeconomic* inequalities (as opposed to those attributable to inequalities between arbitrarily defined social classes), it would appear that much the most substantial weakness in the existing social class data is the extremely poor fit between social class and people's actual socioeconomic circumstances. An indication of how far the Registrar General's social classes are from providing a neat rank ordering of people in terms of their standard of living, can be seen from figures of median occupational income by social class shown in Table 11.1.

It appears that, at least in 1971, there was no clear gradient in occupational incomes from class III non-manual to class V. Not only is there no systematic difference between the earnings of the lower four classes, but the New Earnings Survey (1970) suggests that the dispersion of earnings *within* each occupation is as wide as the dispersion between classes. The extent to which the Registrar General's classes are socioeconomically heterogeneous must call into question the vast number of studies which use them to control for the effects of socioeconomic differences in the population.

If the social class classification provided a clearer ordering of people according to their standard of living, it is hard to believe that the mortality differentials would not appear larger than they do at present. Marmot's work on a large sample of civil servants classified by employment grade confirms this impression. He found more than a three-fold difference in mortality rates between the highest and lowest grades, compared to less than a doubling shown between social classes I and V in the OPCS figures for 1971 (Marmot 1986). The greater differential is no doubt partly due to more accurate occupational information, but it must also be due to the use of employment grades which more closely mirror differences in socioeconomic circumstances than does the class classification of occupations. The weakness of the social class classification is also demonstrated by the fact that classifying by housing tenure or car ownership produces mortality differentials which are almost as large

Table 11.1   Weekly income by social class

Social class	Median income (1971)	% of S.C.V
I	£44.14	200
II	£34.02	154
IIIN	£24.12	109
IIIM	£27.05	122
IV	£22.46	102
V	£22.09	100

Source: Registrar General (1978) OPCS Occupational Mortality 1970–2.

Table 11.2   Changing mortality ratios and the class distribution of the population (*Men, England and Wales*)

Social class		1951	1961
I & II	SMR	91	80
	% Popn.	18%	19%
IV & V	SMR	110	115
	% Popn.	29%	29%
Difference in SMRs		19	35

Note: SMRs are age-standardised mortality ratios which express the mortality in each class as a ratio of the population mean mortality (100) at each date. The social class SMRs have been combined by weighting according to the proportion of the population in each class.
Source: Black Report (1980) Tables 3.1 and 3.16.

(Fox and Goldblatt). Presumably the presence or absence of freezers or fitted carpets would discriminate equally well.

Not only is it likely that the real socioeconomic differences in mortality are larger than the social class figures suggest, but during the period in which we can be slightly more confident that the figures are comparable, it appears that the class gradient in mortality actually increased. If we compare mortality rates for classes I and II combined and IV and V combined, in 1951 and 1961, we are by chance comparing almost identical proportions of the population (see Table 11.2). During the decade the male age-standardised mortality ratio for upper classes improved relative to the average, and that for the lower classes deteriorated. Even the absolute mortality experience of men in most age-groups in social class V actually worsened during this period (Registrar General 1961). That this is a real effect is also confirmed by the known reversal in the social class distribution of heart disease and related diseases which took place partly during this period and seems to have occurred in most other industrial countries. It is likely that this trend is partly a reflection of changes in nutritional and smoking patterns across classes.

Perhaps the most striking feature of class differences in health is how broadly based they are. All the main causes of death – with the single exception of breast cancer – show the lower classes at a disadvantage. This disadvantage occurs in every age group. But it is not only the *incidence* of fatal diseases which shows a class bias. There is also evidence, at least among victims of cancers and heart disease, that case-fatality rates are also higher among the lower classes (Leon and Wilkinson, 1987). In other words, as well as determining who gets a disease, inequalities also determine their chances of dying once they have got it.

Not only are class differences in health broadly based in terms of the wide range of health measures which show a lower class disadvantage, they are also broadly based in terms of causes. Indeed, one is a reflection of the other. Marmot has shown that the class gradient in mortality from diseases unrelated to smoking is just as steep as that for diseases which are related to smoking (Marmot 1986). In addition he showed that even if all the main risk factors for heart disease are taken into account, they can only explain part of the mortality disadvantage in the lower classes.

That inequalities in health are so broadly based raises problems of the nature of their causality. I have argued elsewhere that it is a mistake to think of diseases as having a small number of unique 'causes' awaiting scientific detection (Wilkinson 1983). In practice most aspects of the circumstances in which we live and work are likely to have at least some influence on health, if only we could mount studies large enough, and find the necessary control groups to detect them. In practice we should regard factors labelled 'causal' simply as those aspects of the *causal situation* which researchers have chosen to single out as variables, or capable of variation, rather than those factors which are constant within the population. (In terms of Popper's view of scientific explanation, the idea of a few unique causes falls down with his failure to distinguish between factors nominated as causes and the potentially infinite number of 'initial conditions' which must be satisfied in order for any selected cause to operate. I owe this point to Alex Bellamy.)

In effect then, diseases, like road accidents, are caused by the combination of a vast cluster of circumstances, a list of which might begin: a drunken driver, a wet road, poor visibility, worn tyres, crowded road conditions, the camber of the road, its surface characteristics, distracting advertisements beside the road, tiredness etc. From different perspectives different factors are nominated to the status of causes. The Council highways department focuses on one set of factors, motor manufacturers on another, legislators on yet another, driving instructors, health educators and police on still others. Even then there is nothing to stop epidemiologists adding new causes for themselves such as 'risk-taking behaviour'. With heart disease the list of known causes already includes several aspects of diet, stress, exercise, smoking, water hardness, genetic factors, drug use and personality type.

What are the implications of this view of disease causality for our understanding of class differences in health? Given that most aspects of the myriad of socioeconomic inequalities in our society will have some impact on health, it seems likely that there is no very simple solution to the problem of inequalities in health. Even so, we must ask why it is that the favourable and unfavourable influences of such a large number of different factors do not balance out through the law of averages? When there are innumerable qualitative and quantitative differences between people's ways of life in different classes, why should the net balance of pros and cons work out so systematically to favour those nearer the top of the social hierarchy? The answer can only be that there is still a fairly direct relationship between human preferences and the conditions of life most beneficial to health. Where people have different amounts of freedom, power, money, education and choice, the differences in the way they live will reflect not simply differences, but a hierarchy of preference, and so result in an ordering of health advantage and disadvantage such as we observe.

The task of reducing inequalities in health should not therefore be seen either as a matter simply of reforming one or two aspects of working class life, or alternatively, of getting rid of all differences in an attempt to create uniformity in the way people live. Rather it is a matter of reducing the inequalities in freedom, power, education and money which determine the disparities in the extent to which the way people live is a reflection of their choosing. Essentially, the range of choices open to people must cease to be dominated by their position in society. Only then will the balance of health pros and cons associated with individual circumstances cease to vary so alarmingly from one section of the population to the other.

The same underlying point (that preferred lifestyles are also healthier) follows from the fact that much the most substantial historical improvements in the nation's health have appeared as the side-effects of improvements in the standard of living rather than as a result of health policy itself (McKeown and Lowe 1974). No doubt most future improvements in lower class health will continue to result from the struggle to improve the standard of living for its own sake. The implication of this is the obvious point that in so far as shorter lives result from poorer conditions, there is a double injustice: both the length and the quality of life are diminished. Epidemiologists should remember that though they may concern themselves almost exclusively with inequalities as a health problem, the poor are probably more interested in it as a housing, income, stress, or employment problem.

Many people continue to see the role of behavioural factors in health as an indication that the problem belongs to the realm of freedom rather than constraint in people's lives. But this is to slip into the same error as the eighteenth-century moralists, who commented on the evils of gin drinking, ignoring the fact that behaviour is situational and develops as an attempt to live with, or somehow cope with, circumstances. One might add that it is also a little paradoxical to rely on supposed voluntary factors to explain the greater ill-health of those in lower classes whose lives are distinguished from others primarily by the tighter resource constraints and the diminished range of opportunities and choices open to them.

What then can be done about inequalities in health? Obviously almost any of a wide range of reforms aimed at reducing socioeconomic inequalities may be expected to bring minor, but nevertheless welcome, reductions in inequalities in health. While it is not difficult to suggest social and economic reforms intended to reduce the burden of ill-health in lower social classes, it seems inconceivable that any of our political parties would implement a programme of reforms capable of having a major impact on the problem. While it was a Labour administration which took the initiative in setting up the DHSS working party which produced the Black Report, the Labour

Party was perhaps fortunate to escape the embarrassment of having to respond to the report's recommendations. Yet even if the inconceivable had happened, and the report's recommendations had been implemented in their entirety, most of the problem of inequalities in health would still be with us. When there were suggestions that Swedish society may have developed to a point where inequalities in health had almost disappeared (Black Report 1980, p. 139), there seemed some hope that the problem of class differences in health might be regarded as amenable to policy. But now that we know that even Sweden, with its comparatively egalitarian policies, still has large class differences in health, we are forced to think again (Lynge and Anderson 1985). But my purpose is not to detract from the value of discussing immediate policy issues: even small improvements are better than none. It is instead to look at the broader horizon.

The major impediment to significant progress on this front is lack of the political will – and not just that of governments. To gain wider support for action in this field, it may be helpful to give more consideration to where the inequalities issue might take us in the long run. If research can give us a clearer understanding of the relationship between the social structure and health, it might also clarify our ideas about the wider human implications of the social fabric and the direction in which we should be moving. What I am suggesting is that our social thinking should take more heed of the health effects of different facets of the social structure. This is not because health is the ultimate good, but because it is a powerful social indicator. Indeed, there may be no better unitary measure of human welfare. Familiar summary measures of changes in the standard of living, such as indices of real income, are largely blind to the qualitative changes in the material and social environment which are so crucial to human welfare. Health, on the other hand, is not only sensitive to the qualitative changes in material life, but the research evidence on stress, job satisfaction, depression and lack of close social contact, shows that it is also sensitive to many psychosocial aspects of the quality of life.

Health outcomes often provide objective evidence of the human implications of factors which would otherwise appear simply as matters of subjective judgement. A case in point is the way it took studies of weight gain and cognitive development in monkeys and human neonates to bring about a public recognition that something amounting to love is a necessary component of a baby's well-being. Before that, at least in medical circles, there was a tendency to regard babies as having physical rather than social needs. It now looks as if studies of health may be providing the clearest and most objective indicators of adult social needs and the way in which they are, or are not, met within different forms of social organisation. Epidemiological research may soon provide us with comparatively hard data capable of probing such hitherto hopelessly subjective areas as job satisfaction and the quality of human relations. Though of course we have our intuitions and subjective impressions of the desirable quality of the social fabric, lacking any unifying objectivisation these remain private and ineffective besides the transforming power of economic forces.

To see what inequalities in health can tell us about social reality may make it a little easier to find ways round the major obstacles to change. Presumably the most important reason why the political will to do anything substantial about inequalities in health is lacking, is the belief that it would cost too much money. Coming a close second is the belief that socioeconomic inequalities are good for some people and bad for others. However, in some respects inequalities may be bad for all of us. While differentials in power and prestige may be most harmful to those at the bottom of the social hierarchy, this does not mean that they are wholly beneficial to those at the top. It may well be that there are changes in the structure of social relations which would not only reduce inequalities in health but would improve health throughout society. In so far as opportunities of this kind are most likely to crop up in the field of psychosocial factors in health, such changes may be cost free. Indeed, in fields such as the effects of work satisfaction on health, they may produce considerable economic benefits. Stress, competitiveness, boredom, the distinction between order-givers and order-takers and lack of control over one's work may not only lead to higher mortality rates but also, more expensively, to increased sickness absence and decreased efficiency (Palmore 1969; Grossarth-Maticek *et al.* 1982; Karasek R. *et al.* 1981). Among non-manual workers it is likely that the social organisation of work is now the most important occupational health hazard, and few would deny that there is a close relationship between increased job satisfaction, decreased sickness absence and increased efficiency. In a 15-year American study of ageing, 'work-satisfaction' was a better predictor of longevity than doctor's physical assessments, tobacco consumption or genetic factors. The second best predictor was general 'happiness' (Palmore 1969). A prospective

Yugoslavian study suggested that people identified in the hierarchy as 'active emitters of repression' suffered from more cardiovascular and circulatory diseases, whereas those identified as 'passive receivers of repression' suffered more cancers (Grossarth-Maticek *et al.* 1982).

Outside the field of work there are many studies which testify to the high health costs of divisive social relations and lack of community. Both close personal relationships and a network of wider social affiliations seem protective against the effects of stress (Berkman and Syme 1979).

Stress and the lack of supportive social networks are issues which as well as causing increasing concern throughout society have probably also contributed to the apparent increases in class differences in health since the war. Closely knit working-class communities, such as the Bethnal Green described in Young and Wilmot's *Family and Kinship in East London*, (1957) have been replaced by communities more like the Camberwell described in Brown and Harris's *Social Origins of Depression* (1978). In the latter study, a third of the sample population lived in local authority housing consisting largely of modern high rise flats. Working-class women were considerably less likely to have a 'confiding relationship' and over 30 per cent of those with a pre-school child at home were classed as clinically depressed.

Not only may there be a convergence of class interests regarding some of the psychosocial components of class differences in health, but at least in health terms, the divergence of interests in relation to the distribution of material resources might not be as great as imagined. Let us look briefly at the relationship between income – as a key determinant of the standard of living – and health. My own comparisons of changes in the position of different occupations in the 'earnings league' with changes in their relative positions in the league tables of occupational mortality rates over a twenty-year period suggest that the relationship between income and mortality is causal (Wilkinson 1986b). A move up the earnings league is significantly associated with a move down the mortality league. Reinforcing this point, it also looks as if the narrowing of class differences in post-neonatal mortality which occurred during the early 1970s may well be related to the simultaneous narrowing of class differences in household income (Wilkinson 1986b).

The best fit cross-sectional relationship between occupational incomes and mortality rates in England and Wales is a curve. A simple log transformation of 1970 occupational incomes (from the

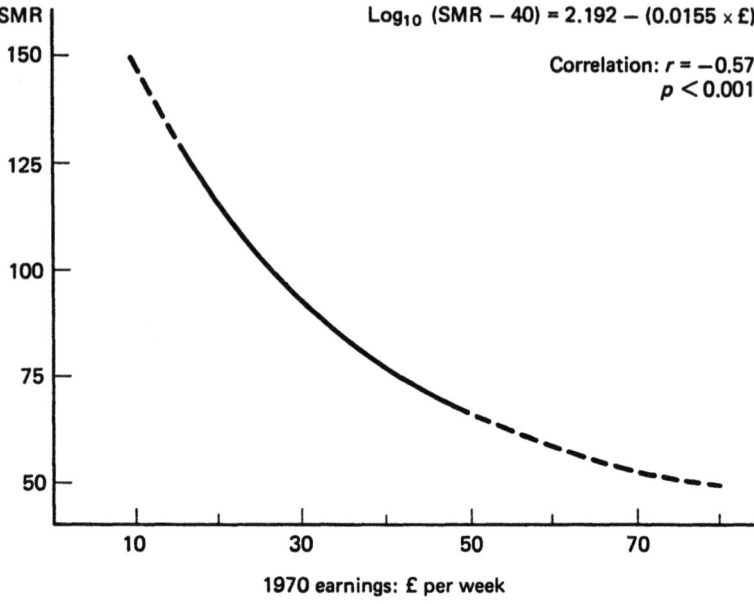

Figure 11.1 Cross-sectional relationship between occupational earnings and standardised mortality ratios

Source: Wilkinson 1986b.

New Earnings Survey) and 1971 occupational mortality rates gives a correlation coefficient of −0.6, a statistically significant improvement on the linear correlation obtained using the raw data. The curvilinear relationship is illustrated in Figure 11.1. Increases in incomes at the lower end of the income range bring large falls in the death rate, while increases at the top end bring little or no improvement in mortality. In short, successive increases in income bring diminishing health returns.

That this is likely to be the case in other countries is indicated by the very close association which Mildred Blaxter pointed out to me between income inequality and overall life expectancy or mortality rates of the populations of developed countries. Across the 11 OECD countries for which there are reliable gini coefficients of income inequality, there is a correlation better than 0.8 between gini coefficients of post-tax income inequality (standardised for differences in household size) and both life expectancy and infant mortality (Figure

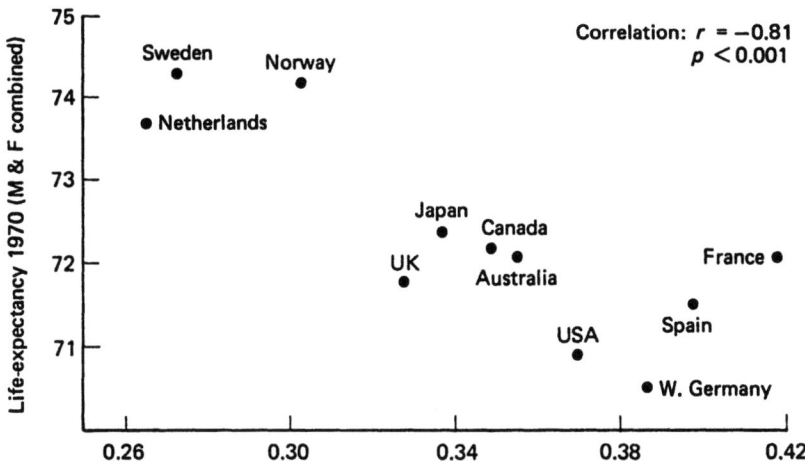

Figure 11.2   Life-expectancy (M & F) and gini coefficients of post-tax income inequality (standardised for household size)

Sources: Sawyer (1976), Table 11; World Bank (1983).

11.2). The correlation is significant at better than 1 in 1000 and suggests that the overall population mortality increases with income inequality. This fits closely with evidence Winter gives in his chapter in this volume that the rapid improvement in British life expectancy during the two world wars was a reflection of decreased inequalities in the standard of living.

A more detailed analysis of the relationship between mortality and income inequality in different countries was carried out by Rodgers (1979). His analysis covers 56 countries, both developed and less developed, and shows that income distribution remains crucial even when the wide variations in average per capita income levels between these countries is taken into account.

Health is then a powerful reason for income redistribution. Given that in 1980 the income distribution was such that the bottom 20 per cent of disposable incomes could be doubled by reducing the top 20 per cent of incomes by only 17 per cent (Townsend 1982), it is clear that the health and welfare of the poor could be substantially improved without the rich suffering any significant worsening of their health.

In so far as health is a good indicator of the material and

psychosocial quality of life, this would suggest that some measure of income redistribution away from the rich need have very little impact on most aspects of their real experience of life. But to command widespread support for such a policy it is probably not even necessary to assume that the age-old question as to whether wealth brings happiness could be answered in terms of diminishing returns. A knowledge of the health benefits alone is probably enough to convince most people that income redistribution should have a high priority.

No doubt class differences in health seem particularly repugnant to us partly because they offend our sense of social justice more than other forms of inequality. That babies in social class V are twice as likely to be born with spina bifida and twice as likely to die in the first year of life as babies in class I, can hardly appear as anything but a gross indictment of society. A number of ideological assumptions help us to see other inequalities as consistent with concepts of social justice. For instance, income differentials are variously assumed to bear some relationship either to the value, or to the responsibility or the unpleasantness of people's work.

At the most general level, acceptance of patterns of inequality is fostered by the notion of equal opportunity. But the irrelevance of the concept of equal opportunity to the problem of inequalities in health shows what a hollow idea it is. Too often it serves merely as a stalking-horse for the maintenance of just those inequalities in power, income, education and status which lie behind the disparities in life expectancy. As far as health goes, equal opportunity simply adds the insecurity and competitiveness of increased social mobility. A German study has found that downward social mobility is an additional risk factor for heart disease (Siegrist 1984) and data from the 1946 cohort of British births suggests that children in families which are upwardly or downwardly mobile are more likely to suffer serious illness (Wadsworth 1986).

Even in areas such as education, where the concept of equal opportunity has some relevance, the existence of major socioeconomic inequalities may make it not only a poor substitute for genuine equality, but also unrealisable. It seems likely that opportunity in most spheres of life will never be insulated – any more than health has been – from the powerful influences of socioeconomic inequalities.

References

Berkman, L. F. and Syme, S. L. (1979) 'Social networks, host resistance and mortality: a nine-year follow-up study of Alameda County residents', *American Journal of Epidemiology*, 109, 186.

Black Report, (1980) *Inequalities in Health*, Report of a DHSS Working Party chaired by Sir Douglas Black (London: DHSS).

Brown, G. W. and Harris, T. (1978) *Social origins of Depression*, (London: Tavistock).

Fox, A. J. and Goldblatt, P. O., *Longitudinal Study: Socio-demographic Mortality Differentials*, OPCS Series LS No. 1 (London: HMSO).

Grossarth-Maticek, R., Siegrist, J. and Vetter, H. (1982) 'Interpersonal repression as a predictor of cancer', *Social Science and Medicine*, 16, 493–8.

Karasek, R., Baker, D. *et al.* (1981) 'Job decision latitude, job demands, and cardiovascular disease: a prospective study of Swedish men', *American Journal of Public Health*, 71(7), 694–705.

Leon, D. and Wilkinson, R. G. (1987) 'Inequalities in prognosis: socioeconomic differences in cancer and heart disease survival', in *Inequalities in Health in Europe*, ed. A. J. Fox, London, Gower. In Press.

Lynge, E. and Anderson, O. (1985) *Mortality: A Comparison of Within-Country Differentials Based on Selected Occupational Groups*, paper presented at European Science Foundation meeting, London, September.

McKeown, T. and Lowe, C. R. (1974) *An Introduction to Social Medicine* (Oxford: Blackwell).

Marmot, M. G. (1986) 'Social inequalities in mortality – the social environment', in Wilkinson, R. G. (ed.) 1986.

New Earnings Survey (1970) Department of Employment (London: HMSO).

Palmore, E. (1969) 'Predicting longevity', *Gerontologist*, 9, 247.

Pamuk, E. R. (1985) 'Social class inequality in mortality from 1921 to 1971 in England and Wales', *Population Studies*, 39, 17–31.

Registrar General (1961) *Decennial Supplement, Occupational Mortality Tables* (London: HMSO).

Registrar General, (1978) *Occupational Mortality 1970–2*, OPCS Series DS No. 1 (London: HMSO).

Rodgers, G. B., 'Income and inequality as determinants of mortality: an international cross-section analysis', *Population Studies*, 33, 343–51.

Sawyer, M. (1976) *Income Distribution in OECD Countries*, OECD Economic Outlook, Occasional Studies.

Siegrist, J. (1984) 'Threat to social status and cardiovascular risk', *Psychotherapy and Psychosomatics*, 42, 90–6.

Townsend, P. (1982) 'An alternative anti-poverty programme', *New Society*, 62(1038), 22–3.

Wadsworth, M. E. J. (1986) 'Serious illness in childhood and its association with later life achievement', in Wilkinson (ed.) 1986.

Wilkinson, R. G. (1983) 'Approaches to research on socioeconomic factors contributing to social class differences in Health', unpublished paper presented to Social Science Research Council Conference on Inequalities in Health, November.

Wilkinson, R. G. (1986a) 'Socio-economic differences in mortality: interpreting the data in their size and trends', in *Class and Health: Research and Longitudinal Data*, (ed.) R. G. Wilkinson (London: Tavistock).

Wilkinson, R. G. (1986b) 'Income and mortality', in Wilkinson (ed.) 1986.

World Bank (1983) *World Tables*, volume II.

Young, M. and Willmott, P. (1957) *Family and Kinship in East London*, (London: Routledge & Kegan Paul).

12 Disadvantage and Mortality: New Evidence from the OPCS Longitudinal Study

A. J. Fox and D. A. Leon

> There is no single state of deprivation or disadvantage. These terms, as well as others like 'social problem' or 'inequality', are widely used and broadly interpreted.
>
> Brown and Madge (1982)

What follows principally is concerned with relative differences in cancer incidence and mortality between sections of the community who are more or less disadvantaged. At the outset, however, we wish to make it clear that most of the socioeconomic measures that we use are not direct measures of disadvantage. There is no simple identity between those who are in any particular socioeconomic category, and those who are 'advantaged' or 'disadvantaged'. Nevertheless, the socioeconomic measures we employ are related to levels of disadvantage, this relationship being best understood in the following terms. Those at the bottom end of a socioeconomic scale are more likely than those higher up the scale to experience disadvantage in various forms, and currently are less likely to experience advantage. The limited pattern of social mobility that exists means that this relationship between current socioeconomic position and disadvantage holds for any point in time, looking either pro- or retrospectively from the present.

1. INTRODUCTION

The DHSS Research Working Group on Inequalities in Health was set up by a Secretary of State who was surprised that wide social class differences in mortality persisted in England and Wales thirty years after the introduction of the National Health Service (see introduction to Black Report 1980).

The Working Group set in motion a continuing and wide-ranging debate on the methods used, the interpretations and explanations of the differentials found and on relationships to policy. We shall look here at the contributions to this debate now being made by our colleagues and ourselves through analysis of data from the OPCS Longitudinal Study. These contributions relate mainly to questions of methodology and interpretation.

The methodological issues considered include a review of the extent to which gradients in mortality as measured in the Decennial Supplements on Occupational Mortality using the Registrar General's Social Classes may be biased, as well as an assessment of criticisms of the social class schema *per se*, which suggests that it is inadequate for the purposes of analysis.

These methodological issues lead on to a discussion of the similarities between differences in mortality produced using a range of socioeconomic measures, which in turn raises important questions of interpretation.

We have already implied that an adequate account of the relationship between mortality and disadvantage has to include consideration of social mobility. This question is discussed at some length in terms of the measurement of mobility itself, as well as with regard to the possible contribution of selection processes to the observed socioeconomic differences in mortality.

Finally, we discuss the relationship of socioeconomic differences in mortality measured on an individual basis to those measured using the characteristics of an area as the basic unit of analysis.

2. THE OPCS LONGITUDINAL STUDY

The OPCS Longitudinal Study covers information for a 1 per cent sample of the population obtained from a number of OPCS statistical sources, including census and vital event records. A general introduction to its design has been given elsewhere (Brown and Fox 1984). Reference will be made here to earlier analyses of socio-demographic differences in mortality (Fox and Goldblatt 1982) and to recently published material on social class differences in mortality (Fox *et al.* 1985), and on differences in mortality between geographic areas

defined in terms of their socioeconomic characteristics (Fox *et al.*
1984). New data on differences in cancer incidence, on differences in
mortality among women and on change in socioeconomic circumstances between 1971 and 1981 draw on current projects (see working
papers by Leon 1985; Leon and Wilkinson 1985; Moser and Goldblatt 1985; and Fox and Grundy 1985).

3. SOCIAL CLASS

Numerator-Denominator Bias

The DHSS Working Group relied heavily on routine data on social
class differences in mortality published by the Registrar General in
his series of Decennial Supplements on Occupational Mortality. In
these volumes the number of people who die about the time of a
census with their occupation or social class recorded on their death
certificates are related to the number of people with that occupation
or social class recorded in the census. One criticism of the data
presented by the DHSS Working Group is based on the many biases
which exist between these two sources. The frequency and nature of
such mismatches have been studied using the LS in a direct comparison of occupation at death with that at census for deaths in 1971
shortly after the census (see Registrar General 1978, pp. 17–23).
These analyses highlighted the potential effect of the treatment of
people who were 'permanently sick' shortly before death. Informants
at death registration would report a prior occupation, whereas at
census only half of the men in this category reported an occupation.
Also, census coders were instructed to ignore this information. An
expected effect of informants promoting the deceased when reporting
deaths was not found, probably because it was counter-balanced by a
tendency among informants to omit employment status when regis-
tering a death. This latter omission was particularly likely to affect
foremen and managers.

Death rates by social class in the LS in 1971–81 have been compared with the Decennial Supplement figures for 1970–2 in order to
assess the overall importance of numerator-denominator mismatches
(Fox *et al.* 1985). These confirm earlier arguments (Fox and Goldblatt 1982; Fox 1980) which suggested that the Decennial Supplement
figures were broadly correct.

Adequacy of Social Class

Much of the debate following the DHSS Working Group Report has focused on the choice of inequality measures used by the Working Group. Commentators, such as Cameron and Jones (1984), Le Grand (1985), Illsley (1986) have questioned the use of the Registrar General's Social Classes. They point to the lack of a theoretical basis for the groupings; to the way in which the location of individual occupations changes between successive censuses; to the degree of heterogeneity within social classes and overlap between social classes; to the failure of the scheme to deal adequately with those out of work, including women, children and the retired as well as the unemployed; and to the difficulties in accounting for changes in the social and industrial structure.

While all of these arguments have validity, it is too easy to exaggerate their importance and to throw the baby out with the bath water. They are not new arguments and were carefully considered by the Working Group who were concerned to make the best use of data which were readily available at the time. Since the publication of their report the LS has been used in a variety of ways to assess whether reliance on social class seriously distorts conclusions concerning the relationship of disadvantage to mortality and cancer incidence.

One of the strengths of the OPCS Longitudinal Study derives from the information it contains about a variety of socioeconomic characteristics. This enables differences in mortality and cancer incidence rates using social class to be compared with those observed using the other socioeconomic measures. In the report on mortality for the period 1971–5, Fox and Goldblatt (1982) compared male socioeconomic mortality differentials on a number of the scales. This work is being extended by Leon (1986) in a systematic analysis of differentials in cancer incidence in 1971–5, and by Moser and Goldblatt (1985) in an analysis of female mortality in 1971–81.

Leon (1986), for example, has considered the ratio of the cancer incidence in low and high socioeconomic groups, defined on the basis of own social class, housing tenure, access to cars, access to amenities and education, for men and women, for a number of individual cancer sites. For women, he also considered husband's social class. Figures 12.1 and 12.2 show the strong correlation between the ranking of each site on individual socioeconomic scales and the median ranking on all scales.

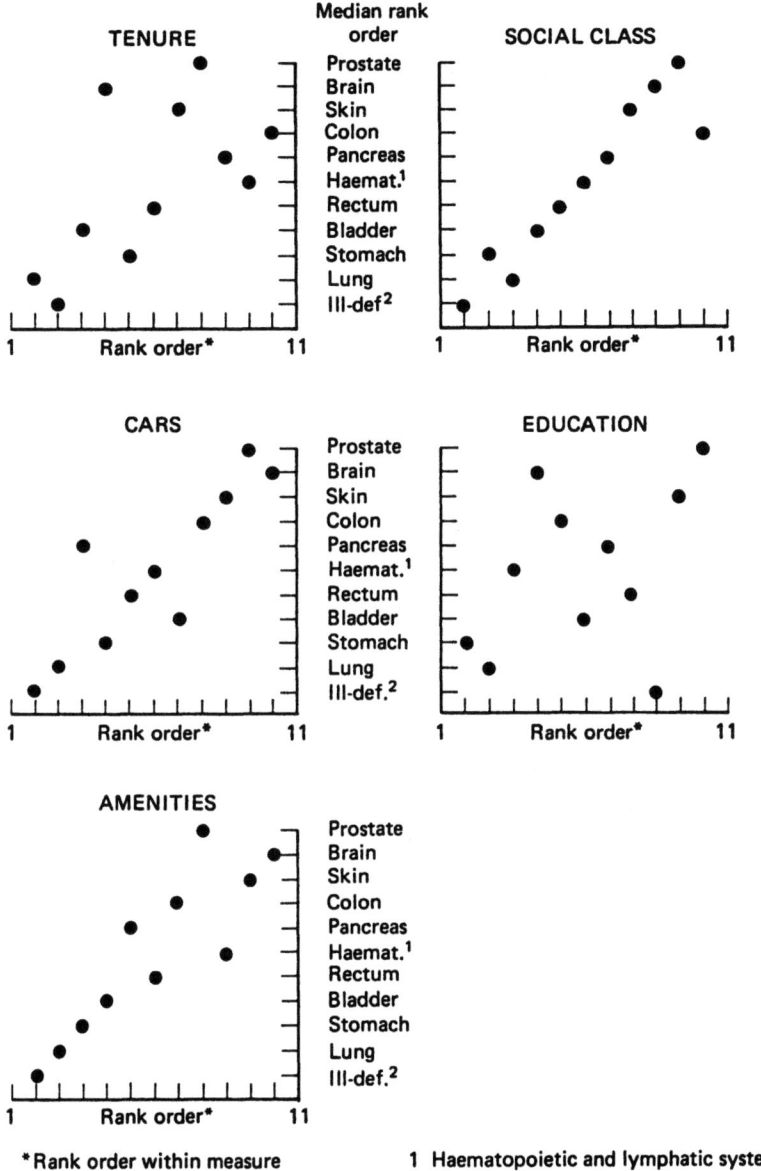

Figure 12.1 Rank order of cancer sites within each measure compared with median rank order of sites for all measures taken together for males

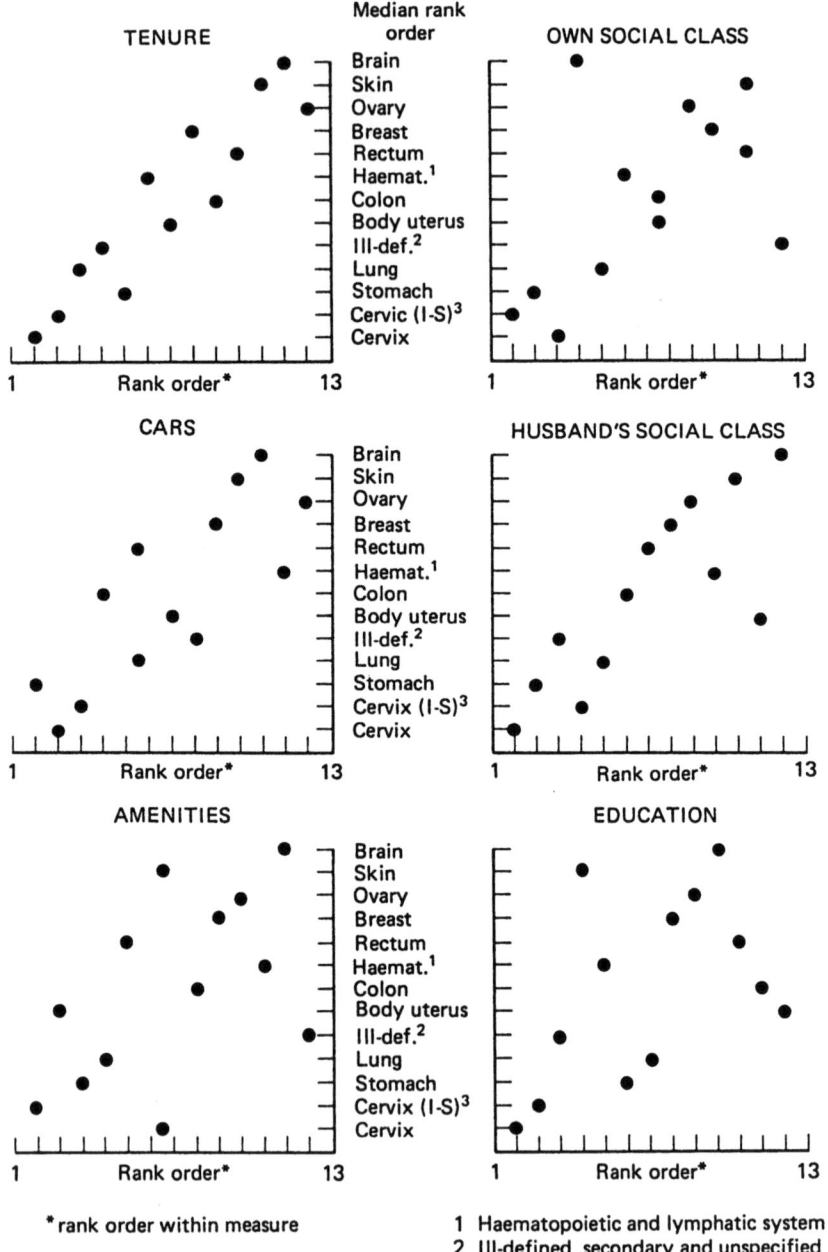

Figure 12.2   Rank order of cancer sites within each measure compared
with the median rank order of sites for all measures taken
together for females

Although each of these socioeconomic scales is defined in terms of one dimension of socioeconomic inequality, each will be strongly correlated with the other scales. More men and women in Social Classes I and II, as compared with men and women in Social Classes IV and V, would be owner occupiers, would be educated and would have access to two or more cars. Leon's analysis shows how scales which group different proportions of the population at the extremes nevertheless provide similar pictures of the ratio between the top and the bottom.

Results similar to those seen for cancer incidence also emerge from analyses of male and female mortality.

Therefore, while one might agree with detailed criticisms about the choice of the Registrar General's schema, the somewhat arbitrary way in which occupations are reallocated between censuses and the failure of the schema to adequately represent those out of employment, these criticisms do not affect the main conclusions about the existence and strengths of relationships between health and disadvantage as measured by social class.

Moving to another area of criticism, the heterogeneity of mortality by occupation within any social class has been taken by some to be a particular weakness of the schema. However, this criticism is misconceived. No socioeconomic measure is expected to explain all the variation in mortality and disease rates in a community. Fox and Adelstein (1978), for instance, have discussed at length the way in which the determinants of 'occupational' mortality can be considered to have two components. One is related to the specific features of the occupation, the other to the more general features of 'way of life', as measured by social class.

Systematic variation in mortality by housing tenure within individual social classes has already been noted (Fox and Goldblatt 1982), the same data showing social class gradients within individual tenure categories. Similar patterns are found when other scales are cross-tabulated (see Figure 12.3). Leon (1986) has suggested that the use of several socioeconomic measures in combination frequently leads to a better definition of 'high' and 'low' risk groups than may be achieved by using each component measure on its own.

4. COMMON OR SPECIFIC EXPLANATIONS

As has already been noted, in an analysis of mortality and cancer incidence the various socioeconomic measures used in the OPCS

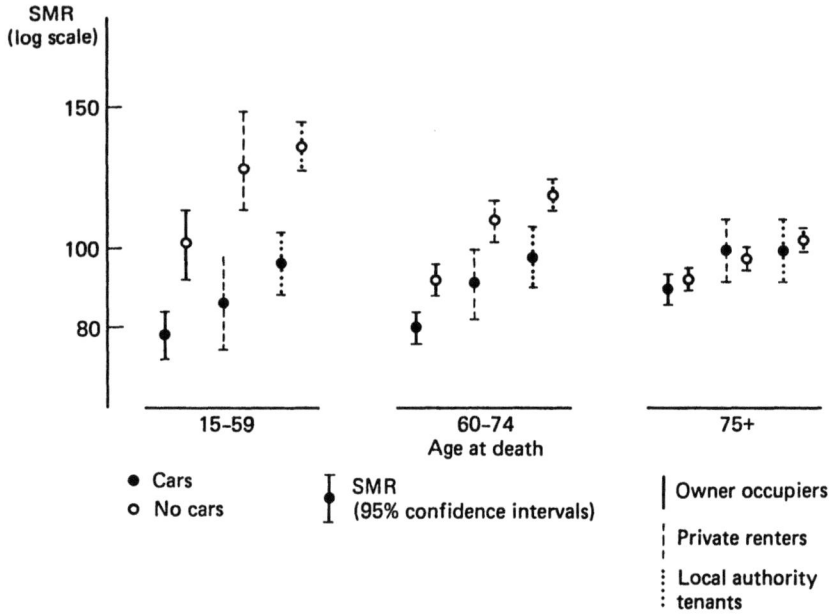

Figure 12.3   Mortality of women 1971–81 by housing tenure and access to cars (Moser and Goldblatt 1985)

Longitudinal Study perform in a similar fashion. For any one cause of death or cancer site, the various gradients produced by the different measures are frequently in the same direction and usually have the same relative magnitude when compared to gradients for other conditions measured on the same scale. In these respects, therefore, many of the socioeconomic gradients observed in the LS and else-where are largely independent of measures themselves. A search for explanations of these gradients has therefore to go beyond the specific features of any single dimension such as education, housing or social class to uncover common elements.

Such common elements might include a general relationship of exposure to a single risk factor with disadvantage. An obvious example of this is the strong negative socioeconomic gradient shown by each measure for lung cancer incidence and mortality. This is principally to be explained in terms of an underlying gradient in tobacco smoking. Despite being obvious, however, and contributing very little to current understanding of etiology, an account of the reasons for the emergence of differential smoking habits in the first place may help to illuminate better some of the structural influences on health and health behaviour (see McQueen 1985).

5. SELECTION BIAS AND MORTALITY DIFFERENTIALS

Stern (1983) described mathematically how it is possible for observed inequalities in mortality between socioeconomic groups to be explained in terms of a process of social mobility in which individuals with better health move up the social hierarchy and those with poor health drift down. This type of explanation is one which has had considerable support from earlier members of the Eugenics Society (Blacker 1950) and has considerably influenced the thinking about policy implications (see for example Szretzer 1984). However, before discussing these arguments in detail, we wish to present some data on the nature and extent of social mobility as seen in the OPCS Longitudinal Study.

Social Mobility in the Longitudinal Study

When the LS was first planned it was recognised that its main contribution to the understanding of socioeconomic differentials in mortality would come when we were able to relate mortality in a period after a census to mobility in the period prior to the census. We have only recently added information from the 1981 Census to the LS and consequently must restrict ourselves here to preliminary observations on the extent and pattern of movement in the last decade. However, over the coming months we shall start to relate mortality after 1981 to socioeconomic mobility during the preceding decade.

The following comments are based on a preliminary analysis of the intercensal material by Fox and Grundy (1985). There are difficulties in interpreting change precisely, mainly because of 'error' and classification changes; issues which are not addressed here (see Fox and Grundy 1985, for further discussion). However, these should not affect the broad conclusions we draw.

First, the degree of continuity from one generation to the next, which varies from class to class, should be noted. The social class origins (in 1971) of sons and daughters (aged 16–25 in 1981) by own social class in 1981 are compared in Table 12.1. Young adults in professional jobs come from a greater diversity of social backgrounds

Table 12.1   Origins of people by sex and class

Grouped class of father in 1971	Sons** in 1981		Daughters** in 1981	
	Professional	Unskilled	Professional	Unskilled
Professional	13.2	0.7	14.4	1.3
Other non-manual	40.3	10.6	42.6	9.4
Manual	35.1	72.8	33.7	74.3
Other*	11.4	15.9	9.4	15.0
Total	817	2229	202	381

Source: Fox and Grundy (1985).
*includes father not present in 1971 (i.e. lone parent family).
**aged 16–25 in 1981.

than those in unskilled jobs who are drawn in the main part from manual classes. This consequence of period changes in the socioeconomic structure, which have led to opportunities of intergenerational upward mobility, has been recognised by students of social mobility (Heath 1980) and voting behaviour (Heath *et al.* 1985) but not incorporated into explanations of the changing relationships between the mortality of men in social class I and social class V.

A high degree of intra-generational mobility is also a central prerequisite of Stern's model, where it is assumed that it is the most healthy who have the greatest probability of rising up the scale after entry to the labour market and the least healthy the greatest probability of falling. Evidence from the LS suggests that early experiences in the labour market are associated with higher frequencies of social class mobility, generally in an upward direction, while mobility at later stages of occupational careers sees a greater balance between upward and downward movement. As is indicated by Table 12.2, the degree of stability depends on the class of origin as well as age. Men in less skilled occupations, whether manual or non-manual, tend to be more socially mobile than those in skilled occupations, almost irrespective of age. In part this would be associated with their obtaining skills, in part with their being promoted, and in part with their moving to other occupations which are located in higher social classes.

These tables, however, should be interpreted with caution. Major

Table 12.2   The fraction[+] of men in a social class in 1971 and 1981 who were in the same social class, by social class and age in 1971

Social Class in 1971	AGE IN 1971					
	16–19	*20–9*	*30–9*	*40–9*	*50–9*	*60–4*
I	31.7	51.3	58.4	59.7	59.4	64.0
II	47.0	69.2	74.1	72.4	69.3	75.9
IIIN	25.3	38.3	46.3	52.1	61.7	69.1
IIIM	62.2	65.9	69.1	67.8	67.1	71.6
IV	32.1	38.5	50.1	57.0	62.5	61.3
V	18.5	27.1	38.3	46.0	46.0	56.9
Total number in a class in 1971 *and* in 1981	8,196	30,071	25,838	26,461	20,440	6,724

[+]Men in particular social class in both 1971 and 1981 divided by men in that social class in 1971 and any social class in 1981, expressed as a percentage.
Note: No account has been taken of classification changes and coding errors.

changes in the classification of occupations between the 1971 and 1981 Censuses, and reporting and coding errors with respect to occupations at the 1981 Census, may well have contributed to the high level of social class mobility observed. For example, the recent report on the Census Post-Enumeration Survey indicates the high degree of 'error' in occupational reporting and coding for the 1981 Census.

Such factors are unlikely to be as important for changes in housing tenure, which demonstrate a far higher degree of stability during adult ages (Figure 12.4). Only among men in the relatively small privately-rented and non-private tenures is there a low degree of stability comparative to that found for social classes. The lower stability noted for the privately rented sector and for younger local authority tenants reflects in part the marked structural changes which have recently been taking place in the housing market, in particular, substantial movement away from privately rented accommodation.

As we argued earlier, position on one socioeconomic scale appears to be strongly related to position on a second scale. To illustrate the way in which this relationship develops we focus now on those men who moved between the two main sectors of the housing market, namely owner occupation and local authority tenure, and consider their social class distribution.

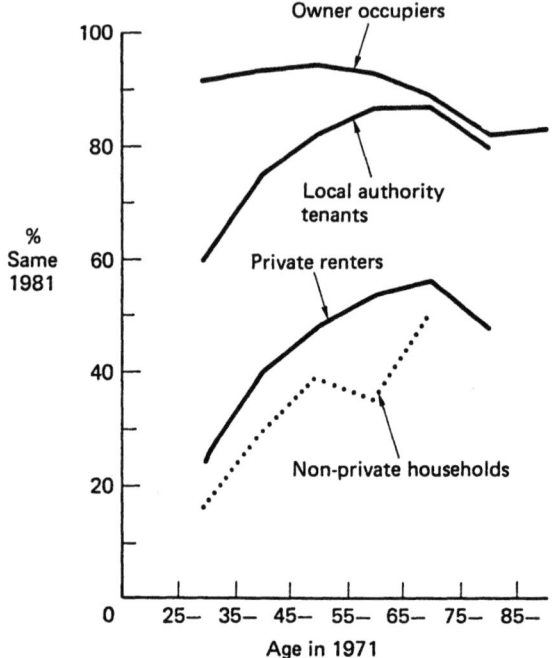

Figure 12.4   Tenure 'stability' 1971–81: Men by age and tenure in 1971

Table 12.3 shows the proportion of owner occupiers in 1971 who became local authority tenants in 1981 and the proportion of local authority tenants who became owner occupiers by social class in 1971 and by age. If we look first at local authority tenants in 1971 we note the relatively large fraction who were owner occupiers in 1981, particularly among those in social classes I and II and at younger ages. Movement in the opposite direction, from owner occupation to local authority tenure, which is substantially less frequent, is also clearly related to social class in 1971. It is less clearly related to age.

These analyses complement those presented by Fox (1985) which show how social class mobility after 1971 (for men becoming fathers) was strongly influenced by position in the housing market in 1971 and migration history prior to 1971.

Although the above discussion indicates the pattern and extent of social class and housing mobility during the 1970s, these data are of more interest to us for the insights which they provide into the extent to which socioeconomic characteristics at one point in time reflect

Table 12.3 Number of men (and percentage of 1971 tenure) changing from owner occupation in 1971 to local authority tenure in 1981, and from local authority tenure in 1971 to owner occupation in 1981, by social class and age in 1971

Social Class in 1971	Type of change	25–34		35–44		45–54		55–64		65–74	
		No. changing	Total no.	No. changing	Total no.	No. changing	Total no.	No. changing	Total no.	No. changing	Total no.
I	Own. Occ. to LAT	9 (0.6)	1525	4 (0.3)	1445	4 (0.4)	976	4 (0.7)	601	– (0.0)	797
	LAT to Own. Occ.	90 (76.3)	118	37 (48.1)	77	20 (31.7)	63	11 (32.4)	34	4	11
II	Own. Occ. to LAT	56 (1.7)	3339	44 (1.1)	4163	44 (1.1)	3935	44 (1.1)	2869	20 (2.4)	844
	LAT to Own. Occ.	289 (64.1)	451	180 (35.2)	912	165 (22.8)	594	63 (19.9)	316	5 (8.3)	60
IIIN	Own. Occ. to LAT	47 (2.1)	2271	39 (2.0)	1986	31 (1.8)	1714	30 (2.2)	1379	22 (2.3)	959
	LAT to Own. Occ	221 (53.8)	411	134 (28.2)	475	89 (15.0)	593	37 (9.5)	391	13 (9.1)	143
IIIM	Own. Occ. to LAT	299 (5.0)	6039	230 (4.3)	5393	138 (3.4)	4082	129 (4.1)	3130	69 (8.9)	773
	LAT to Own. Occ.	1157 (23.8)	3420	871 (22.1)	3949	590 (14.1)	4172	162 (7.7)	2101	20 (3.6)	555
IV	Own. Occ. to LAT	134 (7.5)	1778	113 (6.8)	1651	94 (5.7)	1643	76 (5.2)	1472	40 (10.1)	398
	LAT to Own. Occ.	386 (28.1)	1374	277 (16.6)	1665	220 (10.7)	2064	101 (7.5)	1351	27 (6.2)	437
V	Own. Occ. to LAT	65 (14.9)	436	32 (11.4)	457	36 (7.7)	469	56 (10.4)	538	33 (8.6)	383
	LAT to Own. Occ.	148 (17.9)	826	86 (10.8)	794	59 (6.7)	887	34 (4.4)	766	17 (4.6)	370

Own. Occ. = owner occupiers
LAT = local authority tenants

socioeconomic characteristics earlier in life and predict future circumstances and characteristics.

Selection and Mortality in the Longitudinal Study

As already noted, we are not yet able to study mortality patterns
after 1981 in relation to changes in socioeconomic characteristics in
the preceeding decade. However, in a recent article on mortality in
the period 1971–81 we have attempted to use time trends in SMRs by
social class in 1971 and SMRs by social class for men over retirement
age, to provide a first indication as to how important we might expect
the effects of selection bias to be (Fox, Goldblatt and Jones 1985). It
was argued that, if social mobility were an important factor in
explaining social class differences in mortality, we would expect
differences to narrow with time from the 1971 Census and we would
expect differences at older ages to be substantially narrower than at
younger ages. Since we found neither of these patterns, we suspect
that the net effects of selection bias on mortality differences will not
be large. However, we expect the more sensitive approach using the
post-1981 Census mortality to identify small effects.

Figures 12.1 and 12.2 also shed light on Stern's argument that
socioeconomic differences in mortality could arise as a result of
differential mobility of the sick. Each of the socioeconomic scales
used by Leon (1986) carries different implications with respect to past
and future mobility. In particular, educational gradients are likely to
be dominated by inter-generational change and are affected by mobility after the age of 25 only to the extent that childhood mobility is
predictive of adult mobility. The strong correlation between educational and other socio-economic differences therefore suggests that
these other differences are not greatly influenced by mobility at older
ages.

At first sight these negative conclusions from the OPCS Longitudinal Study appear to be at odds with the results of other studies of
mobility and health. Aside from Stern's theoretical speculations,
strong empirical evidence in support of the selection theory is to be
found in Illsley's (1986) recent updating of his classical study of
health differences between women who marry up the socioeconomic
scale and those who marry down: differences which were then found
to be related to pregnancy outcome (Illsley 1955). Wadsworth (1986)
has also recently documented relationships between parental social
class, childhood health and ill-health, position in the labour market

and early adult health experiences for a cohort of children born in one week in 1946 and followed through to age 26. These studies focus on inter-generational mobility and health and demonstrate clear relationships.

However, the evidence of Illsley and Wadsworth on relationships between health and social mobility does not necessarily conflict with our evidence on the effects of mobility on mortality at older ages. It is possible, for example, that health may be strongly associated with inter-generational mobility, and even with intra-generational mobility, but that the extent of the mobility and the relationship between ill-health and mortality may not be strong enough to influence mortality rates from the major causes of death. It is perhaps striking that little evidence exists for selective mobility explaining the major gradients in lung cancer and ischaemic heart disease mortality nor the gradients for fatal accidents. Only for bronchitis, of the common conditions, has mobility been implicated as a factor contributing to the social class gradient and this, as a cause of death among younger adults, has been declining rapidly.

Finally, with respect to the question of selection bias and mortality, it is appropriate to make a few comments about Stern's theoretical model. This deals with relationships between health and social mobility, but says very little about the environment in which these relationships can change. At the present time, exceptionally high levels of unemployment prevail, the physically and mentally disabled and disadvantaged experience greater difficulty in obtaining and maintaining suitable employment, than at a time when the demand for labour was greater. The location of this group in the socioeconomic hierarchy and its mobility consequently reflect the opportunities afforded by the labour market and not just the qualities endowed to the individual. It is not clear whether Stern would follow the approach of Himsworth (1984) and argue that socioeconomic differentials in mortality were 'natural', or the approach of Goldthorpe (1985) to emphasise the societal/environmental changes.

6. AREA AND INDIVIDUAL DATA

So far we have considered the influence of socioeconomic factors upon health and disease as described on the basis of the characteristics of individuals (e.g. social class) or the characteristics of the households in which they live (e.g. housing tenure). Beyond this it is

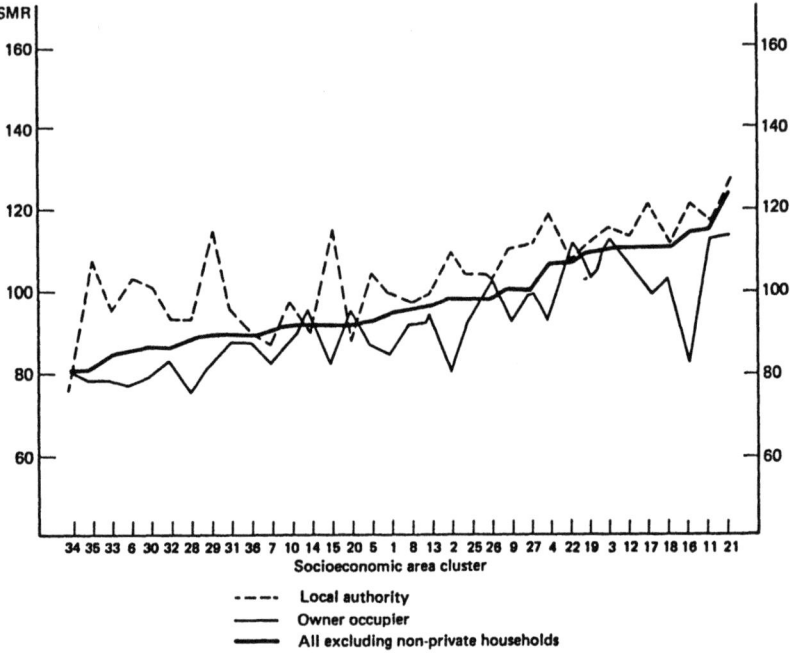

Figure 12.5   Mortality of women in 1971–81 by socioeconomic cluster and
housing tenure (see Fox *et al.* 1984)

worth considering whether the general socioeconomic circumstances
of the area in which individuals and households are located have an
independent effect upon disease rates.

The majority of studies that have looked at the relationships
between disease rates and the socioeconomic characteristics of areas
have been unable to look simultaneously at socioeconomic differences on an individual level. However, the OPCS Longitudinal Study
enables such a simultaneous analysis to be conducted. Data from the
study have been used to address questions such as, whether individual differences in mortality rates can be explained in terms of geographic differences or vice-versa and, are individual differences greater
or smaller in more affluent or less affluent areas (Fox *et al.* 1984;
Jones 1984; Moser and Goldblatt 1985).

Figure 12.5 shows the differences in mortality for women by tenure
within census wards, grouped according to their socioeconomic
characteristics. Clusters of wards have been ranked according to the

mortality level of the cluster. These analyses show that ward differences do not explain, and are not explained by, tenure differences, findings which are similar to those for men reported earlier. Local authority tenants and owner occupiers in 'high mortality' wards tend to have higher mortality than local authority tenants and owner occupiers respectively in 'low mortality' wards. At the same time, in each cluster of wards (except three) local authority tenants have higher mortality than owner occupiers. There is a suggestion that some of the cluster differences are associated with the fraction of local authority tenants in the area. However, of particular interest is the suggestion that tenure differences are not related to the level of mortality of the cluster.

Jones (1984) has started to look further at effects of aggregation in the analysis of geographic differences in mortality. In particular, he has looked at tenure differences in mortality in wards grouped according to the fraction of owner occupiers in the ward; this contrasts with the Craig-Weber grouping which is based on 40 socioeconomic characteristics derived from the census. Jones's preliminary analysis suggests that differences between owner occupiers and local authority tenants are less in wards with a low proportion of owner occupiers than in wards with a high proportion. However, more substantial progress on the topic will only be made when we are able to use more sophisticated statistical methods such as proposed by Aitkin and Longford (1986) which use individuals' records.

7. DISCUSSION

A number of conclusions are apparent from the foregoing discussion. It is clear that mortality rates among the disadvantaged sections of our society are higher, substantially so for particular conditions, than those found among the more advantaged sections. As has been well documented elsewhere, this is not a unique feature of England and Wales, but one which is replicated in Scandinavia as well as in less developed countries (CICRED, 1984; IUSSP 1984). Of greatest interest is a better understanding of the reasons for differentials to be so wide and the extent to which the differences change over time. These issues are not academic issues but are central to national policy. Many countries, for example, are committed to the ideals behind the WHO programme 'Health for all by the year 2000' and some, such as our own, have made major changes to the organisation and distribution of health care resources with the explicit objective of reducing structural inequalities.

We have tried here, using new material deriving from the OPCS Longitudinal Study, to illustrate how our understanding is improving. Some of the questions we have addressed have remained unanswered for approximately a century. Although progress in the last few years on issues such as selection bias has been substantial and is likely to continue to be so over the next few, in the main this has been a negative furrow to follow. We hope that pursuit of the influence of life circumstances will prove more positive and relevant to policy.

Although we have not yet been able to relate change in socio-economic status in the 1970s to post-1981 Census mortality, the material in the LS on change has already strongly influenced our thinking and understanding. At the beginning of this paper we emphasised the multidimensional and longitudinal nature of socio-economic status, in particular its implications for deprivation in the past, the present and the future. This is clearly borne out by the examples we present here on social class and housing tenure change, but could equally well have been illustrated by an analysis of the socioeconomic origins of those who were unemployed in 1981 or the housing distribution in 1981 of those who were unemployed in 1971.

Acknowledgements

It should be clear to readers that this paper reflects the work of a number of colleagues with whom we have been pleased to collaborate. In addition to those referenced directly, we should like to acknowledge the contributions of Helena Pugh and Michael Rosato working on mortality differentials and their impact, supported by the MRC, Raymond Barker and Juliet Webster, who are working on socio-demographic change funded by ESRC grant number H00222001, and Audrey Brown who has done so much to facilitate access to the data.

Our main programme on mortality is funded by the Medical Research Council and David Leon's work on cancer was supported by the Cancer Research Campaign. Crown copyright is reserved. The views expressed are not necessarily those of OPCS.

References

Aitkin, M. and Longford, N. (1986) 'Statistical modelling issues in school effectiveness studies', *Journal of the Royal Statistical Society* A, 149, 1–44.

Black Report (1980) *Inequalities in Health*, Report of a DHSS Working Party chaired by Sir Douglas Black (London: DHSS).

Blacker, C. P. (1950) *Eugenics in Retrospect and Prospect*, Occasional Papers on Eugenics, No. 1 (London: The Eugenics Society and Cassell).

Brown, A. and Fox, A. J. (1984) 'OPCS longitudinal study: ten years on', *Population Trends*, 37, 20–2.

Brown, M. and Madge, N. (1982) *Despite the Welfare State*, SSRC/DHSS Studies in Deprivation and Disadvantage (London: Heinemann Educational).

Cameron, D. and Jones, I. G. (1984) 'Social class – an embarrassment to epidemiology', *Community Medicine*, 6, 37–46.

CICRED (1984) *Socio-Economic Differential Mortality in Industrialised Societies*, vol. 3, Proceedings of meeting in Rome, 24–7 May 1983 (New York: United Nations; Geneva: WHO).

Fox, A. J. (1980) 'Prospects for measuring changes in differential mortality', Proceedings of the UN/WHO Meeting on *Socio-Economic Determinants and Consequences of Mortality*, held in Mexico City, June 1979 (New York: United Nations; Geneva: WHO).

Fox, A. J. (1985) *Social Class and Occupational Mobility*, OPCS Longitudinal Study, No. 2 (London: HMSO).

Fox, A. J. and Adelstein, A. M. (1978) 'Occupational mortality: work or way of life?', *Journal of Epidemiology and Community Health*, 32, 73–8.

Fox, A. J. and Goldblatt, P. O. (1982) *Socio-Demographic Mortality Differentials*, OPCS Longitudinal Study 1971–5, Series LS No. 1 (London: HMSO).

Fox, A. J., Goldblatt, P. O. and Jones, D. R. (1985) 'Social class mortality differentials: artefact, selection or life circumstances?', *Journal of Epidemiology and Community Health*, 39, 1–8.

Fox, A. J. and Grundy, E. M. D. (1985) 'A longitudinal perspective on recent socio-demographic change', Proceedings of Annual Conference of British Society for Population Studies, pp. 15–35 (London: Office of Population Censuses and Surveys).

Fox, A. J., Jones, D. R. and Goldblatt, P. O. (1984) 'Approaches to studying the effect of socio-economic circumstances on geographic differences in mortality in England and Wales', *British Medical Bulletin*, 40, 309–14.

Goldthorpe, J. H. (1985) 'Epidemiology, genetics and sociology: a comment', *Journal of Biosocial Science*, 17, 373–5.

Heath, A. (1980) *Social Mobility* (London: Fontana).

Heath, A., Jowell, R. and Curtice, S. (1985) *How Britain Votes* (Oxford: Pergamon).

Himsworth, H. (1984). 'Epidemiology, genetics and sociology', *Journal of Biosocial Science*, 17, 373–5.

Illsley, R. (1955) 'Social class selection and class differences in relation to stillbirths and infant deaths', *British Medical Journal*, ii 1520–54.

Illsley, R. (1986) 'Occupational class, selection and the production of inequalities', *Quarterly Journal of Social Affairs*, 2, 151–65.

IUSSP (1984) *Methodologies for the Collection and Analysis of Mortality*, Proceedings of Meeting held in Dakar, Senegal, 7–10 July 1981, ed. J. Vallin, J. H. Pollard and L. Heligman (Liège, Belgium: IUSSP).

Jones, D. R. (1984) 'Some notes on the effects of level of aggregation on analysis of mortality in the OPCS Longitudinal Study by area', The City University Social Statistics Research Unit Working Paper No. 20 (London: City University).

Le Grand, J. (1985) *Inequalities in Health: The Human Capital Approach*, Paper No. 1, LSE Suntory Toyota: International Centre for Economics and Related Disciplines Welfare State Programme.

Leon, D. (1985) 'Socio-economic differentials in cancer', a review paper written for the International Agency for Research in Cancer, The City University Social Statistics Research Unit Working Paper No. 31 (London: City University).

Leon, D. and, Wilkinson, R. G. (1985) 'Socio-economic characteristics and cancer survival', The City University Social Statistics Research Unit Working Paper No. 32 (London: City University).

McQueen, D. (1985) 'Behavioural research in smoking: new opportunities', *Quarterly Journal of Social Affairs*, 1, 283–91.

Moser, K. A. and Goldblatt, P. O. (1985) 'Socio-economic differentials in mortality of women using data from the OPCS longitudinal study', The City University Social Statistics Research Unit Working Paper, No. 26 (London: City University).

Registrar General (1978) *Occcupational Mortality 1970–72: Decennial Supplement*, Series DS No. 1 (London: HMSO).

Stern, J. (1983) 'Social mobility and the interpretation of social class mortality differentials', *Journal of Social Policy*, 12, 27–49.

Szreter, S. R. (1984) 'The genesis of the Registrar-General's social classifications of occupations', *British Journal of Sociology*, 35, 522–46.

Wadsworth, M. E. J. (1986) 'Serious illness in childhood and its association with later life achievement', in *Class and Health: Research and Longitudinal Data*, ed. R. G. Wilkinson (London: Tavistock).

Index

MIX
Papier aus verantwortungsvollen Quellen
Paper from responsible sources
FSC® C105338

If you have any concerns about our products,
you can contact us on
ProductSafety@springernature.com

In case Publisher is established outside the EU,
the EU authorized representative is:
Springer Nature Customer Service Center GmbH
Europaplatz 3, 69115 Heidelberg, Germany

Printed by Libri Plureos GmbH
in Hamburg, Germany